MARCO ⊕ POLO

DUBAI
UNITED ARAB EMIRATES

www.marco-polo.com

Sightseeing Highlights

As well as sunshine, azure oceans, fine, sandy beaches, luxurious hotels and shopping malls, a holiday in Dubai, Abu Dhabi and the rest of the Emirates also have museums, medieval forts and oasis towns worth discovering.

❶ ✴✴ Sharjah City

The capital of the third largest emirate is the cultural capital of the United Arab Emirates, with a wealth of museums and art exhibitions. Visitors can look forward to a perfectly restored Old Town, the Heritage & Art Area, interesting museums such as the Al-Hisn Fort and the Museum of Islamic Civilization inside a splendid palace on the Corniche. The latter offers an insight into the history and culture of the Gulf region and Islam.
page 262

building in the world, man-made islands, shopping malls indulging every wish (there is even a ski slope here!) and too many superlatives to mention. The Dubai Aquarium, for example, boasts some 30,000 marine animals, including skates and sharks. South of the city, Dubai Marina has been developed along a 4km/2.5mi artificial estuary.
page 193

❷ ✴✴ Dubai City

Along with Abu Dhabi, the Gulf metropolis on Dubai Creek, the inlet at the heart of the city, is the tourist centre of the UAE. The »Gateway to the Gulf« is famous for seven-star hotels, the Burj Khalifa, the tallest

❸ ✴✴ Abu Dhabi City

The largest, most magnificent mosque in the Arab world, the Sheikh Zayed Grand Mosque of Abu Dhabi, has 80 white domes and a thousand columns decorated with intarsia. On Yas Island, a Formula

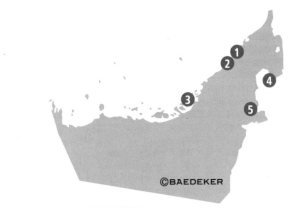

©BAEDEKER

One racing circuit runs under the bridge of the futuristic Yas Viceroy Abu Dhabi Hotel. Saadiyat Island is being developed into a cultural centre with several postmodern museums. **page 150**

❹ ✶✶ Hatta Pools

the ravines south of the oasis town of Hatta carry water all year round in what is one of the most impressive landscapes in the Emirate of Dubai. It is also a wonderful spot in which to go bathing.
page 233

❺ ✶✶ Al Ain

the »garden city« of the Abu Dhabi emirate is located in a watery region at the foot of the Hajar Mountains. the sheikhdom's most important excavation site, the Hili Archaeological Gardens, lies just a few kilometres/miles beyond the city gates, with tombs from the Umm al-Nar culture, dating back over 4000 years. **page 168**

Do You Feel Like ...

... seeing the desert, Islamic architecture, Arabian cafés, camels or wandering through a souk? Discover the seven Emirates according to your own personal tastes.

DESERT

- **Across the Dunes**
  150m/492ft high, glowing red and gold under the sun. Big Red, not far from Dubai, attracts romantics and adventurers alike.
  page 130
- **With a Hot Air Balloon over the Desert of Al Ain**
  Enjoy the serenity and beauty of the desert and oases in a hot air balloon – take to the skies at daybreak.
  page 169
- **At the Desert Hotel**
  (►see above)
  The Qasr al-Sarab on the edge of the Liwa Oasis in Abu Dhabi blends 21st-century luxury with the romance of a Bedouin tent.
  pages 73, 179

ISLAMIC ARCHITECTURE

- **A Traditional Home**
  Courtyard, arcades, a fountain – Heritage House in Dubai reveals all of the aspects of erstwhile Arabian life.
  page 205
- **An Old Administrative Building**
  Bait Al-Wakeel in Dubai is a popular café-restaurant mit a terrace on the bank of the Creek.
  page 208
- **Bait al-Naboodah in Sharjah**
  Walls of coral limestone and ornate carving, a vast courtyard and a wind tower.
  page 265
- **An Islamic Palace**
  the former Al-Majarrah Souk houses the Museum of Islamic Civilization in Sharjah.
  page 270

ARABIAN CAFÉS
- **Water Pipes on the Corniche**
  After sunset, every plastic seat at the Al-Masa Cafeteria, opposite the mosque in Ajman, is quickly occupied.
- **Coffeeshop in the Souk**
  Cardamom and rosewater waft through the air. the coffee shop in the Souk al-Arsah is a popular meeting point for the menfolk.

SOUKS
- **Oriental Souk**
  Souk Khan Murjan on the lower level of the Wafi Mall in Dubai is quite a discovery.
- **Old Arab Style**
  Historical souk with arches and ornamentation: the Souk al-Bahar is actually a replica.
- **Traditional Souk**
  (▶see above)
  The Souk al-Arsah in Sharjah has retained its authentic atmosphere.
- **Most Famous Souk**
  and the most photographed building in the UAE: the Blue Souk in Sharjah in the style of a Belle Époque train station.

CAMELS
- **Market Trade**
  Breeders and traders congregate at the only camel market in the emirates.
- **Famous Race Track**
  The Al-Wathba Camel Race Track in Al Ain plays host to famous camel races.
- **Traditional Circuit**
  Few tourists but big on tradition: the camel race circuit of Ras al-Khaimah in Digdagga.

BACKGROUND

ENJOY DUBAI

Encountering the underwater world in Hotel Atlantis in Dubai

Traditional crafts in Heritage Village in Abu Dhabi City

PRICE CATEGORIES
Restaurants (main dish)
££££ = over £25
£££ = £15 – £25
££ = £10 – £15
£ = up to £10
Hotels (double room)
££££ = over £250
£££ = £150 – £250
££ = £100 – £150
£ = up to £100

Note
Billable service telephone numbers are marked with an asterisk: *0800…

SIGHTS FROM A TO Z

PRACTICAL INFORMATION

Ras al-Kaimah, the northernmost
of the seven emirates of the UAE

BACKGROUND

Most of the United Arab Emira's economic prosperity is still
created by oil. In recent years, however, the Gulf Region has been
exploring the benefits of tourism.

Nature and Envornment

As recently as a few decades ago, the United Arab Emirates (UAE) were amongst the poorest countries in the world. Then oil was discovered – and everything changed. Today, the tallest skyscrapers rise up to the blue sky, artificial islands swim off the coast. Exclusive golf and equestrian tournaments are staged here, there are more luxury hotels, gigantic shopping malls and amusement parks than anywhere else around the globe. And just a few miles beyond the city, the sweeping sand dunes of the desert represent an enticing contrast.

NATURAL ENVIRONMENTS

The United Arab Emirates is situated in the eastern part of the **Arabian plate**. This enormous landmass once covered the southern hemisphere before splitting into several pieces during the Mesozoic Era (250–265 million years ago). When the plates collided in the Tertiary Period (65 million years ago) the sediments of the Tethys Ocean were thrust upwards to form mighty mountain ranges. A separation of the Arabian and the African plates created the Red Sea and the Syrian rift, which today extends from the Ghab basin, through the Jordan rift valley, to the Gulf of Aqaba. According to recent scientific study, the Arabian plate is slowly drifting northward. It has been calculated that the plate has shifted around 100km/62mi over the last 100 million years.

Geology

Around two thirds of the United Arab Emirates is made up of **sandy desert**. The rest of the country is covered by **rocky desert** and savannah-type **semi desert**. The sandy desert consists mainly of **dunes**, which move with the wind away from the sea, constantly building new formations up to 150m/492ft high. **Hajar Mountains** The **Hajar Mountains** are situated along the Oman border in the eastern part of the United Arab Emirates, reaching heights of up to 1,000m/3,281ft. Steep canyons and wide valleys are characteristic of this rugged limestone mountain range. Rainfall and ground water supplies on the western side have led to the settlement of the region, with agricultural areas such as Masafi and ▶Hatta. On the eastern side, a 5km/3.1mi-wide plain stretches out to the ocean. As an extension of the Omani Batinah plain in the southern Fujairah Emirate, it is particularly fertile.

Deserts, dunes and mountains

Shimal near Ras al-Khaimah city was located on an important trade and caravan route in 2000 B.C.

Islands and inlets The coastline is distinctive in its numerous off-shore islands and sandbanks. Off the coast of Abu Dhabi, there are around 200 of these small and sometimes miniature islands, ranging from sandbanks of just a few square metres to larger islands such as **Bani Yas** and **Umm al-Nar**, the latter of which is home to a significant archaeological site, as well as a refinery and a desalination plant. The coastline is characterized by countless inlets or narrow creeks (khor), which sometimes extend far inland. Nearly all coastal towns of the Emirates are situated along these inlets.

MARCO POLO TIP

! *Living desert* **Insider Tip**

Explore the fascinating beauty and vibrancy of the unique desert ecosystem by visiting the exhibitions and outdoor enclosures of Sharjah Desert Park between Sharjah and Al-Dhaid (Sharjah Airport Road, Dhaid Highway, Junction no. 8).

Wadis In the UAE and on the entire Arabian peninsula, there are no large rivers which carry water all year round. During the winter months, the seasonal rain water collects in the wadis or dry riverbeds, which sometimes grow briefly into raging torrents.

Oasis Groundwater reserves from greater depths first fostered the development of **oasis settlements**. Today, the mostly sandy Emirate of Abu Dhabi encompasses two extensive oasis regions, Al Ain and Liwa, both of which are used for agriculture, especially the latter. While the oasis town of Al Dhaid supplies the Sharjah Emirate with agricultural products, the Emirate of Ras Al Khaimah uses the Digdagga oasis to raise cattle and grow dates. The Dibba oasis on the northern coast is shared by the sheikhdoms of Fujairah and Sharjah and the Sultanate of Oman.

WATER

Drinking water is an extremely precious resource in the United Arab Emirates. Constant population growth has led to an enormous increase in the demand for already scarce water supplies. Furthermore, the uncontrolled building of wells caused the groundwater level to sink so dramatically that in 1992 the northern emirates prohibited the drilling of additional wells.

The building of desalination plants was an attempt to satisfy the growing demand for water. Between 1970 and 1995, fresh water production increased from 5 million litres/1.3 million US gal to 212 million litres/56 million US gal per day, and with the implementation of a new desalination plant in Abu Dhabi, the »Al-Taweelah Plant«, the production of drinking water grew to 450 million litres/119 US gal per day.

In earlier centuries, a sophisticated **irrigation system** saw to it that spring water from the oases made landscapes thrive. Canals known as aflaj (singular: falaj), made either of stone or clay and later also of cement, carried precious water to the fields and gardens. However, these **artificial rivers** not only nurtured this »green paradise«, they also provided the drinking water supply for the population (►MARCO POLO Insight p. 215).

FLORA

Vegetation in the UAE is sparse. Both in the coastal and the mountainous regions, the annual rainfall is not enough to support plant cover on the ground. Moreover, the salination of the desert allows only a few particularly resistant plants can thrive. The **acacia** is well adapted to the climate, as can be seen from its fine pinnate leaves and thin thorns.

Equally resistant to the dry conditions is the fast-growing and originally Australian **eucalyptus tree**. The branches of the umbrella tree, from the **Malvaceae** family (Thespesia populnea), form a dense, evergreen canopy resembling the shape of an umbrella. The species sprouts pretty, little yellow blossoms with red dots. Its fruit is not edible, even though they resemble apples. One of the most flashy »newcomers« to the Arabian Gulf is the **Flamboyant tree**. Originally from Madagascar, between February and April it bears fiery red and orange blossoms.

As the United Arab Emirates became increasingly wealthy from oil sales, it began to **green the desert**. Trees and plants that are resistant to extreme heat, dryness and drought were imported. By means of advertising campaigns, the government now tries to convince citizens of the importance of a green country. Schools organize special project weeks where children learn more about native and foreign vegetation, climatic zones and environmental protection.

Every year since 1981, 15 April has been »Tree Day«, a festive event with speeches, dance performances and the planting of numerous trees. The efforts have been a great success: so far, five percent of the land in the Emirate of Dubai has already been covered with greenery. The ultimate goal is eight percent, which corresponds with the inhabited area of the emirate.

Facts and Figures

▶ Arabic spelling

دبي
الإمارات العربية المتحدة

Location:
Arabian Peninsula
Neighbouring countries:
Saudi Arabia, Oman

Area:
77,700 sq km/30,000 sq mi
83,600 sq km/32,278 sq mi with islands

Population: **9.34 million**
In comparison:
New York: 8.4 million

Population density:
111 inhabitants per sq km/ 287 per sq mi

Time:
CET +3 hours

Berlin
4626 km

55°
longitu

25°
latitude

Dub

Abu Dhabi (capital) ■

UAE   OMA

SAUDI ARABIA

©BAEDEKER

▶ **Biggest cities**

Population

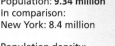

2.28 mil.

1.14 mil. | 900,000 |
| Dubai | Abu Dhabi | Sharjah City | 472,000 / Al Ain |

▶ **Head of state**

President:
Sheikh Khalifa
Bin-Zayed al-Nahyan
(also the Emir of
Abu Dhabi)
Prime minister:
Sheikh Mohammed
Bin-Rashid al-Maktoum
(also the Emir of Dubai)

▶ **Form of governmen**
Federal state
(since 2 Dec 19

▶ **State religi**
Islam

Sharjah City
Dubai

D E   F
G

C

B

■ Abu Dhabi (capital)

■ Al Ain

United Arab Emirates

▶ **Emirates**

A: Abu Dhabi
B: Dubai
C: Sharjah
D: Ajman
E: Umm al-Quwain
F: Ras al-Khaimah
G: Fujairah

| 100 km |
| 62 mi |

Climate

The UAE climate is tropical to subtropical. It is hot all year round. Between June and September, temperatures can rise above 40°C. From October to April, the weather is pleasantly warm, with 8 to 10 hours of sunshine per day. The water temperature in the Gulf is even 19°C in January.

Economy

Chief economic sectors:
mineral oil and natural gas extraction, trade, tourism

Currency

Dirham (Dh) 1 Dh = 100 Fils

Language

Arabic, English

Oil

Average temperatures

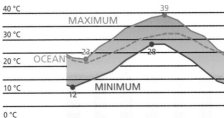

Precipitation

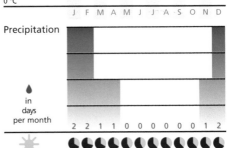

♦ in days per month

2	2	1	1	0	0	0	0	0	0	1	2

in hours of sunshine per day

8	7	8	8	10	10	9	9	9	9	9	8

J F M A M J J A S O N D

The top ten crude oil producers in the world

(2015 in billions of barrels, 1barrel = 159litres)

The ten most productive crude oil reserves in the world

(2015 in billions of barrels, 1barrel = 159litres)

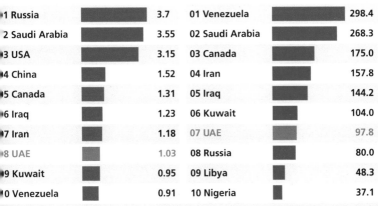

	producers		reserves	
01 Russia	3.7	01 Venezuela	298.4
02 Saudi Arabia	3.55	02 Saudi Arabia	268.3
03 USA	3.15	03 Canada	175.0
04 China	1.52	04 Iran	157.8
05 Canada	1.31	05 Iraq	144.2
06 Iraq	1.23	06 Kuwait	104.0
07 Iran	1.18	07 UAE	97.8
08 UAE	1.03	08 Russia	80.0
09 Kuwait	0.95	09 Libya	48.3
10 Venezuela	0.91	10 Nigeria	37.1

Water is a Scarce Commodity

Although the desert state's freshwater reserves have dropped dramatically, the UAE use more water than most other countries in the world: 70% for agriculture alone, then there are parks, hotel gardens and golf courses requiring artificial irrigation. Drinking water yielded from desalination plants already covers 75% of daily requirements. Water flows to the cities via pipelines from the plants situated on the coast. Here are two of the most important technologies:

▶ **Rapid rise:**
Desalination since 1971 in Abu Dhabi (in million m³)

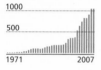

1000

500

1971   2007

▶ **Two methods, one result**
In **multi-stage flash desalination (MSF)** brine is flashed into steam and pure water is distilled. The **reverse osmosis technology (RO)** uses pressure to pass seawater through a fine membrane (e.g. polyamide), holding back the salt molecules.

Seawater supply

Energy supply

Heat

Pressure

▶ **Water consumption per capita, per day**
Although the UAE has such small freshwater reserves, they have the highest water consumption per capita in the world.

in litres

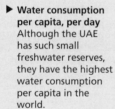

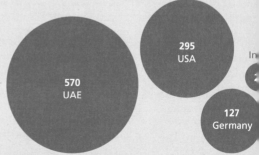

570
UAE

295
USA

127
Germany

▶ **Yield and consequences**
The RO method, with 2 to 4 kWh per ton of drinking water, is far more efficient than the MSF method (up to 100 kWh per ton). In addtion to concentrated brine, the plants flush 24 tones of chlorine, 300 kg of copper and 65 tons of other substances back into the ocean every day. This leads to an increase in salt content and temperature in coastal waters.

ım

water
ling chamber

ım
denses

Pure water

Brine

Multi-stage Flash
Desalination (MSF)

everse osmosis

Semipermeable membrane

→ **Pure water**

→ **Brine**

▶ **Seawater desalination 2008 and 2016**
States with the highest plant capacity in millions m³ per day

Saudi Arabia
UAE
USA
Spain
PR China
Kuwait
Algeria
Australia
Libya
Israel

0   5   10   15   20

■ 2008   ■ 2016 (estimated)

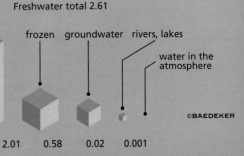

Water reserves
worldwide
in %

Seawater
97.39

Freshwater total 2.61

frozen   groundwater   rivers, lakes
water in the atmosphere

2.01   0.58   0.02   0.001

©BAEDEKER

FAUNA

Besides dromedaries (▶MARCO POLO Insight p. 244), the UAE provides a habitat for around two dozen mammal species, some of which are endemic to the Gulf and some of which originate from other regions of the Arabian Peninsula and Africa. At the top of the food chain is the **leopard**, whose population has shrunk to only around a hundred animals. Indeed, there haven't been any leopard sightings in the UAE in quite some time. The elegant big cat mainly hunts in the mountainous regions of the Arabian Peninsula, and feeds on wild goats, rodents and birds.

Camels in the Rub al-Khali desert

In the UAE, there are numerous species of gazelles and antelopes. The **Arabian mountain gazelle**, which is now only rarely found in the wild, lives primarily in mountainous regions. The **oryx antelope** is one of the most striking, but also most uncommon species. In summer, the fur of this shy animal with two long, pointed horns turns almost completely white. The oryx antelope, once found across the entire Arabian Peninsula and North Africa, nearly became extinct as a result of excessive hunting. At the beginning of the 20th century, only few small herds lived in the Emirates, the Sultanate of Oman and Yemen. In Oman, the last of these animals to live in the wild were killed in 1972. Since then there have been attempts to resettle the oryx antelope, which has been added to the list of protected species. As part of a project financed by the World Wildlife Fund (WWF), animals bred in the US have been resettled in several herds in Oman and the Emirates. Now there are over 4,000 animals living in the UAE.

Gazelles and antelopes

> **?** **MARCO POLO INSIGHT**
>
> *Did you know?*
>
> ... that the »mythical« unicorn is a creature that actually existed? In the 5th century BC Egyptians used to tie the horns of young oryx antelopes so that they would grow together as one. This is how the unicorn, the animal of legend, was »created«.

The caracal lynx, or **desert lynx**, lives all across the Arabian Peninsula and mainly hunts at night for birds and small rodents. During the heat of day the caracal, which survives on very little water, hides in cool dens and retreats. The **red fox** is the most common of foxes. The animal mainly lives in desert regions, but it can also be found at the edge of cities. **Desert hares** and **jumping mice** are among those mammal species which can occasionally be spotted in the Sharjah Desert Park.

Other mammals

Reptiles are perfectly adapted to the Gulf's arid desert climate, which provides ideal living conditions for animals which are able to absorb warmth from their surroundings and survive for days without water. As a result, there are plenty of reptile species living in the UAE. The largest among the lizard family is the **desert monitor**, with a body length of over a metre (3 feet). The reptile with its ser- rated, spiky tail is harmless to humans and mainly feeds on small birds, mice and insects. Do beware of some snake species, however. Among the most venomous are the **horned viper**, which likes to sunbathe in the desert.

Reptiles

Bird life in the United Arab Emirates is enormously diverse. Colin Richardson, author of the standard reference book The Birds of the United Arab Emirates, lists more than 400 different species. During

Birds

»The Noblest Animal of All«

Bedouin works of art and tribal records show that horses were bred on the Arabian Peninsula as early as 2000 BC. Arabian thoroughbreds are considered the world's most beautiful horses; the rather small and delicate animals are intelligent, fast and very attached to people. This noble desert creature is particularly known for its stamina: it is said that a thoroughbred Arabian horse can easily gallop for seven hours without stopping.

Fast and Tough

It must have been significant to the development of the Arabian horse's distinctive features that the Bedouins hardly interfered with nature during breeding, despite the fact that only half of the year's foals survived the difficult climatic conditions on the Arabian Peninsula, with temperatures of over 50°C/122°F. **Systematic breeding** of Arabian hors-es began in Spain after it was conquered by the Arabian army in the 8th century, and reached a climax in the 16th century in the region of what is now Poland. Polish breeding mares became so renowned that even the Spanish court purchased them. Today Arabian horses are bred worldwide. Crossbreeding with other species has brought about the Anglo-Arab horse, which is particularly known for its speed and tenacity.

The Horse Myth

To the Bedouins and the Arabian nobility, horses are true »objects of desire«. Even the Qur'an praises the animals: »Then God took a handful of wind and created a chestnut-brown horse. He exclaimed: I create thee, Oh Arabian. To thy forelock, I bind Victory in battle. On thy back, I set a rich spoil and a Treasure in thy loins. I estab-

Lanfranco Dettori, from Italy, during the Dubai World Cup in 2011

lish thee as one of the Glories of the Earth. I give thee flight without wings.« According to old accounts, **Prophet Muhammad** took 100 horses with him on his departure from Mecca, but only five survived the strenuous journey. These five are believed to be the progenitors of all Arab horses. With his horse, Burak, Muhammad also rode towards heaven. In the Dome of the Rock of Jerusalem a hoof print is still visible in the stone.

The Sport of Kings

Besides camel racing and falcon hunting, horse racing is considered the kings' sport in modern Arabian society. The race tracks in the UAE host weekly races during the winter months. Usually six races are held during the course of one afternoon or evening; winners receive trophy mon-ey or other prizes. Though admission is free, spectators have a chance to win as well. As in all Islamic countries, betting is prohibited in the United Arab Emirates; however, visitors can enter their favourite horse on a card, free of charge. Those who pick the winning horse for all races receive a cash prize from the host.

Dubai World Cup

With prize money of over US$6 million, the Dubai World Cup boasts the highest remuneration in the world. Hosted by the Dubai Racing Club, the race is held every year in March and attracts members of the ruling families of Dubai and Abu Dhabi, as well as renowned breeders and race horse owners. The horses are trained in luxury training stables. Sheikh Mohammed Bin-Rashid al-Maktoum, the UAE's prime minister, is owner of the Zabeel Stables. Around 140 horses are cared for by an equal number of keepers, while two dozen jockeys prepare them for their performance on the racetrack. The animals are kept in air-condi-tioned stables. Their feed – including honeyed oats and vitamin power drinks – are flown in from overseas. The paths between the stables are covered with synthetic flooring to prevent hoof or leg injuries. Veterinarians and horse dentists are on call around the clock. The 2007 Dubai World Cup was won by Invasor, ridden by Fernando Jara and owned by Sheikh Hamdan bin Rashid Al Maktoum.

MARCO POLO TIP

!

A paradise **Insider Tip**

The mangrove reserve south of Fujairah at the Gulf of Oman is a paradise, and not only for aquatic birds. A plethora of coastal flora and fauna thrive in the brackish water area near the town of Khor Kalba. Equipped with a pair of binoculars, enough patience and a bit of luck, it is possible to observe herons, kingfishers and sea cows.

the winter half-year in Europe, migratory birds from Europe, Siberia and Central Asia rest here on their way to Africa and India.

The **greater flamingo** hibernates in Dubai Creek. Up to 2,000 of these majestic birds are counted each year, which makes Dubai the home of the largest flamingo colony on the Arabian Peninsula. Sheikh Muhammad bin Rashid Al Maktoum, the ruler of Dubai and a well-known bird-lover, regularly has the flamingos fed high- carotene food to help them keep their bright pink feathers.

Marine wildlife Over the previous decades, the abundance of marine wildlife has been reduced by poor environmental conditions and increased fishing, yet divers and snorkellers are still presented with a varied and fascinating **underwater world**. Along the eastern coast of the United Arab Emirates, divers can fully appreciate the amazing world of the Indian Ocean with its tropical corals and exotic fish.
The **coral reefs**, covered with colourful brain and plate corals, are particularly stunning. Divers are surrounded by whole colonies of fragile seahorses and, at times, even come across the odd **reef shark**.

Water snakes Be careful with venomous water snakes, which occasionally appear. The various species include the **annulated sea snake**, which can reach a length of up to 3m/9.8ft.

Sea cows The sandy ocean floor all along the western shore of the Emirates is only rarely deeper than 30m/98ft and often covered with sea-grass – ideal living conditions for the rare sea cow, which belongs to the Sirenia family. The Arabs also call it Arous al-Bahr, »**bride of the sea**«. These 3m/10ft-long mammals can reach an age of 70 years old and weigh around 500kg/1,100lb. They feed on plants and live in herds of four to ten animals. Today, the sea cow is a protected species, and the approximately 5,000 animals living in the Arabian Gulf consitute the world's second largest sea cow population after Australia.

Dolphins and whales It is also possible to see dolphins and whales in the Emirates' waters. There are almost two dozen species in the Arabian Gulf and the Indian Ocean, including humpback whales, blue whales, fin whales and false killer whales.

There are numerous animal protection organizations in the UAE. The **Animal** Sharjah Desert Park, for example, was founded in 1992. It now also **protection** includes a museum, which familiarizes visitors with the desert eco-system and its inhabitants. **NARC** The National Avian Research Cen-ter (NARC) aims to preserve rare bird species in the United Arab Emirates. At their research centre in Sweihan, Abu Dhabi, birds from the zoos of Dubai, Al Ain and the priva-te zoos of the royal families are bred and then transferred to nature re-serves. The NARC's essential goal, however, is to breed the houbara, the bird which is the Arabs' prefer-red choice of prey for falcon hun-ting. This timid desert bird can be found in all arid zones of the earth. The **Arabian Leopard Trust** (ALT) is a non-governmental organization whose aim is to explore and improve the living conditions of endangered desert animals.

> **MARCO POLO** TIP | **!**
>
> *Bird-watching in the desert* **Insider Tip**
>
> From Dubai it is just a few miles east to the Ras Al Khor Wildlife & Waterbird Sanctuary, the most important bird reserve in the Emi-rates. A further reserve lies in the middle of the desert: Al-Wathba Wetland Reserve, about 40km/25mi south-east of Abu Dhabi City on the Al Ain Truck Road. About 200 bird species live and nest on the lake, which is about 5 sq km/2 sq mi in size. For further information contact the Emirates Birds Records Committee in Dubai (tel. 04 / 347 22 77).

Population · Politics · Economy

In December 1971, seven sheikhdoms joined together to form a single federal state, the United Arab Emirates as we know it today.

NATIONALS AND EXPATRIATES

The local Arab population, who refers to itself as nationals or locals, are **Locals** of Bedouin origin. Even up until the early sixties, more than half of the population led nomadic lives. The individual emirates were founded according to ancient tribal regions which had developed over centuries. Today, the emirates' inhabitants comprise the members of several tribes, primarily the nomadic **Bani Yas** and the seafaring **Qawasim** who ruled the Gulf region from the 18th century. The Qawasim's preferred tribal area was in the region of Ra's al-Khaymah; the Sharjah settlement, however, also dates back to this tribe. Originally from central Arabia, the Bani Yas always settled around the oases of Liwa during the summer months and eventually founded Abu Dhabi.

Expatriates Of the UAE's population, 85% consists of foreigners, and they are the reason, besides oil, for this new state's current wealth. It is the expatriates who keep the system in the Gulf running: most of the work in the UAE is done by foreigners. Local families often hire several foreign cleaning ladies, nannies and a chauffeur, in addition to a gardener – mostly from India or Sri Lanka – and a chef from Pakistan or Yemen. Bankers and managers from larger firms or hotels are originally from Europe or the US, while managers from small or midsized firms may also come from Arab countries and Asia. Technicians are usually from Europe and the US, as are physicians, though they increasingly come from Egypt and Jordan. Hotel staff is either Indian or Filipino, while arduous manual labour is done by Ceylonese, Pakistanis, Indians or Bangladeshis.

Multicultural Dubai Dubai is distinctly multicultural: the emirate's foreign population originates from 140 countries, primarily from India, Pakistan, Sri Lanka, the Philippines, Egypt, Lebanon and Palestine. The overwhelming majority is forced to live in the Emirates without their wives or relatives. An immigrant worker's family receives a residence permit only with a minimum salary of 4,000 dirham per month as well as a written declaration of consent from the employer. However, foreign workers are willing to accept such re-strictions, as the tax-free wages in the UAE are many times what they would earn in their home country. In addition, residents of the Emirates are entitled to free health care.

RELIGION

State religion Islam, the youngest of the five world religions, is the country's state religion. The Islamic confession of faith proclaims: »I bear witness that there is no god but Allah, and Muhammad is his messenger«, which in Arabic is: »La illaha illa Allah, Muhammad rasul Allah.«

Emergence of Islam The emergence of the world religion of Islam is closely linked to the life of **Prophet Muhammad** who was born in Mecca in 570 as Abu al-Qasim Muhammad ibn ,Abd Allah ibn ,Abd al-Muttalib. At the age of 25, he married the 40-year old merchant's widow Khadija, his former employer. As a caravan leader, he frequently underwent long journeys and occupied himself with religious topics. In 610, »God's Prophet« Muhammad began preaching the messages that the archangel Gabriel had revealed to him. Part of this new doctrine, which Muhammad had founded, was his claim to worship only one god, to free the slaves and to give alms. The initially small number of Muhammad's followers was opposed by an increasing number of Meccan citizens who feared that this new doctrine would worsen their financial position, as they were supposed to pay the regular alms tax while no longer profiting from the »heathen« pilgrimages to the pre-Islamic Kaaba shrine. Eventually, Muhammad left Mecca on 15 July 622 to settle further north in the city of Yathrib (Medina). This date also marks the beginning of the Islamic calendar. In 630, after the victory in Badre over the citizens of Mecca, Muhammad returned to the city and made it the centre of his new religion.

The Prophet's revelations are written in the **114 suras** of the Qur'an. Believers recognize it as »the literal word of God«. The Qur'an provides guidance in nearly all aspects of life, from health care to marriage, even inheritance issues and disputes with neighbours.

Qur'an

The **submission to God**, which is also what Islam literally means, secures believers an afterlife in paradise. This, however, means that the Qur'an commandments must be observed, particularly the five basic duties: the creed of Islam, the five daily prayers, observing the fasting rules during the month of Ramadan, almsgiving and the pilgrimage to Mecca.

Basic duties of Islam

Nationals strolling along Abu Dhabi's Corniche

Welcome to Everyday Life

Sample a little everyday life in the United Arab Emirates, beyond the environs of the hotels. A few suggestions:

FOOTBALL FEVER
First division club Al-Ahli Dubai plays at the Al-Rashid Stadium (usually Fridays, sometimes during the week, in the late afternoon or early evening). Most of the supporters are locals, the atmosphere is fantastic, noisy, fiery but never agressive.

Dubai, Al-Rashid Stadium, admission often free, Al-Nahda Road, Al-Nahda 2. Metro: GGICO

CENTRE FOR CULTURAL UNDERSTANDING
Arabic language classes, guided tours through Dubai's Old Town district of Bastakiya and breakfast with locals – all contribute to better understanding and perhaps the establishment of friendships. Those involved provide an insight into the culture of their Arabic homeland.

Cultural breakfast (Mon, Wed 10am, 70 Dh),Sheikh Mohammed Centre for Cultural Understanding (SMCCU, tel. 04 353 66 66, www.cutures. ae),Dubai, Bastakiya, Bur Dubai; Metro: Al Fahidi

The Cultural Foundation in Abu Dhabi (Abu Dhabi Authority for Culture and Heritage) has the same aim. Here, local residents make good use of the library, courses and a wealth of cultural events. Visitors are always welcome.

Sun–Thu 8am–10pm, Fri 5pm–8pm, Sat 9am–1pm, admission free, Abu Dhabi, Zayed 1st Street/Al-Nasr Street, www.tcaabudhabi.ae

GOLD SOUK
After dark, the womenfolk in black cloaks, some wearing veils, wander through the alleys of the old Gold Souk with their husbands. This is still one of the favourite meeting points for locals, especially the older generation.

Daily 9am–10pm, Sikkat al-Khail, Deira, Dubao. Metro: Al-Ras

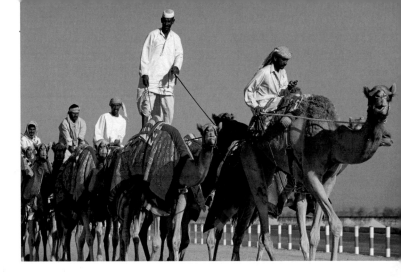

CAMEL RACING

The new camel racetrack in Dubai is an exclusively male domain. Excitement levels are high as the crowds exchange their expert opinions. Foreign spectators – Asian guest workers and a few Western visitors – are more than welcome to join in.

Dubai: Al-Marmoun Camel Race Track, 40km/25mi east of the city, Al Ain Road (E66), turn right after The Seven's Rugby Complex and Esso petrol station; Thu–Sat in the mornings. Abu Dhabi: Al-Wathba Camel Racetrack, 45km/28mi east on the Al Ain Truck Road.

FOOD COURT AT THE FESTIVAL CENTRE SHOPPING MALL

Couples amble through the mall with their kids and Asian nannies, shopping in the boutiques before settling in at one of the many food outlets. Children ask for ice cream, their mothers order sushi – just like the tourists.

Sat–Wed 10am–10pm, Thu, Fri 10am–midnight,Festival Centre, Festival City, Dubai. www.festivalcentre.com

SKI DUBAI

Temperatures around freezing, anoraks and hats at the ready, hot cocoa – a visit to the indoor ski arena is an exotic experience. Conversations invariably begin whilst queueing for the chair lift.

Mall of the Emirates, Dubai, Sheikh Zayed Road, 4th Interchange (p.199).

MARCO ● POLO INSIGHT

Living Without the Veil

The United Arab Emirates and Bahrain are considered the most liberal countries on the Arabian Peninsula. Unlike in conservative Saudi Arabia, where women must wear a veil when in public, they are not required to in the UAE. They can move freely and also study abroad. More than half of all university students in the country are female.

The Western media usually portrays Arab women as oppressed and without any rights. Furthermore, Gulf visitors from Western countries who see women wearing a face mask or veil jump to the conclusion that they have low social status. According to **Islamic law**, a man may have four wives; however, with the exception of the upper class and government circles, monogamy is preferred, if only for financial reasons. The Qur'an states that each of a man's wives must be given the same property and rights. While men represent the family in public, women are the guardians and keepers of the home. They administer their own capital and live a self-determined life, in accordance with the prevailing morals and values.

Marriage and Family

Marriage and family have always had **absolute priority** in the lives of Arabs. In the Arab upper class, it is still mostly the parents who choose the groom as a wedding is primarily a matter between families and not so much of the two individuals involved. The proposal is made by the father of the groom. He and the bride's family negotiate on the dowry, which on average amounts to 100,000 AED (£13,500). From the

In most Arab countries, girls stay unveiled only until puberty

state's wedding fund, instigated by late President Sheikh Zayed in order to restrict marriages with foreign partners, all married couples from the UAE are given a house and 70,000 AED (£9,500).

Domestic Sphere

In Islam, the home is traditionally a sphere of absolute privacy, a kind of untouchable, sanctified world. This also explains why an Arab woman should always wear a veil when she leaves her home. By covering herself, she can then take the protectiveness of her home outside. The Arab expression for house is »dar«, and means private living space. On the Arabian Peninsula, it is deemed indecent to inquire about the health of wives or daughters. The proper and discreet way is to inquire about the well-being of the house, including all family members.

Everyday Life

A woman's most important contacts are her female relatives and friends. When it comes to everyday life in the Emirates, local women are still only vaguely present for tourists and visitors. If at all, they are seen in the lobbies of luxury hotels or in the air-conditioned and shiny chrome shopping malls of Dubai and Abu Dhabi. While most women wear the latest fashion, they like to cover their clothes with a black abaya garment.

Women's Federation

A woman's daily routine is subject to a steady rhythm: they spend most of the day housekeeping and raising their children. However,

In the Emirates, it is mostly only visiting Saudi Arabian women who are veiled

they still have plenty of free time as it is customary to have foreign house servants. The courses organized by the **UAE Women's Federation** are very popular, with subjects including a wide range of art history, art education and languages. The renowned organization was founded by the wife of the former president, Sheikha Fatma Bint-Mubarak. She strongly believes that women should take part in all sections of economy and culture. The UAE is therefore unique among the Gulf States in the fact that women can hold positions in the armed forces and work in many other occupations.

Sheikh Zayed mosque in Abu Dhabi, an architectural highlight of the UAE

Ramadan During Ramadan, the ninth month of the Islamic calendar, every Muslim must fast according to the laws of the Qur'an, as prescribed by the second sura. This means that between sunrise and sunset no one is allowed to eat, drink or smoke. Excluded from these laws are the sick, children, pregnant women, travellers and hard labourers. The fasting period lasts 29 days and ends with a three-day celebration of breaking the fast, »Eid al-Fitr«.

Usually, mosques may not be entered by non-Muslims, even though **Mosques** these buildings – unlike Christian churches – are not sacred but purely meant as **congregation rooms**. The term mosque is derived from the Arabic word »masjid«, which means to bow or to kneel in prayer. The most important place in a mosque is the **»mihrab«**, which is built into the **qibla wall**. It is a semi-circular niche, which is finely ornamented in accordance with its significance. As proscribed by the Qur'an, the qibla indicates the location of the niche and the direction of prayer, facing towards Mecca. Also, every mosque has a **minaret**, a tower from where the muezzin, the caller, reminds his fellow believers to pray five times a day. Even the floor is important: rugs provide protection during prayer, as it is obligatory for the forehead to touch the floor several times. In order to meet the requirements of the ritual cleansing before each prayer, every mosque must always provide a source of water. **Friday Mosque** Although every town can have several mosques, there is one mosque – the Friday Mosque or Grand Mosque – which is the spiritual centre and is usually much bigger than the other mosques.

> **!** *Visit a mosque*   Insider Tip
>
> MARCO ⊕ POLO TIP
>
> Mosques are usually closed to non-Muslims, but in Dubai visitors have the opportunity to see one from the inside. The Centre for Cultural Understanding organizes tours of the Jumeirah Mosque (Jumeirah Road, Sat, Sun, Tue, Thu at 10am, admission 10 AED, information at www.cultures.ae). The Grand Mosque of Abu Dhabi, which was built in memory President Sheikh Zayed in 2004, also allows visits (Rashid al-Maktoum Road, Airport Road; Sat–Thu 9am–11.30am; free admission).

The Islamic faith can be divided into two major religious denominations, which developed as a result of a dispute over the rightful successor of Muhammad. Besides the Qur'an, Sunni Muslims refer in their doctrine to the »sunnah«, the religious principles and laws taught by Prophet Muhammad. Elected successors, i.e. not related by blood, are also considered legitimate successors to Muhammad. The Shiites are regarded as the religious followers of the fourth Caliph Ali, son-in-law and cousin of Muhammad. They only accept direct descendants of Muhammad as the rightful successor of the Prophet. **Religious denominations in the UAE** Around 80% of the Arab population in the UAE are Sunni Muslims; 20% follow Shia Islam. While the citizens of Abu Dhabi are nearly all Sunnis, Dubai is shared by Sunni (65%) and Shiite (35%) Muslims. The Emirates' east coast is mainly inhabited by Shiite communities. **Sunnis and Shiites**

The Islamic calendar is based on the **lunar calendar**. One year consists of 354 or 355 days, i.e. eleven days shorter than the solar year of the Gregorian calendar. According to the Christian calendar, the Is- **Islamic calendar** lamic calendar began on 15 July 622, in the year of the **Hijra**, when Prophet Muhammad withdrew from Mecca and settled in Medina. The year 2011 of the Gregorian calendar, for example, corresponds to the years 1432/1433 AH (anno hegirae) according to the Islamic calendar. The twelve lunar months are defined by the Qur'an, and each of them comprises 29 or 30 days.

Freedom of religion In the United Arab Emirates foreign workers are guaranteed freedom of religion, which means that there are also Christian churches and Hindu temples in Abu Dhabi, Dubai and Sharjah.

STATE AND SOCIETY

Form of state and government On 2 December 1971, the United Arab Emirates was established as a **federal state** consisting of the seven emirates Abu Dhabi, Dubai, Sharjah, Ajman, Ras al-Khaimah, Umm al-Quwain and Fujairah. The state is governed by the Supreme Council of Rulers, made up of the seven emirs. The Supreme Council determines the political direction and governs with support from the Council of Ministers, which is headed by the Vice President, and consists of 21 ministers with portfolios. The Emir of Abu Dhabi, **Sheikh Khalifa Bin-Zayed al-Nahyan**, is President of the United Arab Emirates and Chairman of the Council of Rulers. The Prime Minister is **Sheikh Maktoum Bin-Rashid al-Maktoum**, the Ruler of Dubai. Each of the individual emirates are also run by ministries, which are mostly headed by a member of the royal family. While the seven rulers attempt to reach consensus for the UAE, each emirate is run by an individual feudalistic government: the emir issues decrees, usually with the aid of one or more counsellors. Parties, unions and other forms of political participation of citizens are prohibited in the UAE. Within the framework of the federation, however, the sovereignty of the individual emirates is still very extensive. Common politics and legislation are restricted to foreign affairs and defence policy, matters of health and education, as well as sections of economy and law.

MARCO POLO INSIGHT

?

A brief lesson in colours

The UAE flag consists of a vertical red band covering the left third of the flag, and three horizontal bands of green, white and black (top to bottom). Green is found on most Arabic flags. The first flag of Islam was also green, which is said to date back to the green of the Prophet Muhammad's turban. Red is the colour for Arabic nationality, and white was the prevailing colour for flags of Arabic sheikhdoms in the 19th century. Black is an element of the pan-Arab flag, created in 1918, and therefore an element of many Arab national flags.

The citizens of the UAE live in a welfare state. The ruling families distribute part of their wealth among their subjects and thereby maintain their satisfaction and approval for political actions. The army, ministries and authorities are the most important employers for the local population. According to the tradition of Arab countries, the respective rulers always lend an ear to all questions and issues of their subjects. The »open door« policy of government theoretically offers all citizens of the United Arab Emirates the opportunity to discuss issues in person with the ruler of the emirate or even with the president of the country.

Welfare state

The United Arab Emirates signed the Founding Charter of the **Gulf Cooperation Council** (GCC) with Bahrain, Oman, Kuwait, Qatar and Saudi Arabia in Abu Dhabi in 1981. The goal of this union was cooperation in the areas of foreign, security and economic policy. The political principles of the GCC are defined by the Supreme Council, which consists of the six heads of state. It meets once a year and on special occasions. The rotating presidency is held by one of the member states on an annual basis.

United Arab Emirates

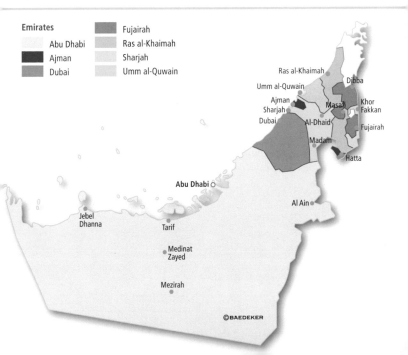

Emir, Sultan and Caliph

What is the difference between an Emir and a Sultan? What was a Caliph? And who may call himself a Sheikh? Delving deeper into Arabian territories, these titles crop up time and again.

Emir

The Emir was a military leader in the 7th century at the beginning of the Islamic Crusades. When a territory had been conquered, the Emir was often installed as governor. Later, the designation became an official title for a regional governor or provincial ruler. The Emir was thus granted administrative and financial powers, but was still subordinate to the Caliph, the highest authority in Islam for religious and judicial affairs. The only Emirates today, besides the UAE, are Kuwait and Qatar.

Sultan

The designation of Sultan derives from the Aramaic »shultana« meaning power or to have power. Abbasid Caliphs were given the Sultan title early on, gradually subsuming religious power into secular authority. Ultimately, Sultan became a recognized rank throughout the Islamic world. Today, alongside the Sultans of Oman and Brunei there are only a few local Sultans in Saudi Arabia.

Caliph

Chosen by the religious community the Caliph was the highest-ranking ruler in the Arab world at the beginning of Islamization. As a successor to the Prophet Muhammed, he held religious and secular power. Finally, various Arab dynasties set their sights on the Caliphate. In the wake of these clashes, the title progressively lost significance and has now disappeared altogether.

Sheikh

The Sheikh, meaning »elder«, was originally a tribal leader chosen by Bedouins, also occupying the highest office of justice. Increasingly, the sons of deceased Sheikhs stood as candidates to succeed their fathers and, over time, the title evolved into a hereditary form of nobility. Hence nowadays, not only the seven rulers of the UAE hold the title, but also their numerous sons and grandsons.

Emirate rulers with British government representatives (around 1960)

In the United Arab Emirates, legislation is largely based on Islamic law, the **Sharia**. Traditionally, it is the sheikh's responsibility to pass judgment. Legal cases involving foreigners, however, are almost without exception tried before a court of law, according to principles of law and order.

ECONOMY

It was Allah who brought **oil** to the Emirates – to faithful Muslims, at least, it is obvious that Allah gave his loyal followers black gold in order to help them find fortune and happiness. The young state does in fact owe its excellent economic circumstances to oil and gas, and its population never needs to worry about money. The per-capita income in the United Arab Emirates is about 38,000 US dollars. However, there are considerable differences between the individual emirates in terms of general wealth and the deposits and quantity of the extracted oil and gas. Abu Dhabi owns the largest oil and gas reserves, followed by the sheikhdoms of Sharjah and Dubai.

The United Arab Emirates is the founding member of **OPEC** (Organization of Petroleum Exporting Countries), which was established in 1974. While only a few years ago oil production and export were the key economic factors in the Gulf region, new business opportunities are now being opened up. Increasingly important for business development are oil-independent sectors, which make up nearly three quarters of the gross national product of the United Arab Emirates. In Dubai in particular, the diversification of the national economy is well ad-vanced: commerce, industrial production and tourism make up about 90% of the gross national product.

AGRICULTURE

At first glance, agricultural efforts seem rather futile in the face of the lack of water, the sandy desert, ground and its continuous salination, and the summer temperatures of up to 50°C/122°F. To counteract such miserable soil conditions, fruit and vege- tables are grown in a mixture of sand, imported fertile soil and peat. For a number of years, agricultural research centres have been funded to experiment with hardy plants that can thrive even under the ex-treme climatic conditions of the Arabian Peninsula.

Due to the extensive **greening** of the desert, the agricultural area of the UAE has in-creased from 18,000ha/44,478 acres in 1972 to more than 300,000ha/741,300 acres to date. Meanwhile, the United Arab

Emirates has become an exporter of fruit and vegetables, and in recent years even exports its grain production surpluses . Parallel to increased areas of cultivation and larger annual harvests, several canning factories have been established. The marketing of tomato ketchup and tinned tomatoes has been particularly successful – nearly half of the production is exported to Europe and to neigh-bouring Arab countries.

Dubai Marina: planned glamour world

Dairy farming is also enormously successful in the UAE. Today, a total of around 30,000 cattle are reared to cover the population's demand for dairy products.

Dairying

Poultry farms are widely spread across the UAE and supply produce for both domestic and international markets.

Poultry farms

The fishing waters of the Arabian Gulf are considered rich in both the amount of fish and the variety of different species. The annual fishing harvest amounts to about 80,000 tons. Most of the 20,000 tons of exported fish are tuna, mackerel and crab.

Fishing

OIL AND GAS

Oil is found anywhere in the world where there is sedimentary rock. Millions of years ago, this rock formed from organic and inorganic sediment under immense pressure. Its numerous cavities were filled with individual oil drops, which had developed over millions of years from residual plant and animal microbes living in water. Dead or- ganisms sank to the bottom of the sea where, as a result of oxygen deprivation, they did not dissolve, but instead created digested sludge. Anaerobic bacteria – which as the name suggests do not require oxygen – turned this digested sludge into oil, which was then covered by sediment. When the Earth's surface hardened, the oil was first pressed into the cavities of the sedimentary rock, then squeezed through until it reached impermeable rock layers, where it formed deposits (▶MARCO POLO Insight p. 40).

Genesis of oil

? | MARCO ⊕ POLO INSIGHT | *Dubai Air Show*

The annual aircraft trade show, the Dubai Air Show, has become increasingly popular among exhibitors and visitors from all over the world. The sheikhdom took this into account and provided grounds of 1.5 sq km/0.6 sq mi near Dubai International Airport, complete with an US$80 million exhibition centre. Over the course of only one year, huge exhibition spaces, a watchtower and 82 guest chalets were built. Several thousand parking spaces can cope with even an unusually high influx of visitors. The Emirate of Dubai has now become one of the world's best locations for aerospace exhibitions.

There is considerable variation regarding the amount of oil in each emirate: **Abu Dhabi** owns 90% of all deposits and produces about 85% of the UAE's output, followed by **Dubai** with approximately 13% of the production. In Sharjah, oil was found only in 1974, and much less than originally hoped. Moreover, oil that is produced on the Sharjah island of Abu Musa must be shared with Iran, which has clai-

Oil deposits

Oil Production

Approx. 10% of the world's known oil reserves are located in the territory of the United Arab Emirates; only Saudi Arabia and Iraq have even larger reserves. The people here are convinced that it was Allah himself who brought oil to the countries of this region, and bestowed wealth upon them. It is true that the annual income per capita of $38,000 is enormous, considering the UAE would be one of the world's poorest countries if it wasn't for the oil.

❶ Oil Rig

The most significant part of an oil production plant is the oil rig. Drill poles of up to 9m/9.9yd each and screw-thread connections are driven up to 10,000m/10,940yd underground. If the pressure of the oil deposit is big enough, the oil is pumped to the surface. If the pressure is not enough, water or steam is pumped through additional bore holes in order to make the oil rise to the top.

❷ Hoist

All drill poles hang on a hoist attached to the steel frame of the oil rig.

❸ Settling Tank

First, a sieving procedure removes rough debris from the extracted mineral oil which is then channelled into the settling tank where the sediment (e.g. sand) settles to the bottom.

❹ Mud Pump

The settled sediment on the tank floor is removed. What remains is pure crude oil, which is channelled through pipelines for further processing.

❺ Drive Units

Engines with a power of up to 4,000 kW start rotating a tray (»lazy Susan«), which is linked to the drill poles. These drill poles are then driven into the ground with an attached boring tool.

A tough job: workers on the oil derrick in the Dubai desert

Pipelines transport the crude oil
to ships or the next oil refinery

sful. Waste
urnt at the

Water or steam injected into the oil
deposit creates pressure and pumps the
crude oil to the surface

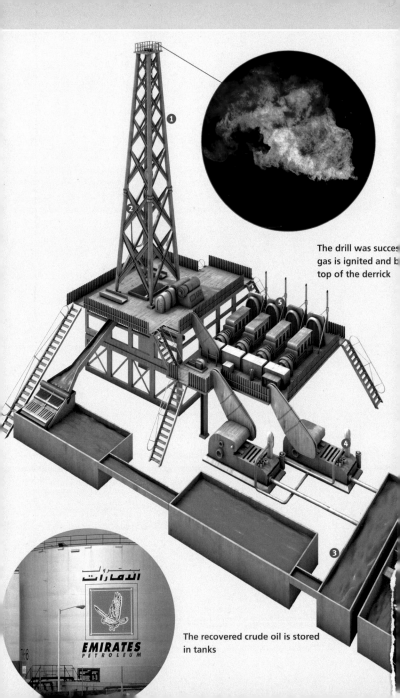

The drill was succes[sful] gas is ignited and b[urns at the] top of the derrick

The recovered crude oil is stored in tanks

EMIRATES
PETROLEUM

med the island ever since 1974. But Sharjah also has large natural gas reserves, which are used to run the local light industry, which includes gas-driven public transport vehicles.

INDUSTRY

Sharjah's industry

The Emirate of Sharjah dominates industry with around half of the industrial production in the United Arab Emirates. The industrial areas of **Layya** and **Al Saja'a** now have the necessary infrastructure to attract new investors and businesses. Each year, over one billion dirham are invested in the expansion of the industrial area of Sharjah. This enormous expenditure, along with government-guaranteed property leases valid for 30–50-year terms, has quickly pro-duced results: currently, Sharjah is home to more than 500 dif- ferent branches of industry.

Jebel Ali Free Trade Zone

The Jebel Ali Free Trade Zone, situated 35km/22mi south of Dubai, is one of the most significant industrial hubs in the country. The headquarters of more than 6,100 companies from 110 dif- ferent countries are squeezed into an area of about 48 sq km/18 sq mi. In addition to a well-planned infrastructure, foreign companies are offered consider-able tax benefits. For example, they are not required to pay income tax or corporate tax for a period of 15 years. Revenue and capital ge-nerated by companies that can be 100% foreign-controlled may be transferred en- tirely. Further incentives are an abundance of adequately skilled staff, mainly from Asia, and low hourly wages. Among the largest manufacturers in Je-bel Ali are Brother, Sony, Honda, Hyundai, Land Rover, Nokia and Reebok. In the world's largest **container port**, companies have a sophisticated container terminal as well as gigantic warehouses at their disposal.

? *Did you know*

MARCO ⊕ POLO INSIGHT

... that the UAE own approximately 10 % of the world's crude oil reserves? Based on current rates of output, these supplies will last for almost 80 years.

TOURISM

Considering the flight time of just under six hours and the pleasant temperatures between October and April, the sheikhdoms in the Gulf region make for an ideal winter holiday for Europeans. Of all six emirates, **Sharjah** was the first to actively embrace tourism. Beach hotels have been erected along the Arabian Gulf coast since the 1970s, and the ban on alcohol was lifted especially for tourists. However, when scantily clad and inebriated tourists started to roam the emirate more and more frequently, in conflict with Is- lamic moral values, the decision was made to ban alcohol in Sharjah once again. In addition it was the urging of King Faisal of Saudi Arabia, who donated a magnificent mosque to the emirate, which caused the emir to re-introduce the ban. But the alcohol-free conditions had a negative impact on the thriving tourism industry. Today, the comparatively liberal Emirate of Dubai attracts the most visitors. For years, the country has been tapping international tourism as a lucrative source of revenue by building luxurious hotels. Abu Dhabi is currently making great efforts to participate in international tourism. It has founded its own airline (Etihad Airways), undertaken a costly modernization of the city, and planned and built the kind of new hotels which cause a sensation, including the luxury Emirates Palace Hotel. The island of **Saadiyat**, which lies off Abu Dhabi City, is being developed into a spectacular site of museums and culture, and a Formula I racing circuit is being built on the island of **Yas**. The island of Saadiyat, which lies off Abu Dhabi City, is being developed into a spectacular site of museums and culture. On the island of Yas, a Formula I racing circuit has joined the F1 race calendar and the »Ferrari World« amusement park has opened its gates.

History

From Desert Kingdom to Economic Centre

Until recently, the United Arab Emirates had neither the means nor the inclination to invest in historical research or archaeological excavation. Therefore many periods of its national history remain largely unexplored.

ARCHAEOLOGY IN THE UAE

The UAE is still quite new to scientific research of the country's pre- and early history. Before oil was discovered, it was mainly foreign research institutions which conducted archaeological studies in the Arabian Gulf. Today, the now wealthy countries have funds of their own. Archaeological exploration of the emirates began in 1953, with a discovery on **Umm al-Nar**, a small island off the coast of Abu Dhabi. The many flints found in the sand, which were once employed as tools, gave the island its name: Umm al-Nar, meaning **»mother of fire«**. Today, this expression is synonymous with the period between 2500 and 1800 BC. Ancient settlements were discovered; ceramics, jewellery and weapons were found in communal graves. Numerous gravestones displaying drawings of camels were an indication that even at this early point in time, pack animals were domesticated in the Gulf.

EARLY HISTORY (4000 BC – 6TH CENTURY AD)

4000–2000 BC	Mesopotamian settlements on the east coast of the Arabian Peninsula
1000 BC	Incense trade with Oman leads to the expansion of settlements inland.
2nd century AD	With the breaching of the Marib dam, more set-tlers move to the area of the present-day UAE.

The first inhabitants of the Arabian Peninsula were presumably hunters and gatherers who lived in this area toward the end of the **Old Stone Age** (17000–8500 BC). The earliest settlements in the area of

First settlers

Depiction of pearl diving in the Dubai national museum

Ceramics finds from Hili and Jebel Hafit in the Al Ain National Museum

the UAE, from around 4000 BC, were located in Ras al-Khaimah . Round stone graves found north of the Khatt hot springs, as well as flint tools and arrowheads, give an indication of an ancient culture. Grave findings on the island of Umm al-Nar are evidence for extensive trade relations of an already developed civilization. During the **Bronze Age** (2000–1300 BC), the area of what is now known as the United Arab Emirates was the main supplier of bronze to Mesopotamia (Iraq). Archaeological excavations have shown that the traditional »arish« style of housing was already in use then.

Mesopotamia | Mesopotamia, the country situated between the Euphrates and Tigris rivers, is one of the most ancient civilizations of Arabia. Apart from references in the Old Testament mentioning a thriving region, nothing was known about this early society for a long time. In 1765, the German geographer Carsten Niebuhr discovered cuneiform writings in the Persian imperial city of **Persepolis** that were composed by the Achaemenid kings Darius (521–485 BC) and Xerxes (485–465 BC). The texts were deciphered in 1802 by linguist Georg Friedrich Grotefend . Eventually thousands of clay tablets were found, which belonged to Assurbanipal, King of Assyria (668–626 BC), and in- cluded accounts of the Sumerians, Assyrians and Babylonians. The Babylonian-Assyrian cuneiform tablets of the Mesopotamians also revealed information about ancient civilizations in the Gulf region.

Sumerians | As early as 3200 BC, the Sumerians, a non-Semitic people, settled in Mesopotamia and established city states along the lower reaches of the Euphrates and Tigris rivers. In 2900 BC, the Sumerians deve- loped cuneiform writing, which is considered the oldest known form of written expression. Cuneiform was written on clay tablets, and the symbols were carved in with styluses.

Around 2350 BC Semitic Akkadians started to settle in Mesopotamia. They founded the harbour city of Akkad, which also became the Akkadian capital, and traded with numerous remote cities and nations. Clay tablets include accounts of King Sargon of Akkad, who boasted that fully loaded ships from Meluhha, Dilmun and Magan berthed at his harbour. Meluhha was located in Pakistan, Dilmun was a region in the western part of the Arabian Gulf, and Magan was located in the area of what is now the UAE and Oman.   **Akkadians**

Along the Gulf coast, people settled in village communities surrounded by protective walls. One of the most significant sites from the Bronze Age is Shimal, in the Emirate of Ras al-Khaimah. Several communal graves were discovered here as well as in Qusais, Jumeirah and along the hills of Jebel Hafit near Al Ain.   **Shimal**

In Ad Door near Umm al-Quwain stand the **ruins** of a **temple** from around 100 BC, in the vicinity of which pottery from India and Mesopotamia as well as Roman glassware have been found.   **Ad Door**

THE ISLAMIC EMPIRE (6TH CENTURY – 15TH CENTURY)

570	Birth of Prophet Muhammad
622	Beginning of the Islamic calendar and the Islamization of South Arabia
632	Death of Prophet Muhammad
644	Written summary of the Qur'an
661	Sunni and Shia schism

Islam, the youngest of the great monotheistic world religions, was first preached by **Muhammad Ibn Abd Allah** (570–632), later known as Prophet Muhammad, a merchant from Mecca. The year 622, when Muhammad and his followers retreated to Medina, also marks the beginning of the Muslim calendar. After Muhammad's death in 632, his father-in-law, **Abu Bakr**, was made his successor (632–634) and first caliph. In 635, the Arabian Peninsula became fully Islamized after the Battle at Dibba, a region which today belongs to the Emirate of Fujairah, and where local tribes had initially rejected the new religion. When Ali, cousin and son-in-law of Muhammad, became the fourth caliph in 656, the centre of Islam shifted   **Development of Islam** from Medina to Iraq . With Ali's assassination in 661, Islam split into the two rival religious groups of **Shiite** and **Sunni** Muslims (►p. 31); the caliphate moved from Arabia to Damascus and with it the centre of Muslim power. The Holy Cities remained only spiritual centres.

The elected caliph was succeeded by the **Umayyad** dynasty, which produced a total of 14 caliphs. In 750, it was overthrown by the Abbasid dynasty in Baghdad, which ruled until 1258. During the reign of **Harun al-Rashid** (786–809), one of the most famous Abbasid caliphs, Islamic cul-ture became increasingly sophisticated.

For almost a thousand years, the harbour city of **Julfar** dominated the history of what is now known as the United Arab Emirates. The first references to this city can be found in Arab chronicles, which give accounts of a Mesopotamian army that stopped there in 696 on its way to Oman. In the following centuries, the city be- came a frequent site of battle. In 942, Julfar troops succeeded in freeing the cities of Baghdad and Basra from Persian invaders. Chinese and Vietnamese potsherds found in Julfar are indications of the extensive Asian trade of Arab sailors.

PORTUGUESE PERIOD
(16TH CENTURY / 17TH CENTURY)

1507	The Portuguese conquer Muscat (Oman) and erect forts on the eastern coast of the Arabian Peninsula.	
1618	Founding of the British East India Company on the south-west coast of Yemen	
1680	The Dutch establish trading posts on the Arabian Gulf.	

Portugal as a colonial power

In 1498, the Portuguese discovered the sea route to India. Nothing now stood in the way of their territorial expansion in Arabia. In 1507, they conquered Muscat and gained control of the entrance to the Arabian Gulf, the Strait of Hormuz. Numerous forts were erected along the coast, but unlike Oman, the Portuguese found the southern part of the Gulf coast insignificant and useless for their strategic purposes. The European colonial power only occupied what is now called **Khor Fakkan** whose deep natural harbour aroused Portugal's interest. From there, they dominated the coast until far into the 17th century.

Piracy on the Gulf Coast

The great power of the Portuguese didn't stop piracy along the Gulf coast, but it did diminish it considerably. The pirates were members of the Qawasim tribe, whose settlement area was in what is now the

Sheikhdom of Ras al-Khaimah. In the early 19th century the **Qawasim** owned a fleet of over 800 ships crewed by about 20,000 men.
Slavery Slavery also thrived: Central African captives were carried off to gathering points along the coast where slave traders sold them to South Arabia.

TRUCIAL STATES
(17TH CENTURY – 20TH CENTURY)

18th century	Bedouins settle on the coasts of what is now the UAE.
1761	Foundation of Abu Dhabi
1841	Protectorate Treaties between the Emirates and Great Britain
1958	Oil is found in Abu Dhabi.
1971	Foundation of the United Arab Emirates

Great Britain's influence on the Gulf coast must be viewed in connection with the world power's increasing commitment to India. In 1608, the first ship of the British East India Company landed at the coast of

Influence of Great Britain

Kalba Old Fort from the 16th century, south of Fujairah city

the subcontinent. After the establishment of a **trading hub**, the British quickly began to explore the Gulf region. Under Shah Abbas, Persia allied itself with the East India Company in 1622, which led to the British successfully ousting the Portuguese from the Gulf region.

Development of the Sheikhdoms

During the 18th century, the Sheikhdoms of **Umm al-Quwain**, **Ajman** and **Sharjah** became the new settlements of the Bedouin tribes in the hinterland. Then **Abu Dhabi** was founded in 1761; and in 1833, under Sheikh Maktoum, Bedouins from the Bani Yas tribe first settled along the Creek of **Dubai**.

»Pirate Coast«

When British ships were repeatedly attacked by the **Qawasim**, Europeans began referring to the Gulf region as the »Pirate Coast«. With support from the Sultan of Oman, the British government dispatched several warships. In 1819, they attacked Ras al-Khaimah, the Qasimi base, and burnt down forts in Umm al-Quwain, Ajman, Sharjah and Dubai. Eventually Great Britain and the Qawasim tribe negotiated. In the treaty of 1820, the rulers of the sheikhdoms on the Arabian Gulf agreed to stop raiding ships of the East India Company; in return, the British offered the sheikhdoms military protection. Several other truce treaties and agreements followed.

»Trucial Coast«

Due to the lack of clearly defined borders and a comprehensive country name, the emirates on the Arabian Gulf came to be called the **Trucial Coast**. In 1892, the sheikhdoms signed **»Exclusive Agreements«** thereby committing to deny other states the right to settle along their coasts, which was practically equivalent to status as a British protectorate.

»Trucial States Council«

In 1951, the British founded the »Trucial States Council«, the »Council of Emirs«, where controversial political issues were dis- cussed. Nearly two decades later, in 1968, the British began to with-draw from all regions »east of Suez«, which suddenly forced the emirates to make decisions about their political future; vastly differ-ing interests had to be taken into account. Great Britain urged them to form a federation.

Founding of the UAE

The prospect of oil improved the chances of collaboration. Indeed, Abu Dhabi had been exporting crude oil since 1963. On the initiative of Abu Dhabi and Dubai and thanks to the negotiating skills of Sheikh Zayed Bin Sultan al-Nahyan (ruler of Abu Dhabi; 1918 – 2004), the founding of the United Arab Emirates was confirmed on 2 December 1971, a federation of states including the seven sheikhdoms of Abu Dhabi, Dubai, Sharjah, Ajman, Ras al-Khaimah (since 1972), Umm al-Quwain and Fujairah. »They became a catalyst for economic development and for new social freedoms in the region.«

The neighbouring sheikdoms Qatar and Bahrain, which until then had also been under the British protectorate, decided to establish states of their own. Bahrain proclaimed independence on 15 August 1971, Qatar on 1 September in the same year. In 2004 the ruler of Abu Dhabi and president of the UAE, the charismatic Sheikh Zayed (Famous People) passed away. He was succeeded by his son Khalifa. Following the death of the Emir of Dubai in 2006, his brother Mohammed Bin-Rashid al Maktoum became ruler of Dubai and Prime Minister of the UAE.

The discovery of oil in the 1950s and 1960s unleashed an unprecedented wave of building activity in the UAE. Today, its harbours and airports are amongst the biggest in the world, hubs for global trade. Dubai was perhaps the first of the emirates to harness the potential of globalization for itself as it grew into a hypermodern metropolis. This development culminated not only in Burj Al Arab, the hotel shaped like a sail and known the world over, but also in the highest building in the world, the Burj Khalifa, opened in 2010.

Development until today

Dubai suffered massive financial problems when the global financial crisis hit in 2009. Countless building projects were halted or even scrapped. Wealthy neighbour Abu Dhabi stepped in with millions in credit to cover Dubai's debts. If anything, the crisis drew the emirates closer together and it will be interesting to see what lessons are learned from the most recent developments. In 2013 the Emirate of Dubai was successful in its bid to stage the World Expo in the year 2020 (www.expo2020dubai.ae). To cope with the anticipated influx of visitors, Dubai is expanding its infrastructure, heralding the next phase of intensive construction work.

Thus far, the Arab uprisings in neighbouring states have not encroached on the UAE, already forty years old. The government's politics are, in fact, »one of the few success stories known in the modern Arab world.« (R. Hermann).

Arts and Culture

A Brief History of Art

**Islamic culture has bestowed upon the world a highly develo-
ped form of decorative art. There is an extremely rich variety
of techniques, the most highly regarded of which is calligraphy, with its different scripts and arabesques.**

ISLAMIC ART

»Angels do not enter a place in which there is a picture of God's creatures.« According to this admonition by Muhammad Islamic art ex-
cludes images of people or animals from painting and sculpture. This
is usually justified with regulations from the Qur'an – which states
that imitating nature is apostasy –, but there are probably other reasons as depictions of living beings were common in early mosques
and other Islamic structures.

Ban on images

The self-portraits of wealthy benefactors probably got out of hand
and became symbols of wealth and luxury. At the same time, it became clear that it was impossible to compete with the wealth of images
and expression in Byzantine art. So the principle of aniconism took
over in Islam. But the prohibition was only followed strictly in religious art (and exceptions can be found there as well). In Persia and
India figurative art in miniature painting developed especially at
court.

In the Islamic world, painting and sculpture are less significant art
forms than the richly ornamental decorative art. Besides floral and
geometrical motifs, this art form mainly employs Arabic writing, as
Islamic law forbids the visual representation of God or people. In the
Qur'an, however, there is no indication of such a prohibition; it is
actually based upon a declaration by Muhammad that men and animals may be created by God alone.

Ornamen-
tation

The art of calligraphy has always been highly valued in the Islamic
world and is considered far more important than any other fine art,
for »nothing is more rewarding than to write down God's words«.
The formula »bismi allah« (»in the name of Allah«) is used repeatedly, as are the words »Allah« and »Muhammad«, in numerous dif- ferent ways. Besides the sura of the Qur'an, lines of poetry, famous
names and significant dates are also rendered in calligraphy. Almost
every building in the Islamic world has some form of **calligraphy**

Calligraphy

Arabian gold jewellery is also richly ornamented

decoration – lines of writing in flowing styles are used to frame windows, doors and niches.

For scripts there is a distinction between italics and the older, kufic form of writing, which was simpler, less curved and therefore particularly suitable for writing on parchment or stone. The close connection between calligraphy and geometry be-comes evident in the proportions of calligraphy, which vary accord-ing to geometrical figures and principles.

Arabesque   Alongside calligraphy, the arabesque was a preferred artistic form of expression . The decorative pattern contains **plant forms**, primarily tendrils, forming intricate lines in great numbers and variations. Floral forms are often combined with geometrical structures or characters.

Al-Bidiya mosque in Fujairah emirate, the oldest mosque in the UAE

ISLAMIC ARCHITECTURE

Local orientation was typical of Islamic architecture. Unlike medicine or music, architecture was not considered to be a scientific discipline but rather a trade, knowledge that anyone could gain. Since construction workers were not organized in guilds and did not travel there was little trans-regional exchange of construction technology in the Arab world.

Arches have dominated the structures of Islamic architecture since the construction of the Great Mosque in Damascus in the early 8th century. During the same period, Islam's **decorative architecture** developed out of the building style in which columns were connected to form arcades, so that the area in between the arches could be decorated with ornaments and patterns, both vertically and horizontally. Mosque architecture always follows consistent decorative principles. The interior, usually covered by a dome, is decorated with ornaments and characters and often laid out with several layers of rugs. The **minaret** is a slender and often richly decorated tower rising a-bove the mosque, from which the muezzin calls the faithful to prayer five times per day. The key elements of the interior architecture are the prayer niche facing Mecca (**mihrab**) and the pulpit (**minbar**). There is often also an outer courtyard of the mosque, usually surrounded by arcades, which is where the facilities for ritual washing are located.

Mosques

Islamic architecture typically developed on a local basis. Unlike in medicine or music, architecture was not considered an academic discipline, but a trade – knowledge that could be learnt by everyone. As builders were not organized into guilds and didn't tend to travel, knowledge about construction was hardly ever exchanged within the Arab world.

The design of **residential buildings** is based on the **principles of sacral architecture**. While the exterior seems fairly unadorned, the interior of the building unfolds in almost prodigal splendour. Arab housing areas and settlements are much more secluded than western cities or villages, and therefore largely hidden from passing tour-ists. The seemingly chaotic streets and alleys are arranged every which way, often ending in cul-de-sacs or narrow courtyards, but the apparent chaos is there for a reason: the alleys which end suddenly in a complex of interlocking houses allow residents and clans the privacy they desire. To western tourists, Arab homes often seem surprisingly large. The extensive houses, however, also accommodate the numerous in-laws of a family, including their children. Small windows provide protection from the hot and often hostile environment out-

The Wonderful World of Musical Nuance

Music has always been highly appreciated in Arab culture, aptly expressed by the words »tarab« (music) and »mutrib« (singer), originally meaning joy or giver of joy. Even when reciting Qur'an verses, the melodiousness of the presentation is important. In fact, numerous well-known Arab singers started their career as Qur'an reciters.

Distinct Arabic music only emerged after the establishment of Islam, as a new musical tradition evolved over the course of the 7th and 8th centuries with Byzantine, Greek and Indian influences as well as elements from an Arab-Semitic musical culture.

Foreign World of Sound

Unlike the western 12-tone system, the Arab system comprises more than 24 tones. To European ears used to the 12-tone system, a melody with more than twelve tones within one octave and with intervals smaller than a semitone may sound rather foreign. One major difference from European music is the size of the interval, which to those accustomed to European music sounds rather like »sharp« intonation.

Sigah and Saba …

Another element of Arabic music is heterophony: the multiple variation of a song or melody. Those who can deliver unique interpretations are considered creative musicians, or even composers.

… Love and Pain

Arab music theorist al-Faruqi compares the tool of artistic ornamentation to the principle of musical improvisation: »Just like using an unlimited amount of motifs to create visual arabesques, the musical vocabulary of improvisational Arab instrumental or vocal artists is practically unrestricted.« Furthermore, Arabic music is based on the principle of maqam. Originally the term only referred to the place where music was played. Today maqam expresses the improvisational method for carrying a melody, and also which vocal style, rhythm and instruments are used for the performance. The maqam is also associated with particular emotions: bayati stands for life energy and joy, sigah for the feeling of love, and saba for pain and sadness. In Syria and Iraq, there are more than one hundred traditional maqamat. Experienced listeners can recognize the underlying maqam even by hearing just the beginning of a musical performance.

Impact on Europe

Arabic music was also brought to Europe via Mauritanian Spain. Whether at the Sicilian court of Frederick II or at the dukes' courts in Christian Spain – Arab singers and musicians were always welcome and popular guests. Euro-

Cultivating traditions: a men's dance with music

pean music also adopted elements from Arabic singing and mel-ody, as can be seen by the impact on troubadour poetry.

The End of Originality?

Today a performer's repertoire comprises folklore, national and love songs. The music interprets the lyrics by choosing a particular maqam, which depends on the mood and material. However, since westernization has also penetrated Arabic music, the once widespread singing techniques are slowly disappearing, as is the traditional ensemble consisting of four to six in-struments: lute (ud), zither (kanun), reed pipe (nay), violin (kamancheh), tambourine (daf) and goblet drum (darbakeh). Now modern compositions even make use of European instruments, upon which it is almost impossible to play traditional Arabic music. The consequence of this was a transformation which ultimately meant rhythmic simplification. In recent years, Arabic music has been greatly compromised to match international tastes by incorporating western dance rhythms and melodies. But maybe the move westwards will attract even more listeners.

side, while the thick walls keep the rooms cool in summer. One room is reserved exclusively for men, the **mafraj**, which is traditionally located on the top floor. Here, the men of the house lounge on rugs and cushions after an opulent meal, drink tea and smoke a water pipe, while the ladies sit together in the rooms reserved for women. Even today, this tradition is still prevalent.

Forts

Even before the common era, settlers from the Umm al-Nar period erected stone towers, most likely used for observation and defence. With the Islamization of the Arabian Peninsula in the 7th century, the number and size of **watchtowers** increased. They were round and consisted partly of a very solid stone foundation, while the rest of the tower was made of air-dried mud bricks. The entrance was located on the level of the first floor and could only be reached via ladders or ropes. Over time, several towers were connected by stone or mud walls and created a **safe fortress** with an interior courtyard. Soon the Emirates had an extensive network of forts, which were often located on a hill or in the mountains overlooking the villages and oases. However, it proved necessary to extend the protected area in order to provide a sanctuary for citizens in the event of attack. The forts were increasingly based around water; living and storage rooms were built, as well as stables, and the interior courtyard was extended. Some forts were even traversed by a canal system, the aflaj (▶MARCO POLO Insight p.228), to irrigate the garden. In the 17th century, defence buildings that were originally designed as forts also came to be used as **governors' residences** for the imam or emir. They included representative rooms, some of which where decorated with ceiling paintings and carvings. The mighty wooden gates to the fortress were decorated with iron and brass nails. Of many forts, only the stone foundations as well as a few collapsed mud walls have remained. Today, these ruins are considered national monuments and have been elaborately restored using only original materials.

ARTS AND CRAFTS

Silver
jewellery

Silver jewellery has a long and important tradition in Arab countries. The silver **Maria Theresia thaler**, which was introduced in South Arabia in the 18th century, was used as payment for coffee and remained the valid currency in Yemen until 1968, but also served as material for creating masterpieces of filigree art. The 28g/1oz coin with a portrait of the Austrian Empress, first minted in 1741, was often incorporated into pieces of jewellery. Opulent earrings, necklaces and belts were adorned with corals and ochre and milk-coloured amber.

Ornate piece of jewellery in the Dubai gold souk

Besides the traditionally Arabic and Islamic shapes, silversmiths took inspiration from the Asian and African cultures, incorporating finely crafted petal or leaf shapes. This filigree effect was increased by one special characteristic of the precious metal: silver oxidizes very quickly. Even when silver is polished, the dents in the finely chased jewellery keep their dark stains. The resulting three-dimensional effect gives silver its particular charm. In the neighbouring state of Oman silver jewellery is still very popular. In the silver city of **Nizwa**, dozens of silversmiths are still processing the precious metal using tradition-al methods. One centuries-old tradition has it that silver jewellery possesses magical powers. **Amulets** are said to protect their wearers from doom or the »evil eye«. Even children were given an amulet, a tradition which is to this day still widely practised on the Arabian Peninsula.

In parallel with changing tastes over the past decades, the silversmiths of the Emirates have be-come **goldsmiths**. The centuries-old design tradition meant for oxidized silver brings about different results when applied to gold. For this reason, Arab gold jewellery hardly ever appeals to European tastes. Only very few workshops have developed a simpler vocabulary of design more suitable for gold.

Ceramics · Ceramics are mainly produced in Ras al-Khaimah . The local red clay is processed into ceramic vessels for storing food, as well as jars, pots, cups and mugs. **Mabkhar**, clay pots that are used as incense burners, make popular souvenirs.

ARAB FOLKLORE

Folk music (►MARCO POLO Insight p.56) and folk dance play a significant role at most traditional celebrations, particularly at weddings . Aside from a few exceptions such as the »hair dance«, performed by young, unveiled women in colourful dresses, it is only the men who dance. The groups aren't fixed; every man is invited to participate. The dancers move in a line or circle and clap their hands to the rhythm of the drums or a tambourine.

TRADITIONAL CLOTHING

Male clothing · Traditional clothing in the Arabian Gulf is influenced by religious laws and climate. The male population of the United Arab Emirates prefers the »**dishdasha**«, an ankle-length, long-sleeved white caftan – also coloured or striped in winter – usually made of cotton. For special occasions, a black or brown cape-like garment, embroidered with a wide golden border, is worn over it. The head is always covered by a white, loosely worn scarf, a **keffiyeh** or **ghutra**, which is held by a black wool rope known as a **agal**; a small skull-cap, a **taqia**, helps hold the scarf in place.

Curved dagger · Men wear the traditional curved dagger only on special occasions. Just a few decades ago, the curved dagger, its blade beautifully decorated with silver thread or disks, was an essential part of the outfit. The handle of the dagger, often decorated with silver, is made of horn, animal bone or – in the case of the more valuable specimens – of ivory. Daggers that are sold to tourists mostly have a plastic handle; the blade, once made of steel, now often consists of sheet metal and is hollow and blunt. The matching belt used to be made of leather with silver embroidery, and is now of plastic with brocade-like trim.

Female clothing · A typical garment for women is the **kandoura**, a long dress with elaborate embroidery on the neckline, sleeves and hem. Over the kandoura, women often wear a rectangular cloth, the **thaub**, with holes for the head and arms; underneath the kandoura they wear long trousers (**sirwal**) with embroidery on the hem. Outside the house, women dress in a long black cloak, called the **abaya**, abba or shaili. In Dubai, Abu Dhabi and Sharjah only older women cover their

Henna tattoos: exotic souvenir of an Arabian holiday

faces, while women in other emirates prefer long silk veils. A shiny, black, sometimes golden mask covering eyebrows, nose and mouth (**burqa**) is mainly worn by women from Saudi Arabia and Qatar visiting the Emirates.

Henna paintings are part of the traditional jewellery for Gulf women, which are worn for special occasions such as weddings, births and religious holidays. The powder of the henna bush is mixed with fragrant oils and essences and processed to form a reddish paste. Hands, arms, feet and legs are then painted with artistic patterns symbolizing beauty, purity and fertility. The jewellery-like tattoo stays on the skin for several days or weeks until it fades. Today, numerous cosmetic studios offer female tourists the chance to decorate their hands with traditional henna paintings.

Henna painting

Famous People

AHMED BIN-MAJID (1432–1500)

Born in Julfar in 1432, Shihab al-Ahmed Bin-Majid al-Najdi was one   *Navigator*
of the best navigators in the Arab world. He went to a Qur'an school
and later studied geography, astronomy and Arabic literature. Majid,
who titled himself »Lion of the Sea« and helped the Portu-guese find
their way to Mauritius, was recruited up by the Portu-guese explorer
Vasco de Gama in 1498 to join him on his journey to India from the
African west coast. Majid navigated around the Cape of Good Hope,
sailed north along the east coast of Africa and crossed the Indian
Ocean. He documented his knowledge of seafaring in dozens of
books. The Benefits and Principles of Oceanography, published in
1489, is an early reference work about the origins of navigation, com-
passes and astronomical meteorology.

IBN BATTUTA (1304–1377)

Journeying further than any of his contemporaries, Ibn Battuta lived   *Legal scholar*
to travel: he covered a total of 120,000km/73,000mi. The faithful
Muslim's greatest ambition was to see the most significant places of
the Islamic world with his own eyes. Born in Tangier in 1304, a jurist
from a wealthy family, Ibn Battuta first travelled the world at the age
of 21. Over the next 30 years he travelled continuously to India, the
Maldives, China and Africa. After a visit to Mecca in 1326/1327 Ibn
Battuta took the sea route from Jeddah (Saudi Arabia), along the Red
Sea coast to Aden (Yemen). From there he continued via Salalah and
Sur (Oman) to the east coast of what is now the UAE. In his accounts
he describes that, in the spirit of Allah, he meets fellow Muslims everywhere; they support him and help him in emergencies. His longest
journey, between 1333 and 1346, was through India, where for some
of the time he worked as a judge for the Sultan of Delhi. His last journey in 1355/1356 was a risky crossing of the Sahara desert, from Tangier to Mali and Timbuktu. It was the Sultan of Morocco who finally
urged Battuta to dictate an account of his extensive travels and experiences to a scholar, compiled in a book titled Rihla (journeys). Ibn
Battuta died in 1377 (other sources state 1369) in his birthplace, Tangier.

SIR WILFRED THESIGER (1910–2003)

To this day, the desert crossings of Sir Wilfred Thesiger are an inspi-   *Explorer*
ration to anyone travelling in Arabia. The embodiment of the eccen-

Sheikh Zayed Bin-Sultan al-Nahyan, first president of the UAE

tric British world traveller, Thesiger received an excellent education: born on 3 June 1910 in the Ethiopian capital Addis Ababa.he at- tended Eton College and Magdalen College, Oxford, and later pursued a career in the government administration of Sudan. Thesiger first travelled to the Arabian Peninsula in 1945. He began his first desert crossing in Salalah (Oman), and travelled across the wide Rub al-Khali desert to Doha (Qatar). Four years later Thesiger was the first European to cross the dreaded Wahibah Sands east of Oman. With Arabian Sands, his book about his second desert crossing, he gained international fame. He was knighted in 1995. On invitation of the Sultan of Oman and the President of the UAE, he returned to South Arabia in the years 1977, 1990 and 2000 where he received several honorary awards. He died in London on 24 August 2003.

SHEIKH ZAYED BIN-SULTAN AL-NAHYAN (1917–2004)

First Presi-
dent of the
United Arab
Emirates

The ruler of the Emirate of Abu Dhabi was also the late Head of State and President of the United Arab Emirates. Born in Al Ain in 1917 (or 1918), his al-Nahyan family is a member of the Al Bu Falah section of the Bani Yas Bedouin tribe, to which the Dubai dynasty also belongs. Between 1946 and 1966 Sheikh Zayed held the post of governor of the east province of the Abu Dhabi Emirate. After a revolt in 1966 his brother Sheikh Shakhbout Bin-Sultan al-Nahyan succeeded the emir, who had been in power since 1928. Sheikh Zayed contributed significantly to the establishment of the UAE in 1971 and became its first President the same year; his office was confirmed by the Supreme Council of Rulers every five years. He knew how to balance the emirates' opposing interests within the federation, even if it meant »buying« the smaller emirate's approval. The border conflicts between Saudi Arabia and Oman were settled mainly through his efforts. His generosity in sharing the blessings of the »black gold« with the population also fostered social peace. Social interests inclined him to found the first school for girls in 1966, and mandatory education finally became statutory in 1972. The elaborate and expensive landscape management of the Abu Dhabi Emirate also dates back to the emir's initiative, as do numerous social benefits for the sick or disabled, widows, and those intending to marry. The generous benefits of the UAE welfare system are practically financed by the Emirate of Abu Dhabi. In 1975 the ruler's wife, Sheikha Fatima Bint-Mubarak, founded the Abu Dhabi Women's Society, which still today runs a handicraft cooperative in the capital. Sheikh Zayed died on November 2nd, 2004. His eldest son, Sheikh Khalifa Bin-Zayed al-Nahyan, became his successor.

SHEIKHA LUBNA KHALID SULTAN AL QASIMI

For many young women in the Emirates, Sheikha Lubna Al Qasimi is a role model. The popular Minister of Economy and Planning is the UAE's first woman minister ever, and moreover occupies a key senior position in government. A member of the Al Qasimi royal family, the ruling family of Sharjah, Lubna was a voracious reader as a girl and a keen pupil at school. She excelled in her studies, going on to study computer science at the age of 17, and gaining her Bachelor of Science from the University of California. Returning home, she started a career as a computer programmer, working long hours and eschewing the privilege her background could have provided. She subsequently held a variety of senior positions, and in 2000 became the head of the Tejari, the UAE's leading electronic business-to-business marketplace. In 2001 Lubna headed the executive team responsible for e-government initiatives in Dubai's public sector. In November 2004, she assumed her position in the cabinet – the first woman in the Emirates' history to achieve this. Despite her Western education, Lubna wears the black abaya and shayla robes traditional for Emirate women. Today, she is one of the UAE's most influential figures, and admired to the extent that, during public appearances, young women approach her to have their photographs taken with her, tell her their dreams – and ask for career advice.

Government minister

ENJOY DUBAI AND THE UAE

What are the typical dishes you really must try? Which festivals and events are the most famous? Find out more about the national sport of camel racing. Read all about it here – ideally before your trip.

Accommodation

Where to Bed Down for the Night

Few regions in the world can compete with such offers: the most luxurious (and expensive) hotels, some of them quite extraordinary, are located in the emirate of Dubai.

In addition to hotels which belong to the ruling family, most international chains are represented in Dubai with four and five-star establishments. The most popular luxury hotels for Europeans and families are dotted along Jumeirah Beach, which extends for more than 20km/12.5 mi. Coveted addresses in the city include the new Downtown Dubai district and the area around Dubai Marina. Mid-range hotels in the three or four-star categories are mostly situated in the city centre. As an attractive alternative to the larger hotels, some smaller ones in the 4-star range are located in historic wind tower houses which can still be seen in the renovated district of Bastakiya, for example, in Bur Dubai.

Inexpensive, basic hotel accommodation attracts predominantly Asian and Eastern European guests in Dubai, as well as a younger contingent using the emirate as a stopover en route to Asia. Hygiene is generally fine in these basic hotels, which are usually located in the centre (in Dubai, for example, in the historic district of Bur Dubai, close to Dubai Museum and near the Gold Souk in Deira). European visitors are something of a rarity here, as they tend to gravitate towards luxury accommodation more befitting their vision of a Gulf holiday dream.

Inexpensive hotels

As far as prices are concerned, the UAE in general and Dubai in particular are expensive holiday destinations. At peak times, namely from November to March, hotel prices in the upper segment are amongst the highest in the world. This can be attributed to the high standard of accommodation, sometimes reaching the six star segment, and to the high level of demand. Around Christmas and Easter, hotels are likely to be fully booked. The remainder of the year, the high volume of bookings is reflected by capacity around the 80% mark. Prices drop in the summer months when temperatures exceed 40 degrees and many locals go on holiday to Europe. Rooms can then be found for 60% of the regular rate. Furthermore, hotel prices can vary from one emirate to another, although Dubai and Abu Dhabi

Top dollar prices

Burj Al Arab in Dubai, one of the most famous hotels in the world

Another famous address in Dubai: Jumeirah Beach Hotel

consistently command top dollar charges. It usually makes sense to book accommodation via an agent before leaving Europe. For those who prefer to go it alone or are planning a few days as a stopover in Dubai, an overview of close to 200 hotels is available on the Dubai Tourism website (www.dubaitourism.ae).

Abu Dhabi is also renowned for its luxury hotels, some three dozen at present, with numbers still rising. Flagship is Emirates Palace, opened by the Kempinski group in 2005 and a tourist attraction on its own merit, hence the many non-guests who turn up to take a look. The hotels on the Corniche are increasingly augmented by establishments in Khor al-Maqta'a and on the recently completed Yas Island.

? **UAE Youth Hostel Association**

MARCO ● POLO INSIGHT

Youth hostels can be found in Dubai, Sharjah, Fujairah and Khor Fakkan. For further details:
Al Nahda Road 39, Al Nahda 1
Qusais, P. O. Box 94141
Dubai
Tel. 04 298 81 51
www.uaeyha.com

Youth hostels   Youth hostels (bait al-shabab) can be found in Dubai, Sharjah, Fujairah and Khor Fakkan, often very comfortable and well maintained by an energetic organization. Men and women are sometimes required to sleep in separate rooms; one night costs between 65 and 90 Dirham per person. With a family pass, couples and families can book a room of their own (a double room in Dubai costs 250 Dh).

Sojourns in Luxury Hotels

The United Arab Emirates are famous for their luxury hotels – no other city has more than Dubai. And as luxury comes at a price, costs are equally high everywhere.

Burj Al Arab, Madinat Jumeirah and Jumeirah Beach Hotel – Dubai's most prestigious hotels belong to the Jumeirah Group portfolio. The internationally successful hotel chain was founded as recently as 1997 and is owned by Sheikh Hamdan bin-Rashid al-Maktoum, brother of Sheikh Mohammed, ruler of Dubai. It is named after the district of Jumeirah, one of Dubai's most expensive residential areas.

Owned by the Ruling Family

Jewel in the Jumeirah crown is the Burj Al Arab or »Arabian Tower«, the most prestigious hotel in Dubai. Completed in 1999, the hotel was an international media sensation, firmly placing Dubai on the world map (p.202). Dubai's landmark is referred to as a seven-star hotel, even though official hotel ratings only award up to five stars. An artificial island was specially created for the blue and white hotel tower which stands 321m/1053ft tall, shaped like a sail billowing in the wind. If the exterior is spectacular, the interior is no less resplendent: the 180m/591ft high lobby is a futuristic dome of light and gold, with imposing columns adorned in gold leaf and sweeping golden canopies. The balconies spanning the different levels resemble a vast honeycomb. When ascending the un-

commonly broad escalator to a higher floor, gigantic fountains suddenly begin to spray on either side. Guests reside in suites, the smallest of which measure 170sq m/203 sq yd, each with its own butler in attendance around the clock. Chief designer Khuan Chew from Singapore grasped the »once in a lifetime« assignment with both hands, encouraging her crew to use their full creative energy for the interior design. Antique marble was bought from shut-down quarries, exotic woods were imported from Sumatra and Java and rare blue granite was acquired in Brazil for 1300 Euro per square metre.

The **Jumeirah Beach Hotel**, the first hotel opened by the group in 1997, stretches out like a stylized wave – a breathtaking sight for Skyview Bar guests in the Burj Al Arab. Modernized several times in recent years, it remains one of the most renowned addresses of the Emirate (££££; Jumeirah Road, www.jumeirah.com).

Jumeirah Beach is especially popular with families thanks to a particularly attractive bonus: free admission to the adjacent Wild Wadi Water Park (which also belongs to the Jumeirah Group), a delight for children of all ages.

A sojourn at the **Madinat Jumeirah** (££££; Jumeirah Beach Road, www.jumeirah.com) guarantees unrivalled luxury and opulence in an

Arabian fairytale, a »city« comprising three hotels – madinat is the Arabic word for city. Dozens of restaurants, cafés, several clubs and discos are on site, as well as a stylish oriental souk. Featuring heavy, carved wooden doors, stone alcoves and plush curtains, the large hotel rooms (50 sq m/538 sq ft upwards) in Al Qasr (The Palace) and Mina A'Salam (Harbour of Peace), the two outstanding hotels here, are equally splendid. The most luxurious accommodation at Madinat Jumeirah is to be found at Dar al-Masyaf, with villas in the style of traditional Arab summer palaces containing different suites (starting at 60 sq m/645 sq ft). Hotel guests are ferried around the

4km/2.5mi of waterways in electric abras. Dubai's answer to Venice is a tourist attraction in its own right, one which non-residents can also enjoy if they pay for the privilege.

Palaces in the Desert

The desert with its tall sand dunes presents an attractive contrast to everything else the UAE have to offer. This is particularly true with regard to the megacities of Dubai and Abu Dhabi, where the desert has been pushed back by the construction boom. Fortunately, some desert hotels still exist, providing accommodation at the heart of magnificent natural landscapes. Guests stay on average for three nights in the five-star hotels in the

A palace in the desert: Qasr al-Sarab

sand, some of which are described hereunder; more can be found in the »Sights A to Z« chapter.

The pioneer among the desert hotels was the **Al-Maha**, still the most beautiful and stylish of its kind. Approximately 25 sq km/10 sq mi of desert in the Emirate of Dubai have been established as a protected natural landscape where indigenous desert plants and palms have been cultivated and wildlife such as the oryx antelope (Al-Maha in Arabic) encouraged to settle. A subterranean natural reservoir not only supplies water to the waterholes created for the animals which come to drink in the early hours of morning and at dusk, but also helps to maintain the resort's large pool and the private pools of the guest villas. Indeed, the Al-Maha combines the luxury of the 21st century with the romance of a Bedouin tent. Arabian accessories evoke just the right mood: handcrafted kilim cushions lie on elegant, dazzlingly polished wood parquet floors, heavy doors and chests decorated with intricate inlay reflect old customs with their iron nails on display. The cuisine sets new standards in the Emirates, whilst the programme of entertainment and excursions will not disappoint. Two activities per day are included in the price – safaris, riding Arab horses or camels, wildlife observation, falconry demonstrations and archery. At sunset, for example, one might ride a camel out into the desert to be greeted by a hotel employee with a glass of chilled champagne. Or one might choose to take 5 o'clock tea with Earl Grey and scones in the opulent library, amongst riches of historical travel literature and Arabian classics.

The resort places great emphasis on ecological sustainability: solar power is used, water is collected, rubbish recycled and natural air-conditioning is achieved through traditional construction techniques.

Location: approx. 40km/ 25mi along the E66 highway towards Al Ain (Exit 47) then roughly 10km/6mi along sand tracks.££££; www.al-maha.com; Tel. 04 832 99 00

The **Bab Al Shams**, literally the »gateway to the sun« in Arabic, is a renowned desert resort beyond the gates of Dubai. Resembling a Bedouin palace, the hotel wins many admirers thanks to its fantastic location, nestled among sweeping sand dunes. Rooms are luxurious, with all modern comforts, but the traditional clay architecture of centuries past is also respected – a nicely balanced contrast.

Location: approx. 70km/43mi southeast of central Dubai; ££££; www.meydanhotels.com; Tel. 04 809 64 98

Since 2010 Abu Dhabi has been enriched by a hotel resort in an extraordinary location: **Qasr al-Sarab** (►p.179) stands on the edge of the »Empty Quarter«, the legendary Rub al-Khali desert, and the Liwa Oases which belong to the Emirate, some 150km/93mi from the capital of Abu Dhabi. The hotel, owned by the luxury Thai chain Anantara, is evocative of a desert palace and has attracted a succession of international photographers who are keen to use the magical setting for photo productions.

With crenellated battlements, towers and sand-coloured walls, the hotel resembles an Arab fort, complete with numerous secluded courtyards and panoramic terraces which offer romantic views of the sand dunes up to 200m/656ft high. Nature could not be closer at hand.

Two hours from Abu Dhabi, a desert experience awaits visitors, promising exotic dreams of adventure in a world of luxury and stylish design. Rooms feature antique artworks alongside iPod docking stations, bathrooms entice with rainforest showers and cavernous bathtubs, some rooms even have private pools. Desert safaris by jeep or quad, hot air balloon tours, chic spa facilities and an oriental hammam add up to the stuff of dreams. Standing on a rooftop terrace, looking out across the dunes, the Qasr al-Sarab name makes perfect sense – it translates as Palace of the Mirage.

At the heart of the nature reserve

In the middle of the nature reserve Ras al-Khaimah Emirate: Hotel Banyan Tree Al-Wadi fits perfectly into the landscape.

in the Emirate of Ras al-Khaimah: the Banyan Tree Al-Wadi hotel blends perfectly into the landscape.

Few international tourists have discovered Ras al-Khaimah thus far, in spite of the Emirate being just an hour's drive from Dubai. **The Banyan Tree Al-Wadi hotel** opened in 2010 (p.250) on 100 hectares/247 acres of land between sand dunes and the Hajar Mountains, with a 60 hectare/148 acre nature reserve where antelopes and gazelles roam. The enchantingly spacious guest villas (starting at 150 sq m/1614 sq ft) are pleasantly uncluttered, with antiques from the Gulf region adding a delicate note here and there. The luxury Banyan Tree chain, renowned for its commitment to environmental conservation and social projects, brings a touch of Asian minimalism to the UAE. One of the resort's most compelling attractions is its Beach Club, approximately 30 minutes ride from the hotel. Guests can sleep in newly constructed beach villas right on the ocean and visit the hotel to enjoy the Rain Forest health and wellness spa or to see the wildlife centre where falcons and antelopes are bred.

Exceptional Addresses

Full descriptions of the following recommendations can be found in the Sights from A to Z section of the book.

PRICE CATEGORIES
Hotels (price per double room)
££££ over £ 250 £
£££ £150 – £250
££ £100 – £150
£ up to 100 £

ABU DHABI CITY
Emirates Palace ££££
Resembles a palace from an Oriental fairytale (▶p.156)

QASR AL SARAB **££££**
A desert resort styled like an Arab Bedouin settlement, undoubtedly the emirate's most romantic and evocative hotel (▶p.74, 179).

AL AIN
Mercure Grand Jebel Hafeet ££
Stands like a modern castle on Jebel Hafeet at a height of 915m/3,000ft and boasts a unique panoramic view of Al Ain and the surrounding desert (▶p.170).

DUBAI CITY
Atlantis ££££
Crescent Road, The Palm Jumeirah, www.atlantisthepalm.com
Dubai's largest hotel is located on the Palm Jumeirah, a man-made island off the coast. Welcome to a holiday in a fantasy world (▶p.217).

HATTA
Hatta Fort Hotel £££
Comfortable chalets in a beautiful garden which is rich in birdlife. Extensive range of sporting activities (▶p.232).

FUJAIRAH CITY
Royal Beach Hotel ££££
A hotel with a beautiful sandy beach, 7km/4mi south of Dibba. Diving lessons and trips to Musandam and other locations on offer (▶p.237).

OMAN
Six Senses Hideaway Zighy Bay ££££
This luxury hotel lies north of Dibba in a wide bay, two hours' drive from the airport. Some of the villas have direct access to the sea. A wide range of water sports activities and excursions available. Excellent cuisine (▶p.143).

Golden Tulip Resort £££
Al-Khasab
Set a little higher up from the sea, the hotel has lovely views. No beach. Diving trips, dhow tours and excursions into the mountains all on offer (▶p.143).

RAS AL-KHAIMAH CITY
Banyan Tree Al-Wadi ££££
Asian-inspired design meets the ultimate nature experience. The luxury hotel was opened in 2010, some 20km/12.5mi south of RAK City at the heart of the Wadi Khadiya nature reserve which covers 100 hectares/247 acres. Here and in the hotel's beach club villas half an hour away from the main site, guests can enjoy the best of both worlds, the desert and the sea (▶p.75, 250).

SHARJAH
Radisson £££
Guests staying at this hotel on the Corniche can look forward to a variety of restaurants, private beach and numerous water sports activities (▶p.264).

KHOR FAKKAN
Oceanic Hotel £££
Shaped like a star, this comfortable hotel with a beautiful beach and a long list of water sports activities, including the hotel's own diving station (▶p.280).

Children in Dubai

Lots of Variety

Camel rides, ocean and sandy beaches, desert expeditions, numerous amusement parks on a par with anything found in the USA – there is no shortage of activities for the younger ones.

Kids are curious to see the desert. Tours give them the opportunity to see camels, climb sand dunes and experience the thrill of a wild desert expedition in an off-road vehicle. They will be similarly delighted by the three gigantic water parks in Dubai and Abu Dhabi, which are sure to keep them entertained all day long. Parents might find them rather daunting, but the vast shopping malls feature amusement arcades with hypermodern computer games and cutting-edge simulators. In Sharjah, the Desert Park and the wonderfully designed zoo in Al-Ain will not only delight children, but also introduce them to animals they have never seen before. It is well worth paying a visit to Dubai Museum, where life-size puppets offer a playful insight into how people lived centuries ago.

Curiosity and the kids

Dubai's »Kids go for Free« is a summer campaign geared towards families. Children up to twelve years of age accompanied by two parents paying the full rate can sleep and eat for free in more than 80 hotels until the end of September. Plane tickets are cheaper at this time and admission to many attractions is free.

Kid-friendly prices

The Top Attractions (a selection)

Wild Wadi
Jumeirah Beach Road, Dubai
Daily, Nov–Feb 10am–6pm,
March–May, Sept, Oct until 7pm,
June–Aug until 8pm,
tel. 04 348 44 44, www.wildwadi.
com, admission: 275 Dh, children
(up to 110cm/3ft 7in) 215 Dh
Styled like a desert village, the
park alongside the Burj Al Arab
will delight parents as well as their
offspring. Water slides run
through wadis or drop down artificial hills (particularly busy at
weekends).

Aquaventure
Crescent Road, The Palm
Jumeirah, Dubai
Daily 10am–7pm, tel. 04 426 00
00, www.atlantisthepalm.com;
admission 250 Dh, children (up to
120cm/3ft 11 in) 205 Dh
Centrepiece of the Aquaventure
complex is the 30m/98ft »Ziggurat« pyramid with seven water sli-

Fun at Aquaventure, the water park at the Atlantis Hotel, Dubai

Meeting maritime neighbours at the Atlantis Hotel, Dubai

des emerging from the structure, one of which passes through a shark tank. Hotel Atlantis guests may use the water park and the well-groomed beach at their leisure, free of charge.

Yas Waterworld
Yas Island, Abu Dhabi
Tel. 02 414 20 00
www.yaswaterworld.com
Daily 10am–7pm; admission 240 Dh, children (up to 110cm/3ft 7in) 195 Dh
Waterslides for children, youngsters and adults, learn how to stand or lie on a surfboard; various expensive shops and cafés.

Iceland Water Park
Al Hamra, Ras al Khaimah
Tel. 07 206 78 88
www.icelandwaterpark.com
Daily 10am–7pm; Fri 8pm–midnight Ladies Night; admission 150 Dh, children (up to 120cm/3ft 11 in) 100 Dh
The park (less architecturally spectacular than Dubai's water parks) is worth a visit when in the area and the kids would like to cool down and have some fun at the same time.

Sharjah Discovery Centre
Al-Dhaid Road km 15 (9mi)
4th Interchange (opposite the

airport), Sharjah
Tel. 06 558 65 77
www.sharjahmuseums.ae
Sun–Thu 8am–2pm, Fri and Sat
4pm–8pm; admission 10 Dh,
children (up to age 17) 5 Dh
A paradise for kids who are interested in technology and like to
try out experiments.

Sharjah Desert Park

Al-Dhaid Road (E88), 8th Interchange, 28km/17mi east of the
centre of Sharjah, tel. 06 531 19
99
Daily except Tue, 9am–5.30pm, Fri
from 2pm, Sat from 11am; admission 15 Dh, children (aged 12-16)
5 Dh
As well as the numerous enclosures (Arabian Wildlife Centre) where
animals from the Arabian Peninsula, Africa and Asia live, there are
also excellent exhibitions, a petting
zoo (Children's Farm), a natural
history museum, aquarium and
café on site. The cafeteria comes
complete with views of camels and
other four-legged friends.

Dubai Aquarium & Underwater Zoo

Dubai Mall, Financial Centre Road,
off Sheikh Zayed Road, 1st Inter-
change, Dubai
Metro: Dubai Mall
Tel. 04 448 52 00
www.thedubaiaquarium.com
Sun–Wed 10am–10pm, Thu to
Sat until midnight; admission 70
Dh, children (aged 3 to 12) 55 Dh
In typical Dubai style, a fascinating
underwater world is presented to
visitors here: this gigantic aquari-
um spans different levels of the
Dubai Mall.

Mantras glide gracefully through
the water, whole armies of seahorses swim alongside parrotfish.

Ski Dubai

Mall of the Emirates, Sheikh Zayed
Road, 4th Interchange
Metro: Mall of the Emirates
Tel. 04 409 40 90
www.theplaymania.com
Sun–Wed 10am–11pm, Thu
10am–midnight, Fri 9am–midnight, Sat 9am–11pm
Admission: 200 Dh, children (up
to the age of 12) 170 Dh for 2
hours, each additional hour 50
Dh, day pass 300 Dh, children 275
Dh
Anoraks and ski pants are available for hire. Take the lift up to the
ski slope or make a snowman,
drink a hot chocolate. If it gets
too warm in the desert, this is the
perfect place for some recreational pleasure.

Kidzania

Dubai Mall, Level 2, Financial
Centre Road, off Sheikh Zayed
Road, 1st Interchange
Metro: Dubai Mall
Tel. 04 448 52 22
www.kidzania.ae,
Sun–Wed 9am–9pm, Thu until
11pm, Fri, Sat 10am–11pm, admission 95 Dh, children (aged 4
to 16) 140 Dh, 2–3 years of age
95 Dh
Fly an aeroplane, direct traffic:
here, kids can do what they enjoy
most: dress up as doctors, pilots,
salespeople or fire chiefs and experience the world of adults as
they play.

A Day at Ferrari World

200,000 square metres/49 acres of flame red pavilion roof emblazoned with the Ferrari logo span portions of Yas Island. Here at Ferrari World, fathers are more than happy to share in the kids' activities as they make their way through Abu Dhabi's biggest leisure park.

Opened in 2010 on Yas Island, one of the largest natural islands of the Emirate, the theme park is devoted to the legendary race car and its Italian homeland.

Attractions

Ferrari World offers visitors a whole range of attractions for all ages, guaranteed to raise adrenalin levels. Opened to an international fanfare, the Formula Rossa ride, for example, is acclaimed as the »world's fastest rollercoaster«. Sixteen passengers takes their seats in a single vehicle which looks like an over-sized race car. Accelerating from 0 to 217kmh/135mph in 2.5 seconds, the adventure lasts a mere minute and a half, which is nevetheless time enough to set knees wobbling and stomachs churning.

Centrepiece of the park is the »G-Force« free fall tower, which pierces the tent root to reach up to a height of 62m/203ft. Original Ferrari seats inside a glass cabin catapult guests to the top through the pavilion roof to give them magnificent views of the island and ocean before hurtling back down to the ground.

The Fiorano GT Challenge roller-coaster simulates a race between two Ferrari F 430 Spider replicas on parallel tracks – another ride which lasts 90 seconds, enough to get a real feel for extreme braking manoeuvres and subsequent acceleration.

Younger children will be attracted to the »Junior Grand Prix« where little Ferraris drive around at up to 6kmh/4mph. Kids are first given instruction and they can earn a Ferrari driving licence on completion. There is a also a traditional carousel, but with futuristic racing cars instead of wooden horses and carriages. 3D simulations will transport children and their parents to unknown worlds, whilst simulators offer the chance to put one's racing driver skills to the test.

Italian restaurants, pizzerias and café-bars offer a full array of refreshments. In contrast to Maranello, Ferrari's home in Emilia-Romagna, close to the city of Modena, there is every chance of securing a table at »Mamma Rossella« without having to reserve in advance. Michael Schuhmacher was not the only diner to say »Mamma« to Rosella Paolucci, owner of the original restaurant which is such a legend in Maranello, graced by Ferrari glitterati tucking into lasagne and tagliatelli.

Abu Dhabi, Yas Island, daily 11am–8pm, www.ferrariworldabudhabi.com, admission 240 Dh, children (up to 130cm/4ft 3in) 195 Dh, premium ticket for fast-track access to attractions 440 Dh / 365 Dh.

Ferrari World on Yas Island, Abu Dhabi, a vision in red

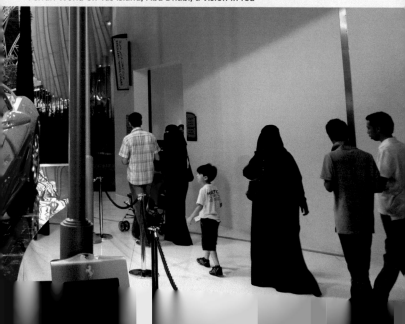

Festivals, Holidays and Events

Calendar of Events

Camel racing, Dubai shopping, pop concerts, golf tournaments with rich prizes and Formula 1 races – action all year round, particularly in Dubai and Abu Dhabi.

Dozens of events have been developed in recent years and decades, complementing traditional Arab festivals which date back centuries, along with Islamic holidays.

Colourful calendar of events

Most important to the local population is Eid al-Fitr, immediately after the four weeks of Ramadan. The end of the fast is celebrated throughout the Arabian Peninsula with great pomp. Families exchange presents. Hotels and restaurants are fully booked, whilst countless musical and cultural events are held at this time. Shops promote special Eid al-Fitr offers and hotels often advertize discounted package deals for the festive period.

The Dubai World Cup, an annual fixture since 1996, is famous the world over. Staged in March, it boasts the most generous prize money of any horse race, a princely US $10 million.
The ruler of Dubai, Sheikh Mohammed Bin-Rashid al-Maktoum, is always on the scene. He owns some of the most expensive thoroughbreds and his horses have won the Dubai World Cup on more than one occasion.

Most of the events and holidays in the United Arab Emirates are based on the lunar Islamic calendar; only a few holidays are based on the Gregorian calendar. The Islamic year is approximately eleven days shorter than the solar year of the Gregorian calendar. Islamic calculation of time begins in the year AD 622, called Hijra, on 15 July 622, the day Mohammed left Mecca; therefore, the year 2017 is the year 1438/1439 AH according to the Islamic calendar (Anno Hijra).

Islamic Holidays

Easter, Christmas, New Year and other expatriate events and holidays – from St Patrick's Day for the Irish to Thanksgiving for the US Americans – are celebrated at the larger hotels.

Expatriate holidays

For more information on events and the bigger hotels' entertainment programmes, take a look at the monthly publications »What's On«, »Time Out Abu Dhabi« and »Time Out Dubai«.

Programme of events

Two Arab football fans before kick-off

Off to the Camel Races!

The ruler of Abu Dhabi and owner of a racing camel worth in excess of one million US dollars watches the race without batting an eyelid.

Euphoria is not in evidence, but he seems pleased enough that his steed has come in first. The final of the 8km/5mi event may only take 12 minutes, but the Grand Prix of Al-Wathba is the most important race on the UAE calendar.

Camel Racing is a National Sport

Camel racing is a national sport throughout the entire Arabian Peninsula. Each Emirate has at least one or, in some cases, several camel racetracks. During the winter months, from October to March, races in the emirates are staged every Thursday and Friday (and increasingly on Saturdays). Fans come from all over to watch, causing traffic jams on highways and local roads alike.

The day begins early. Young Bedouins, Pakistanis and Bangladeshis check the animals one last time to see that the valuable creatures are in good health and fit to run. They then lead the camels to the starting line. The crowd is made up of spectators from the emirates, Saudi Arabia, Bahrian and Qatar, men in sandals, white dishdashas and colourful headdress, denoting where they come from. They take their places on striped Empire chairs in the grandstand, using their phones, discussing the prospects of race favourites, studying the programme intensely. Foreign guests will also get a sense of the tension and excitement.

The crowd grows more animated as the race begins. Fully-grown camels can reach speeds of 60kmh/37mph or more. Some owners rev up their heavy all-terrain vehicles and drive along the adjacent track, twice the width of the racing strip, keeping pace with their animals. It is too much for them to sit still and wait, they need to get as close as possible to the action and spur their camels on. Material gains are not so important in camel racing – betting is frowned upon in Islamic tradition – but honour and glory are paramount. Rathar than money, certain important races may offer prizes to the winning camel owner such as a luxury limousine or villa.

From Child Jockeys to Robots

How much, or how little, the jockey weighs can be a crucial factor in winning or losing. Hence children were often commandeered in days gone by. A law was passed in 2005 to ban child jockeys. Mounting international pressure and intervention by human rights organizations did much to stigmatize exploitative practices in Arab countries. Children as young as five or six years of age had actually been purchased from parents in Sri Lanka or Bangladesh.

Thousands of children were returned to their homes in a repatriation campaign, where they would receive psychological support and a school education. The enforcement of the ban can, in all likelihood, be traced back to an invention: jockeys no longer strike their camels with a whip, instead little robots in human form are deployed. Regulations are ignored less and less, but in the course of their research, human rights organizations happened upon ten year old children still being coerced into participating in camel races in the UAE.

In Dubai, the Nad al-Sheba track on the edge of the city has been replaced by the Al-Marmoun Camel Race Track, Al-Marmoun, Al Ain Road (E66), 40km/25mi east of Dubai (turn right after The Sevens rugby complex and Esso petrol station). In Abu Dhabi the Al-Wathba Camel Racetrack is 45km/28mi east of the capital on the Al Ain Truck Road.

The camels enter the arena in Al-Marmoun, Dubai

Holidays and Festivals (a selection)

ISLAMIC HOLIDAYS
Weekly day of rest
Friday is the official weekly day of rest. On this day, banks, government offices and most businesses are closed; believers meet at the mosques for noon prayer. Weekends in the UAE – in contrast to the rest of the Arab world – extend to Fridays and Saturdays.

Eid al-Adha
The end of the ten-day Haj period, when Muslim believers embark on their pilgrimage (Haj) to Mecca, is celebrated with the three-day sacrificial feast of Eid al-Adha. A ram is slaughtered by many families to mark the occasion (dates: 31 August – 2 September 2017, 21 – 23 August 2018, 11 – 13 August 2019).

Eid al-Fitr
Immediately after Ramadan, the end of the fast is celebrated with three days of opulent meals and the exchange of gifts. Restaurants stage themed evenings and erect party tents, children are dressed up in their finest clothes and everybody is out and about. The importance of the feast is often compared to the Christian holiday of Christmas (dates: 25 – 27 June 2017, 15 – 17 June 2018, 5 – 7 June 2019).

Ramadan
In the holy month of Ramadan, Muslims commemorate the religious revelations of the prophet Mohammed. They do not eat, drink or smoke from sunrise to sunset. Non-Muslims are also expected to forego these pleasures in public. Many businesses and museums have shorter opening hours; restaurants do not open until after sunset (dates: 27 May – 25 June 2017, 27 May – 24 June 2018, 6 May – 5 June 2019).

NATIONAL HOLIDAYS
6 August
Accession Day: the day on which the first president of the UAE, Sheikh Zayed Bin-Sultan al-Nayan, took office (1972)

2 December
National Day: the day the seven emirates joined together (1971); on this day, a rich programme of cultural events can be enjoyed throughout the UAE.

SPORTING EVENTS
Dubai Desert Classic
This high-class golf tournament takes place annually at the end of January/beginning of February (www.dubaidesertclassic.com).

Dubai World Cup
Ten million US dollars in prize money make this the richest horse race in the world. Staged in March of each year (www.dubaiworldcup.com).

Camel races
Camel races take place during the winter months, from November to March, every Thursday and Friday and now more often on Saturdays. Begins at 7am, even on the national holiday (2 Dec).

Eid al-Fitr: women celebrate the breaking of the fast

Horse races

Horse races offering large prizes are organized in Dubai under the patronage of the ruling family, whose members themselves own many race horses. Six race meetings are staged each week between November and April, starting at 7pm.

EVENTS
Theatres and concerts

The theatre and concert scenes are not so highly developed in the UAE; the focus is more on sun, fun and shopping. There is a small theatre with 442 seats in Madinat Jumeirah (Dubai) near the Burj Al Arab (tel. 04 366 65 46, www.madinattheatre.com). The Dubai Community Theatre & Arts Centre, run by expatriates, hosts art exhibitions and performances (Mall of the Emirates, Level 2, Al-Barsha, tel. 04 341 47 77, www-ductac.org).

Dubai Air Show

The annual Dubai Air Show (www.dubaiairshow.aero) is a magnet for exhibitors and spectators from all over the world. This is reflected by the gigantic new exhibition arena of the Dubai World Central Aerotropolis.

King of the Desert

The Arabian thoroughbred, the oldest pure-bred horse in the world, embodies power, stamina, beauty and physical perfection, coupled with nigh indestructible health. Horse races in the emirates provide an opportunity to admire these magnificent specimens in action.

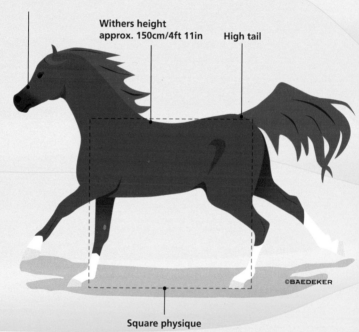

Small head, broad forehead, deep-set eyes, concave »dished head«.

Withers height approx. 150cm/4ft 11in

High tail

©BAEDEKER

Square physique

▶ **Millionaire in two minutes**
The **Dubai World Cup** is the most valuable horse race in the world in terms of prize money. It is staged by the Dubai Racing Club every year in March. The winner can look forward to collecting $10 million.

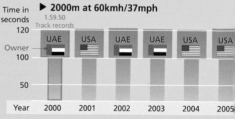

▶ **2000m at 60kmh/37mph**

Time in seconds
1.59.50
Track records

	2000	2001	2002	2003	2004	2005
Owner	UAE	USA	UAE	UAE	USA	USA

120
100
50
Year

Arabian breeds

Asil Arabian
A thoroughbred Arabian whose lineage can be raced back to the Arab horses bred by Bedouins on the Arabian Peninsula. The original, authentic Arabian.

Pure-bred Arabian
The pure-bred Arabian has, as the description suggests, no foreign, crossbred blood whatsoever. German breeders add the ox suffix to its name.

Arab
Arab horses are labelled thus to distinguish them from actual thoroughbreds on the one hand and the Shagya or Anglo-Arabs on the other, that is they are neither pure-bred, nor half-bloods.

Shagya Arabian
The Shagya Arabian's origins go back to the k.u.k. monarchy, pure-bred for over 200 years. It is recognized as a distinct breeding type amongst Arabian horses and is generally stronger than a thoroughbred Arabian, with greater bone strength and calibre.

Anglo Arab
The Anglo-Arab comes from France and is a crossbreed between an Arabian and English thoroughbred. These horses must have at least 25% Arabian ancestry in the fourth generation.

▶ **Emirates Racing Authority race tracks**

Meydan (Dubai)

Start | Finish
Dubai World Cup

Jebel Ali

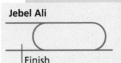

Finish

Sharjah

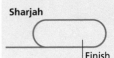

Finish

Abu Dhabi | Finish

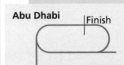

Starting postions vary according to length of the race

UAE	UAE	USA	USA	BRA	JPN	UAE	USA	UAE	IRL	USA
2006	2007	2008	2009	2010	2011	2012	2013	2014	2015	2016

A Real Pleasure …

Whether eating out or at home, food is one of the great pleasures of the Emirates, as is acknowledged in the Qur'an. Locals delight in copious buffets with a rich array of meat, fish and vegetable dishes. Hospitality in the Gulf region is legendary, guests are invariably offered more food than they could possibly eat. In contrast to Europe, it is not the done thing to clear one's plate entirely. Leaving a last morsel confirms sends the message to the host that one's hunger is satisfied.

Arabs are not vegetarian, as a rule. The Qur'an forbids the eating of meat from animals which have died naturally. Muslims are not allowed to ingest blood, hence animals are ritually slaughtered. Pork is prohibited by religious law. Chicken and lamb are the most commonly consumed meats in the UAE, beef to a lesser extent. Camel dishes continue to enjoy popularity among the local population, but are seldom seen on restaurant menus. Exotic fish dishes are for more likely to be found. *Arab cuisine*

Bedouin Dinners often provide the perfect finale to an extensive desert safari in the UAE. Diners sit on rugs and cushions, as tradition dictates. The main course consists of meat cooked in spicy vegetable sauces, crispy meat skewers, hot flatbread fresh from stone ovens, a vast spread of tomato and cucumber salads, lentil and bean dishes, spicy yoghurt sauce and vegtables pickled in vinegar.

The waters of the Arabian Gulf boast an abundance of fish and shellfish. The number one fish found on every menu in the UAE is hammour, a type of perch which is usually steamed and prepared in a tomato sauce. Guests who prefer to use cutlery will be glad to learn that it is readily available: the days when everyone helped themselves from a common platter using their fingers are largely consigned to the past. Nevertheless, only the right hand is used for eating since the left is regarded as unclean, and the flatbread used to scoop up rice, fish or meat serves as »disposable cutlery«.

Lunch and dinner traditionally begin with a selection of cold appetizers, known as mezze and bookended with sumptuous, sugary-sweet desserts. These are often enriched with rosewater, honey, pistachios and little pieces of dates. Delicious puddings prepared with coconut milk and cream are inevitably rich in calories. However, the classic dessert still consists of dates, which are served pitted and filled with almonds, marzipan or chocolate. *Starters and desserts*

Coffee prepared the traditional way – a national drink in the UAE

Ethnic variety and prices
In all likelihood, nowhere else in the world can lay claim to such a wide variety of ethnic restaurants as Dubai and the Emirates. Expatriates from over 100 different countries have not only proved a source of manpower, they also brought their culinary traditions to the Gulf and soon began opening their own restaurants. In addition to the variations on Arab cuisine, there are also Indian, Thai, Chinese, Philippine, Pakistani, Afghan, Russian, German, French, Italian, Polynesian and Mongolian restaurants.

Indian and Pakistani establishments are among the cheaper places to eat, predominantly frequented by Asian expatriates and their families. It is worth checking out restaurants which may look rather nondescript on the outside – the reward is consistently delicious food, fresh and authentically prepared. Thanks to rigorous inspections, hygiene standards are excellent across the UAE, even in the smallest, most basic restaurants.

The bigger and more expensive the hotel, the wider the variety of cuisine on offer tends to be. Five star hotels are likely to have not only Arab restaurants, but also Chinese, Japanese or European (French or Italian), as well as locales famed for fish or seafood specialities and cafés based on European coffeehouse culture. There are also bistros, open around the clock, serving American-style snacks.

> **MARCO POLO TIP**
>
> ! *Dinner Cruises* **Insider Tip**
>
> Dinner Cruises in Dubai are a special experience. Seated on the top deck of a traditional dhow gliding across the Creek, diners look out onto the beautifully illuminated night-time metropolis which provides the perfect backdrop to their meal. Such dhows can be found at Quay 1, Dhow Wharfage (tel. 04 280 78 60, www.creekcruises.com), on the bank of the Creek on the Deira side between the Radisson Blu and the Sheraton, on the Bur Dubai bank before Bastakiya and in the Al-Boom Tourist Village (tel. 04 324 14 44, www.alboom.ae).

Food courts
The shopping mall food courts present an alternative to restaurants. Generally found on the uppermost level, these self-service outlets offer Arab and Asian dishes, as well as burgers, pizza, pasta, salads and baguettes. They are usually very busy around lunchtime, but a full meal can be found for around 15 Dirham, typically served on plastic plates.

Dining culture
Guests are served before the host. Few words are exchanged during the meal itself. Having eaten, diners go into an adjacent room for coffee. When drinking coffee, the following rules apply: refusing a cup of coffee is an insult to the host. If you do not indicate that you have had enough after the first cup, it will be refilled a second and third time. Coffee is served in small cups without handles, only filled to one-third.

Nightlife outside of the hotels is scarce, which accounts for the popularity of theme nights organized several times a week in many hotels, attracting locals as well as tourists. Themed buffets – for example »Seafood Night« or »Italian Night« – are accompanied by a musical or cultural programme.

Theme nights

Arab breakfasts are very rich. Locals like to eat houmous, a chick pea puree dressed with sesame oil and some garlic, ragouts cooked with white beans, tomatoes, and meat, with flatbread and tea. Tourist hotels serve conventional breakfast buffets, but houmous and bean dishes are also available.

Breakfast

At noon, hotels provide sumptuous lunch buffets: appetizers consisting of tomatoes, cucumbers, fennel and spicy salads are followed by meat and fish dishes as the main course. A large selection of vegetables, potato dishes and rice round out the meal. A certain amount of restraint is advised when it comes to the desserts: mousse au chocolat, Italian panna cotta, crème caramel and delicious sorbet, accompanied by fresh fruit and a full complement of Arab sweets: puff pastries dripping with honey and filled with pistachios and walnuts, as well as candied figs and oranges.

Lunch buffets

Counting the calories is not the done thing here

Five Typical Dishes

Here are a few dishes you should definitely try in the United Arab Emirates

Houmous, a chick pea puree, is an inimitable speciality, rich in calories. Traditionally, chick peas are soaked in salt water overnight, then cooked in fresh water the following day, first boiled and then simmered until they are soft. The resulting mash is added to a mixer with finely chopped garlic, lemon juice, salt and sesame oil. Once smooth, it is served on flat plates.

Moutabel is a thick **aubergine mash**, originally from Syria. It is prepared by baking aubergines in the oven until they are completely soft and their flesh can easily be scooped out of the skin. The creamy mash is made by mixing the aubergine pulp with garlic, sesame oil and whole milk yoghurt, sometimes with crushed chili pods stirred in. Usually served in Dubai with pomegranate seeds on the plate.

Nobody is really counting, but it still common knowledge in the emirates today that a woman can only marry when she has mastered at least 50 aubergine recipes.

Shawarma is the Arabian answer to American fast food. Sold for just a few Dirham at street stalls, but also listed on the menu of luxury hotels, this is the region's favourite snack. Crispy flatbread is filled with slices of chicken, veal or lamb from a revolving spit, coated in yoghurt sauce and served with tomato and onion. The peerless taste is down to the marinade which always contains garlic, vinegar, chili and cardamom.

Umm Ali is the favourite dessert of Dubai and the Emirates. »Ali's Mother« is a sweet pudding served fresh from the oven, made from white bread, milk, sugar, rosewater, nutmeg and ground almonds, the Arabic version of English bread pudding. Umm Ali is often seen amongst the desserts offered in hotels – if so, do not delay, or it will soon be gone!

Ful medames, fava beans in spicy tomato sauce with onions, chili pepper and a variety of spices is a popular breakfast dish, but is also often found on the table at lunch or dinner. Originating in Egypt, it has appeared in records since the fourth century. Traditionally served with small, round beans, it is cooked at a low temperature in an open pot.

Spice Culture

This delicious aroma which makes Arab cuisine so distinctive, an irresistibly fragrant blend of cumin, coriander, fennel seeds, garlic and cinnamon, lending dishes their special character.

Arab cuisine without spices would be like a sky without stars, a meadow without flowers, so they say. Indeed, spices are the very essence of Arab cuisine. The Spice Souk, where cinnamon and cardamom are sold straight from open jute sacks, entices with delectable aromas and a veritable wealth of colours and forms: ground chili peppers and pods light up in signal reds and deep greens, tamarind powder shines in golden yellow, there are black cumin seeds and cardamom pods in light green and ochre. Baharat, a blend of spices, is available in the souks of Dubai and the other emirates, but most people in the UAE prefer to mix their own favourites. Dried lime is a popular flavouring agent, used whole or in powdered form.

Sesame seeds occupy an important place in culinary tradition. They are used in making oils and pastes or added, roasted, to garnish dishes. Meat and fish are popularly marinated in a mix of spices and yoghurt sauces for many hours, which not only ensures a delightfully spicy flavour, but also helps to keep the meat tender. Further characteristics of Arab spice culture are the subtle combination of sour and sweet, as well as the intense use of spices in virtually all foodstuffs, bread included. Cardamom pods are served in coffee. Nutmeg, cloves and lavender add a fragrant note to tea. Local women brew delicious spice tea which they even drink in summer months, made from milk, cardamom, saffron, cinnamon and black tea.

In addition to the spices commonly known in the West, there are many which are more or less exclusive to the region: sumac for example, is gleaned from the crushed seeds of the Rhus chinensis plant. Its sweet, tangy flavour is used to spice up lentil and poultry dishes or, mixed with thyme, is added to flatbread dough during the baking process. Kamoun is the Arabic word for cumin (Cumincum cyminum), an indispensable accompaniment to virtually every dish.

The seeds are the most commonly used part of the plant which grows in North Africa and India. Their strong flavour is both spicy and bitter, with an aromatic, exotic scent. Pimento (Pimenta officinalis), known in Dubai as bohar, is afforded similar status in Arab countries to pepper in Europe. The small dried berries of the pimento tree which is cultivated in India and Central America are used to spice up meat and vegetables. Their taste is a mixture of pepper and cloves.

Tahina is a thick, oily cream, a by-product of sesame oil production used throughout the Middle East and North Africa. Mixed with finely chopped garlic, it is used as seasoning for fish and meat dishes.

Spices are a distinctive feature of Arab cuisine.

Cinnamon (Cinnamomum zeylanicum), known as kirfa, is used far more widely in Arab countries than in Europe, where it is associated primarily with Christmas baking. Sprinkled sparingly, it adds a spicy, sweet touch to lamb and vegetables. It also goes well together with other spices such as pepper, pimento and garlic.

As noted in the Bible and the Qur'an, it was the legendary Queen of Sheba who travelled to Jerusalem in the 10th century, laden with precious stones and spices to pay her respects to King Solomon. At that time, spices were as valuable as gold and jewels. To own them was a sign of great wealth. Thanks to her commercial connections to Asia, the people of Arabia were able to savour exotic spices long before their European counterparts. The veritable monopoly which developed is now long gone, but a predilection for liberal use of spices in Arab cuisine remains.

RECOMMENDED RESTAURANTS – A SELECTION

The following suggestions are designed to whet the reader's appetite. More detailed descriptions can be found in the Sights from A to Z section under the corresponding headings.

PRICE CATEGORIES
££££ = over £25
£££ = £15 – £25
££ = £10 – £15
£ = up to 10 £

A stroll past the cafés and restaurants of Dubai Marina

ABU DHABI CITY
Al-Dhafra £££
Dinner cruise with fish and steak specialities: board a dhow for a journey down the Corniche with a view of the skyline (▶p.153).

Chinoy Haven Chinese Restaurant ££
Delicious Chinese fare such as stir-fried vegetable and meat dishes with ginger and garlic, or hot and spicy soups (▶p.156).

LIWA OASES
Suhail ££££
High quality Arab and international food, matched by a superb view over the desert and wadi from the roof garden (▶p.179).

AJMAN CITY
India House ££
Vegetarian food, such as exotic vegetables from the tandoori oven (▶p.186).

DUBAI CITY
At.mosphere ££££
The highest restaurant in the world in the Burj Khalifa. Prices are similarly lofty – Arabic and international dishes are on offer, but the absolute highlight is the spectacular view (▶p.200).

Bayt al Wakeel ££
This trading house, built in 1935, stands directly on the creek. Arabic and Western cuisine can be savoured here whilst watching boats sail to and fro on Dubai's inlet (▶p.200).

Spectacular view from a height of 442m/1450ft in the rarified At.mosphere of Dubai

Food Court £
A food court as a recommendation? Perfectly reasonable in Dubai. Enjoy Arabic specialties whilst looking down from the balcony at the hustle and bustle on the creek (▶p.200).

FUJAIRAH CITY
Breeze £££
Beach restaurant belonging to the Hilton Fujairah, a stone's throw from the Indian Ocean. Fresh fish a speciality (▶p.237).

SHARJAH CITY
Caesar's Palace ££
www.marbellaresort.com
Elegant restaurant with lovely views of the lagoon, serving international cuisine, in particular Italian specialities (▶p.264).

KHOR FAKKAN
Taj Kohrfakkan £
Best spot on the ocean promenade. This Indian restaurant is open for lunch and dinner. The fish and prawn curries are absolutely delicious (▶p.280).

Sharjah nightlife with the 60m/200ft Eye of the Emirates big wheel

Evening
dinner

Dinner at the hotels is usually celebrated as an event of extraordinary beauty; in some cases, served outdoors by candlelight. Guests help themselves from the buffet, attractively presented with tropical flowers and fine table linens, or they make their selection à la carte. If hotel management has organized an accompanying musical programme, dinner can extend from sunset until midnight. In the most exclusive hotels, food meets the highest culinary standards; however, it is also very good in mid-range establishments.

Fruit and
vegetables

Fruit and vegetables are integral to Arab cuisine. The most popular vegetables include cucumber, green beans, eggplant, white turnip, carrots, chard, fennel, cauliflower and chick peas, either cooked, steamed or pickled in a vinegar marinade. Grilled and roasted meat dishes are traditionally served in a sauce with vegetables. In Arab culture, eggplant has long been given almost magical importance.

Spices

MARCO POLO Insight p.98

DRINKS

Alcohol

Alcohol is forbidden to a large extent throughout the UAE, although it is open to debate whether or not the Qur'an actually proscribes alcohol altogether. What is clear, however, is that drinking sessions and drunkenness are taboo. As tourist numbers have increased, hotels and restaurants catering primarily to non-Muslim guests have been granted alcohol licences. Beer, wine and other drinks can be ordered in all of the emirates today, with the exception of Sharjah. Supermarkets cannot and will not sell alcohol drinks. It remains an offence to consume alcohol in public, for example on the beach.

Alcoholic
drinks

Bars and clubs in luxury hotels serve all the finest and suitably expensive drinks. The menu of the Skyview Bar of the Burj Al Arab promises not only exclusive long drinks, champagne and 25 year-old Cachaça, but also boasted the »most expensive cocktail in the world« until it sadly sold out. The 55 year-old Scottish malt whisky was enriched with gold leaf. All is not lost, however, as the malt in question, Macallan, can be sampled for 14,500 Dirham, roughly 3000 Euro.

Non-alcoholic
beverages

The most common beverage is mineral water, bottled in the Emirates of Fujairah and Ras al-Khaimah and served with every meal. For more demanding clientele who expect to find European water on the table, French and Italian imports are also available. Fresh juice made from tropical fruits and vegetables (mango, orange, papaya, pomegranate) can be found on every menu. Often run by Asian expatriates, the little juice bars located in souks and Dubai metro stations also serve milkshakes, fruit shakes, energy drinks and fresh fruits to eat as well as regular juice.

Alongside tea, the national Arab drink is coffee. It is served in small cups or glasses without handles, both before and after meals, when meeting with friends or indeed on any occasion. Across the UAE today, especially in Dubai and Abu Dhabi, there are cafés serving Italian style specialities such as cappuccino and latte macchiato. Nevertheless, the traditional way to make coffee has survived over centuries. Finely ground coffee is heated with water and sugar in a copper pot, then poured into the cup in such a way that the grounds remain in the pot. Coffee is usually just spiced with cardamom. Tea is very sweet. Indian tearooms and small restaurants serve chai with hot milk, cinnamon and other spices.

Coffee and tea

Try a Kiwi Cooler, a popular drink in Dubai with kiwi juice, lemon, elderflower, crushed ice and fresh peppermint. A mocktail, so to speak. Non-alcoholic beverages are quite the fashion in Dubai and Abu Dhabi, prepared with fresh juices and syrups, spiced with ginger and cardamom, resulting in deliciously exotic creations. Every restaurant, every bar creates its own blends, some even have a special mocktail menu. The mocktail culture is especially celebrated in luxury hotels, who go so far as to publish mocktail recipe books. The most appealing mocktails are the ones with clearly defined layers of colour: thick strawberry puree at the bottom of the glass, for example, lighter mango and orange juice on top. Saudi Champagne is a classic, a mix of apple juice, sugar syrup and tonic water with fresh mint leaves.

Mocktails and more

Shopping

Shoppers' Paradise

In the Emirate of Dubai, consumerism is afforded lofty status. So deeply is it ingrained in public life, that the very name of Dubai is sometimes understood as an example of nominative determinism – do buy.

Indeed, buying and selling, the very essence of trade, are traditional activities for the people of Dubai, exercised with a passion for centuries. In former times, pearls and gold were traded and sold in Asian countries, promoting the first era of wealth in the Gulf region. In the souks as well, centres of social life and much more than mere shopping arcades, trade was brisk and animated at all hours. Folk congregated in the labyrinth of narrow, shadowy alleyways to exchange news and, of course, to do business. Shops here are usually just single units, rows and rows of them squashed together, many in a single alley purveying similar goods to their neighbours. Where the customer ultimately chooses to make his purchase is hard to predict, the game of life unfolds as only it can. The shopkeepers take it in their stride.

Due to the low levels of customs duty and no great levying of taxes, many international brand name items – especially clothing, electronics and cosmetics – are often significantly less expensive than in Europe. In addition, beautiful handicrafts can be found in the United Arab Emirates, though these usually come from neighbouring countries. **Shoppers' paradise**

Shops are usually open Sat–Thu 8am–1pm and 4pm–8pm, souks often stay open until 10pm. **Opening times**

The Gold Souk is still very much a centre of trade in Dubai. Around 300 jewellers can be found in the covered streets of the City of Gold, part of the larger Deira Souk which stretches along the creek from Nasser Square to Al-Khor Street. The biggest gold souk in the Emirates continues to attract tourists, but is only of secondary importance as an actual place to shop. Gold here is designed to cater primarily to Arab and Asian tastes, the chains and bracelets on offer tend to be too filigree, too skittish for European customers. **Souks**
In Abu Dhabi and Sharjah, souks and shopping complexes have dedicated departments for gold jewellery.
When the aromas of cinnamon and cardamom, cumin and frankincense (▶MARCO POLO Insight p.98) waft through the air, the spice

The design of the Ibn Battuta Mall is inspired by the voyages described in the journals of the famous 14th-century seafarer

? *The Best Shopping Locations*

- Abu Dhabi Mall: elegant stores, cafés and restaurants
- Kinokuniya Book World in the Dubai Mall: the largest book-shop in the UAE
- Blue Souk: the top floor of the Sharjah Souk offers the most beautiful antiques and old handicrafts
- Majlis Gallery: Dubai's number 1 store for handicrafts
- Bur Juman Centre: the most exclusive of Dubai's many shopping malls, with boutiques on four levels
- Souk at Central Market: a new souk at Abu Dhabi's World Trade Center attracts visitors thanks to its unique architectural design (Foster & Partners).

souk cannot be far away. Traders sell their wares directly from open jute sacks. Nuts, pistachios and spices are complemented by scented oils and resins, cloths from India and the Far East, plastic toys and decorative cosmetics.

The UAE has a vast array of shopping malls, also known as commercial centres, based on their American counterparts. Air-conditioned shopping complexes rising up several levels are often exercises in architectural grandeur. Everything from supermarkets to Armani boutiques, American cosmetics to French lace underwear can be found here, all the most famous brands from the West and food courts hosting self-service restaurants, usually located centrally.

Duty free   The duty free sections at the airports of Abu Dhabi, Dubai and Sharjah present an astounding wealth of goods, sometimes with attractively discounted prices also available to transit passengers on their way to or from the Far East. The duty free area at Dubai Airport really is a shoppers' paradise on account of the huge range of products. Before and after flights, customers can wander through 15,000 sq m/160,000 sq ft of retail space stocked with quality goods at reasonable prices.

Antiques   Most of the antiques offered for sale in the United Arab Emirates come from foreign countries, usually Iran, Syria and India. Items genuinely crafted in the UAE are very rare, whereas imports from Oman and Yemen are commonly found.
Old wooden chests called sanduks are beautifully carved and decorated.

Bedouin   Most of the silver, wood and leather Bedouin jewellery offered in the
jewellery   UAE comes from Oman and Yemen. The best selection and prices can thus be found in Buraimi (Oman) near Al Ain.

Books   English-language books, mainly about the UAE, and illustrated volumes are available in shopping mall bookstores and Family Bookshops.

Many stores in the United Arab Emirates offer (illegal) knockoffs and forgeries of designer goods and brand-name products – watches, jewellery, bags and clothing – with logos and tags mimicking the originals. In Dubai there is an entire shopping district, the Karama Bazaar, of shops offering imitation designer items (Gucci, Dolce & Gabbana, Prada, Calvin Klein, DKNY) for a song. If you are in the market for a Cartier, Rolex or Breitling watch for 25 £ upwards, you will probably have to ask the storekeeper and will then find yourself ushered into a back room. Importing such forgeries into the EU is prohibited, however.

Designer imitations

Curved Arab daggers are available in every conceivable variation, from plastic imitations to silver works of art. Most of them are produced in Yemen and Oman, where they are called either janbiya or khanjar.

Curved Arab daggers

An Arab coffee pot (dallah) made of sheet metal or steel with the typical beak-shaped spout makes a charming souvenir that is available everywhere.

Coffee pots

Most crockery in the UAE comes from Ras al-Khaimah, where it is still made from local clay and fired in traditional kilns.

Ceramics

Sharjah in particular is home to a lively arts scene that promotes local artists; it is centred around the Sharjah Arts Area with the Sharjah Arts Museum and galleries.

Arts and crafts

Traditional silver jewellery is imported from Yemen and Oman and is therefore more expensive than in the originating countries. Silver from the Maria-Theresia thaler, which reached Yemen as payment for coffee in the 18th and 19th centuries, was melted down to create finely engraved silver jewellery. Incense (luban) and other tree resins as well as bokhur mainly come from Oman, but are also prepared in the UAE. Incense burners for resin or pot-pourri are called mubkhar and can be found in antique and art shops. Dates and oriental spices make tasty souvenirs.

Souvenirs

Countless shops in Dubai, Abu Dhabi, Al Ain and Sharjah sell rugs and fabrics, most of which are brought in from Iran, Pakistan and Central Asia. All souks have a section dedicated to oriental and Asian spices, sold from bulk bags or pre-packaged at excellent prices. The best selection can be found at the Iranian Market near the port of Abu Dhabi.

Rugs and fabrics

Consumer Frenzy Deluxe

Shopping malls are the »cathedrals of modern leisure society« and have replaced classic tourist sites in foreign lands, as sociologists have observed. Visitors to Dubai are on a mission to shop at the world-famous shopping centres where designer labels wait to be snapped up at bargain prices.

At the Aquarium

Some of Dubai's shopping malls are not immediately recognizable as such. Take the Dubai Aquarium, which extends over two levels of thick glass walls. Divers swim among the giant rays, sharks and other sea creatures, controlling the feeding stations and cleaning the underwater paradise. The Dubai Aquarium (according to Dubai, the largest in the world) does not belong to a zoo but is part of the Dubai Mall, which was the world's largest shopping mall when it was opened. Designed to impress, striking works of art adorn the avenues of the vast, 220,000 sqm/ 263,000 sq yd complex. Shopping has become an end in itself as 1200 stores entice all those who enter with a sophisticated strategy of persuasion.

»Potemkin Palaces«

The eyes of 21st-century shopping nomads will light up when they enter the »Mall of the Emirates«. Its distinguishing feature is the gigantic »Ski Dubai« indoor ski arena. Several cafés and the adjacent Kempinski Hotel (in Alpine style, naturally) make it possible to drink a hot cocoa and look through windows into the winter wonderland, whilst temperatures outside pass the 40 degrees mark. There are more than 450 shops, including the Emporio Armani Boutique and neighbouring Armani Café with exclusively Italian staff, a popular rendezvous for Dubai's fashion conscious trendsetters. It is also worth paying a visit to the upper class British store Harvey Nichols, where elite British brands and deluxe fragrances much loved by the Queen are on display. Everything expensive and extravagant can be found here.

In addition to the Dubai Mall and the Mall of the Emirates, Dubai has dozens more shopping malls, all several storeys high, styled in glass, granite and chrome. These extremely undercooled consumer temples gather together hundreds of boutiques and branches of French, British or American luxury stores. Simulacra of Florentine Renaissance palaces, Venetian canals and bridges, copies of historic fountains grace the Mercato Mall, where 120 shops sit beneath an enormous glass dome.

Another noteworthy example is the Ibn Battuta Mall, named after the 14th-century Arabian seafarer (Famous people), its design inspired by the notes he made on his historic voyages. Visitors thus pass through patios resembling medieval Andalusia, sit in cafés watched over by an Egyptian sphinx or ad-

Mall of the Emirates: almost 500 stores, 70 cafés and restaurants

mire facades in the style of Chinese and Persian palaces, surrounded by Indian Mughal structures.

The luxurious Wafi Mall, meanwhile, resonates with contemporary flair, its spectacular pyramid architecture shining in glass and chrome. Outside, replicas of Egyptian statues catch the eye, while atria and colonnades dominate the opulent interior. As well as hosting over 300 stores, many designer boutiques among them, the Wafi Center is also known for the exquisite Cleopatra's Spa on the upper level and a traditionally styled souk (Khan Murjan) on the lower level. For the addresses of all the malls mentioned above, plus further details, see p.198.

Dubai Shopping Festival

»Unwrap the exceptional« and »Fabulous malls, fabulous savings« give a clear indication of what the Dubai Shopping Festival is all about. Famous brands at the lowest prices anywhere in the world is the raison d'être of the DSF, an event known by the locals as Layali Dubai.

First staged in 1996, the shopping festival has proved a resounding success, becoming one of the busiest events on the calendar. Timing undoubtedly has much to do with the numbers it attracts: the annual event takes place at the height of the season in January/February when hotel occupancy exceeds 90%.It also coincides with prestigious tournaments such as the PGA Golf Dubai Desert Classic and the Dubai World Cup, the world's most expensive horse race, which attract visitors to the Emirate from all over the world. Seasonal sales, offering discounts of up to 60 per cent, ensure that demand is high in all stores, from small Indian textile purveyors of saris and cloth by the metre to electronics stores packed with televisions and cameras, all the way to designer boutiques where the latest Prada range can be picked up at reduced prices. In the souks, water pipes are sold for half price, there are two for one offers on cuddly camels and price tags on Gucci watches drop.

The Only Way is Up

The DSF, as the spectacle is known to insiders, attracts over 3.5 million visitors per year, twice as many as in its inaugural year. Over the past few years, cash registers rang to the tune of 2 billion Euros over a four week period, an astronomical sum which is sure to rise even higher in the future. VIsitors from Europe and Asia, Australia and the USA pour into the hotels, along with tourists from the richest regions of the Gulf. In recent years, tour operators have begun organizing short trips to the DSF at competitive prices, combining an attractive shopping experience with perfect weather in the winter months.

There is more to the festival than four weeks of shopping for bargains, however. The real magnet is a comprehensive programme of cultural events, amusements and entertainment. Dubai locals and expatriates alike love the daily raffles with top prizes, either as cash or expensive gifts. At no other time of year can such an unparalleled cast of international top stars be seen on stage in Dubai, as a wonderfully diverse series of concerts features everything from classical music and opera to Hollywood variety and Irish song. Exclusive fashion designers also parade their creations on the catwalk. The »One world. One family. One festival« slogan underlines the multicultural, family-friendly nature of this huge event. Large numbers of families head straight for the »Global Village« (part of Dubailand): some 50 countries are represented in this cultural amusement park with pavilions and miniature versions of their most famous national

Shopping festival street performance

landmarks. Al fresco restaurants serve culinary specialties from the respective countries, stalls sell typical handicrafts from the regions. All the fun of the fair is here, with rollercoasters, dodgems and a ferris wheel. Live shows are staged in a 6,000 capacity amphitheatre. The festival's immense popularity owes much to its propensity to cater to guests on different budgets. Those less keen on shopping can enjoy a range of free events, details of which are listed in the DSF Official Guide. At the Dubai Heritage and Diving Village on the creek, for example, traditional Arabic dishes are prepared, street artists perform in the shopping malls, concerts are staged in parks and gardens, tea and dates are served. Younger visitors will be thrilled to see the likes of Pharrell Williams and N.E.R.D.

Dubai Summer Surprises

Dubai Summer Surprises represent a ten week-long counterpart to the winter shopping festival. Shops again offer discounts between June and August, enhanced by a wide variety of accompanying events. Fresh surprises are announced each week, including firework displays, a Chinese circus and pyrotechnics.

Due to the almost unbearable heat which descends on the UAE in summer, participation is perhaps slightly less fun than might be anticipated. Air-conditioned rooms are undoubtedly more appealing at this time of year in Dubai.

Sport and Outdoors

No Time to Get Bored

Camel races, ice skating, golf and diving, polo and car racing – the sporting spectrum of the UAE could scarcely be more colourful.

Even ski fans will find their wishes granted in the desert Emirate of Dubai. Between October and April – thereafter it is simply too hot – a jaunt across the sand dunes on mono-skis is all the rage. »Sand boarding« involves careering down the dunes, some as high as 150m/492ft, on skis or snowboards. There are no ski lifts – at least not yet – so the ascent is negotiated by jeep. In summer, when temperatures are too extreme, the Ski Dubai indoor arena provides an appropriately alpine alternative. Artificial snow guarantees a wintry atmosphere all year round.

Dubai and the other emirates can fulfil every promise of a relaxing holiday on the beach when winter takes hold in Europe. Swimming, sailing, waterskiing or surfing – Dubai above all is a luxurious oasis for holidaymakers who enjoy the good life. The country has miles and miles of fine sandy beaches, especially well maintained in the vicinity of the four and five-star hotels. Natural vegation is scarce on the beach, but palm trees and similar tropical greenery adorn the hotel complexes. City hotels often have their own beach clubs with sun loungers, parasols, toilets and cafés. Non-residents can purchase day passes to gain admittance to hotel beach clubs in Dubai; alternatively, the Jumeirah Beach Park (Jumeirah Road, daily 8am–11pm, Mondays women and children only, admission 5 Dh) with 700m/2297ft of private beach, restaurants, cafés, volleyball courts and barbecue areas. In some spots, however, camel droppings can be a nuisance, whilst the roar of jet skis can be equally irksome to swimmers or anyone seeking peace and quiet. In Abu Dhabi City, the western half of the Corniche is a white sandy beach with all the requisite tourist infrastructure. In the west, on the Arabian Gulf, most beaches are wide and blessed with fine sand. They slope gently down towards the sea, making them ideal for children. The beaches of the east coast, in Khor Fakkan and Fujairah, for instance, are not so wide and are sometimes stony. Underwater life here is hugely popular with divers. Water sports facilities and other activities vary from hotel to hotel. Surfboards and catamarans may be available for hire and lessons offered on how to use them. The more adventurous might wish to take to the skies by parachute, to-

Relaxing beach holidays

Skating on sand in the desert, an alternative to snow

Dubai's Wild Water Parks

Take a deep breath, close your eyes, cross your arms across your chest, then lie back and hurtle down at 80kmh/50mph to the depths at the foot of the Burj Al Arab, level with the gigantic ocean wave facade of the Jumeirah Beach Hotel which reaches up from the coast to the sky.

Wild Wadi

Jumeirah Sceirah is a spectacular water slide which drops 33m/108ft at speeds approaching free fall. The park's design is both striking and elegant, with unusual and spectacular attractions to thrill visitors of all ages. Imagine a Walt Disney park with the flair of Aladdin's Lamp: dizzyingly tall water slides are mounted on mighty stone blocks, waterfalls cascade down imaginatively crafted ravines. The charming view from the park is no less memorable: the ocean shimmers in shades of turquoise blue, dotted with palms in the foreground and yachts on the water.   In spite of its size, the park is easily navigable. It is divided into different sections, with two dozen water slides of all shapes and sizes at its centre. One quirky ride promise a guaranteed fun factor: a »Family Ride« in oversized yellow rubber tyres, big enough for several people at once, uses water pressure to shoots passengers up the slide. As the name suggests, the »Breaker's Bay« pool features tremendous artificial waves.

Avoid visiting Wild Wadi after Ramadan, as the water park is usually full to bursting at this time. July and August are also best avoided, when temperatures considerably higher than 40° render any outdoor activity a strenous undertaking (further information p.217).

Aquaventure

Exciting as it is, Wild Wadi is topped by Aquaventure, the water park at the Atlantis Hotel (details, ▶p.222). The location alone, at the apex of the Palm Jumeirah, is unique. This unrivalled waterworld was developed at enormous expense as part of the spectacular themed Atlantis hotel resort (whose guests enjoy free admission to the water park).

Centrepiece of the Aquaventure complex is the 30m/98ft »Ziggurat« step pyramid , starting point for seven wild and wonderful water slides. The »Shark Attack« slide is truly remarkable in that it descends from a height of 13m/42ft into a shark tank – no need to worry, the ride passes through a glass tunnel, so it is not as dangerous as it sounds. The »Leap of Faith« slide, meanwhile, sets the pulse racing with a drop of 27m/88ft. As in Wild Wadi, almost all of the attractions here are interconnected: visitors can sail on air cushions along two kilometres/over a mile of white water rapids and gentle streams which wind their way through the park's 17 hectares/42 acres. Conveyor belts catapult guests up

Lots for the little ones to do: the Aquaventure park at the Atlantis Hotel in Dubai

to the slides and back to the start again.

If this sounds like a maritime nirvana, then Dolphin Bay brings matters back down to earth with a resounding thud. Here, two dozen South Seas dolphins are confined to a pool which they can cross with just a few flicks of their fins. They are expected to jump through hoops and kiss their trainer. Neither this ordeal nor the »swimming with dolphins« attraction should be supported. Aquaventure states that it donates a portion of its income to an organization which strives to maintain maritime ecosystems – perhaps this is an attempt to redress the balance.

Golf on the Gulf

Colin Montgomerie, Ernie Els, Tiger Woods and their colleagues at the top of the world golf rankings have clearly demonstrated that golfing conditions could not be better in Dubai.

Paradise for Golfers

Fantastic golf courses in a region dominated by desert, this is a contradiction which has long since been overcome in Dubai. International golf architects have designed the courses and desalination plants ensure that irrigation is not a problem. Armies of gardners and helpers keep the manicured greens pristine. Still, the Emirates Golf Club was quite a sensation when it was opened in 1988, the first grass golf course on the Arabian Peninsula to host championships. Interest in what had previously been a little known sport also burgeoned among the local population when the Dubai Desert Classic became a permanent fixture on the PGA calendar in 1989. It is the only tournament on the PGA European Tour to take place on the Arabian Peninsula.

Today, Dubai has secured its status as a golfer's paradise. In the near future, Dubai will be able to boast a dozen world-class golf courses, exotic verdant oases with luxurious clubhouses and splendid restaurants. Special offers on green fees can be found in the summer months, when golfers relish swinging their irons under floodlights late into the night. Guests are welcome in all clubs, equipment can be hired. Men require a handicap under 28, woman a maximum of 36. Dubai Golf takes bookings for all clubs (www.dubaigolf.com, tel. 04 380 12 34).

The Most Beautiful Golf Course

Dubai Creek Golf & Yacht Club (Garhoud, tel. 04 295 60 00, www.dubaigolf.com, green fees from 500 Dh) is said to be Dubai's most beautiful course. Situated on the Deira bank of the creek, the 18-hole, par 72 championship course is also the most famous course in Dubai, with fascinating views across the creek (particularly from the 17th and 18th holes). The club has four restaurants, including the Boardwalk with a popular terrace and the Aquarium, an exquisite fish restaurant. The club house, right on the edge of the creek, is an architectural highlight, shaped like the sails of an Arabian dhow. For those who would like to stay close by, the Park Hyatt is a luxurious option between the greens and the water.

Emirates Golf Club

Visible from afar, the defining feature of the Emirates Golf Club is the clubhouse, six impressive structures of concrete and glass, designed in the style of Bedouin tents. Next to the 18-hole Majlis course, Dubai's oldest, lies the Faldo, designed by golfing legend Nick Faldo and characterized by a wadi which

The clubhouse of the Dubai Creek Golf & Yacht Club

meanders through the 18-hole course.

The Badia

The Badia (Dubai Festival City, Al-Badia, www.albadiagolfclub.ae, green fee from 395 Dh) is an 18-hole course designed by Robert Trent Jones Jr. Numerous waterways thread their way through the course which combines challenging tee shots with Dubai skyline panoramas, plus wellness facilities in the clubhouse.

The Els Golf Club

The Els Golf Club (Dubai Sports City, tel. 04 425 10 10, www.els-clubdubai.com, green fee 795 Dh, »twilight specials« from 295 Dh) is conveniently situated on Emirates Road in Dubai Sports City. This is Dubai's classiest course: South African Ernie Els has designed the championship layout with dazzling white sand bunkers, lush Bermuda grass and incorporating the adja-cent desert dunes into the lands-cape. The club also runs the highly acclaimed Butch Harmon School of Golf.

Nad al-Sheba Golf Club

Characterized by deep bunkers and double greens, the 18 holes of Nad al-Sheba's par 71 course (Nad al-Sheba, southeast of the centre, tel. 04 336 36 66, www.dubaigolf.info/nadalsheba, green fee 22 Dh) are famous for being the chosen playground of the famous – a veritable high society course. Its fame is also due to the fact that the world's richest horse race is staged here. The 6861m/7503 yard-long course was designed by star architect Karl Litten who drew inspiration from Scottish links courses. When it gets too hot during the day, golfers meet after sundown instead. Playing under the floodlights which line the entire course is a different experience altogether.

wed along by boat. Thanks to perennially warm waters, divers and snorklers will enjoy ideal conditions, notably off the east coast in the Emirate of Fujairah and in Khor Fakkan, an exclave of the Sharjah Emirate.

Camel and horse races

The most popular pursuit for many local men and expatriates from Asia is a trip to the camel racing track (►MARCO POLO Insight p.118). Horse racing enjoys an equally rich tradition, yet in contrast to camel races, the equestrian variety constitutes a society event with the ruling family often in attendance.

Polo tournaments are no less glamorous, as can be witnessed at the Ghantoot Racing and Polo Club (www.grpc.ae), one of the world's most prestigious clubs, located between Dubai and Abu Dhabi.

BIRDWATCHING

Mainly in early spring and autumn, the estuaries and lagoons of the Emirates of Dubai, Sharjah, Ajman, Ras al-Khaimah as well as the mangrove swamps of Umm al-Quwain make ideal places for birdwatching. Tours are organized by the Birds Records Committee in Dubai (www.uaebirding.com).

DESERT DRIVING

By car through the desert

Self-organized desert tours are always something of a risk. Be sure never to drive off-road in a car without four-wheel drive capability. Even in an all-terrain vehicle, the chances of getting stuck in the soft sand are relatively high. The general rule is: the darker the ground, the firmer the surface. For those who choose to leave the tarmac roads, it is important to remember to let some air out of the tyres: on hard, rocky ground the tyre pressure should be around 75% of the recommended air pressure, in soft desert sand a maximum of 50%, so that tyre have better grip. Driving with decreased tyre pressure, however, requires great caution. Always take to the road with at least two fully fuelled vehicles. Essential equipment includes a spare fuel canister, water supply, a spare tyre, a tow rope, tools, a plank to jack the vehicle, sand shovels and a large piece of sheet metal to put under the wheels if the car gets stuck in the sand. To prevent the car from overturning, sand dunes should be approached straight on, not diagonally.

Plenty of tour operators offer »desert driving courses«. An all-day course costs between 250– 300 Dirham.

Sports Addresses

ICE SKATING RINKS
Abu Dhabi Ice Rink
Zayed Sports City
Airport Road
Abu Dhabi
Tel. 02 403 43 33
www.zsc.ae
Daily 10am–10pm
Admission: incl. skate hire 40 Dh

Dubai Ice Rink
Dubai Mall, Metro: Dubai Mall
Tel. 04 448 51 11
www.dubaiicerink.com
8am–4.30pm, Sun from 10am
Admission 55 Dh (2 hrs)

FITNESS CENTRES
Al-Nasr Fitness Centre
Al-Nasr Leisureland
Umm Hureir, Bur Dubai
Dubai, Metro: Oud Metha
Tel. 04 337 12 34
www.alnasrll.com
Daily 9am–10pm
Large amusement park with nu-
merous sports facilities, including
squash, bowling, go-karts and ice
skating rink.

Flamingo Beach Resort
UAQ Tourist Club
Umm al-Quwain
Tel. 06 765 00 00
www.flamingoresort.ae
Leisure centre and water sports
club

GOLF
Dubai Golf Office
Tel. 04 380 12 34
www.dubaigolf.com
Central booking service for Dubai
golf courses

Emirates Golf Club
MARCO POLO Insight p.116

Dubai Creek Golf & Yacht Club
MARCO POLO Insight p.116

Abu Dhabi Airport Golf Club (Al Ghazal Golf Club)
Channel Road
(beyond the new airport on the
road to the suburb of Umm Al-
Nar)
Abu Dhabi
Tel. 02 575 80 40
www.alghazalgolf.ae
The 18-hole course, which comprises 125ha/300 acres, is irrigated underground by an artificial
lake of desalinated seawater.

HORSE RIDING
Abu Dhabi Equestrian Club
Saeed Bin-Thanoun Street
Mushrif, Abu Dhabi
Tel. 02 445 55 00
www.adec-web.com
90 school and rental horses, from
70 Dh per hour.

Dubai Polo & Equestrian Club
Emirates Road
Arabian Ranches, Dubai
Tel. 04 361 81 11
www.poloclubdubai.com
Private horse riding lessons for
250 Dh per hour.

Sharjah Equestrian & Racing Club
Al Dhaid Road
Interchange 6, Al Atain, Sharjah
Tel. 06 531 11 88

Underwater paradise Musandam

www.serc.ae
The club operates a riding school and a race track.

SAND SKIING

Sand dune skiing is becoming increasingly popular. Many travel agencies in the UAE organize tours and rent out equipment.

Arabian Adventures
Emirates Holiday Building (1st floor)
Sheikh Zayed Road, Dubai
Metro: Business Bay
Tel. 04 303 48 88
www.arabian-adventures.com

DEEP-SEA ANGLING

Several charter firms operate tours for deep-sea angling. The alternative is to hire a boat and organize one's own expedition. Ocean Adventures in Sharjah rents out a 12m/40ft boat for up to six persons for angling trips (half-day 1830 Dh, full day 2750 Dh) as far as the east coast and Oman.
Ocean Adventures
Marbella Resort
Buheira Corniche, Sharjah
Tel. 06 568 08 86
www.oceanadventuresuae.com

SAILING

In Dubai the following hotels have their own sailing boats and offer sailing lessons: the Jebel Ali, Hilton, Jumeirah Beach, Meridien, Oasis, Royal Mirage and Dubai Marine.

DIVING

The sandy, shallow west coast of the UAE is unsuitable for diving, whereas the east coast has a wealth of underwater flora and fauna to offer. Its offshore reefs and rocky islands are understandably popular among the diving community. Expeditions to the spectacular scenery of the Musandam Peninsula, which belongs to Oman, come highly recommended. UAE diving centres offer diving trips and courses.

Emirates Diving Association

P.O. Bix 33220
Diving Village
Shindagha Area
Bur Dubai, Dubai
Tel. 04 393 93 90
www.emiratesdiving.com
The Diving Association provides information on diving in the UAE.

Sandy Beach Diving Centre

Sandy Beach Motel
Dibba – Khor Fakkan Highway
Dubai
Tel. 09 244 55 55
www.sandybm.com
The diving centre is on the beach of Al Aqqa, halfway between Dibba and Khor Fakkan. It runs courses for PADI qualifications.

AL-BOOM DIVING

Dubai, Al-Wasl Road, close to the Iranian Hospital
Tel. 04 342 29 93
www.alboomdiving.com
This Dubai diving school offers PADI instruction and organizes trips to the east coast and Musandam Peninsula.

WATER PARKS

MARCO POLO Insight p.114

Dreamland Aqua Park

Umm al-Quwain
Tel. 06 768 18 88
www.dreamlanduae.com
Sun–Thu 10am–6pm, Fri and Sat until 7pm, (Fri, Sat for families only)
Admission: 135 Dh, children 85 Dh
The water park lies 14km/9mi north of the UAQ Roundabout on the road to Ras al-Khaimah.

WATER SKIING / WINDSURFING

Most of the larger beach hotels offer their guests the chance to go water skiing or windsurfing.

TOURS

You have not yet decided where to go? Our tour suggestions help you – tips for the best routes an suggestions for the best accommodation.

Travelling in the United Arab Emirates

The Emirates have plenty to offer besides beaches and shopping malls. It is therefore highly recommended to venture outside the tourist centres of Dubai, Sharjah and Abu Dhabi and take a closer look at the many beautiful features of this country. Al Ain and Muscat can be reached by bus, the northern emirates by collective taxi. All other destinations can be visited in the ubiquitous organized tours. Renting a car is the easiest option – the streets are safe and in excellent condition.

Tour 1　**Dubai by Metro**
A fully automated ride, four metres / thirteen feet high above the streets of Dubai
▶page 128

ARABIAN
GULF

** Abu Dhabi

Tarif

National
Auto Museum

TOUR 3

Medinat
Zayed

Bu Sahan

Oases of Liwa

©BAEDEKER

Mezirah

* Oases of Liwa

Hamim

SAUDI　ARABIA

Tour 2 Dubai to Al Ain

Palm trees, bougainvilleas, golden-red desert sand and grazing camels along the desert highways to Al Ain. The date palms and clay houses are characteristic of the Buraimi oasis in Oman.

▶page 130

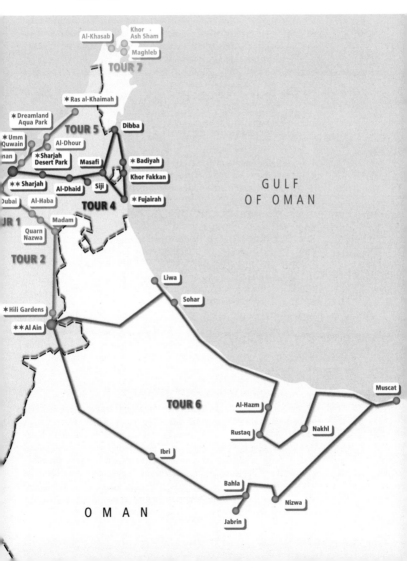

Through Deserts, Wadis and Mountains

Preperations for your trip

Within the space of just a few years, Dubai has become a synonym for luxury vacations. The region is unrivalled among medium- distance destinations: Sunshine almost around the clock, well-kept beaches, and a tourist infrastructure that amazes even spoiled jet setters. For a long weekend or the two-week family vacation – Dubai and the Emirates are ideal travel destinations for the **winter months**: exotic, free of health risks, and almost one hundred percent safe. The beach hotels along Jumeirah Beach and the elegant city hotels are ideal starting points for an eventful stay. And all types of water sports are offered, from jet skiing to diving courses.

Those interested in architecture can find pre-Islamic and Islamic gu-ard towers and forts, mosques from the entire Islamic era all the way to grand neo-Islamic mosques, Portuguese forts and the most modern residential and office buildings. In Dubai and Sharjah, old Souks were reconstructed in detail and historical villages and downtown areas were restored or recreated as »Heritage Villages« – outdoor museums. They offer **insight into traditional Arab life** before the oil boom and a tranquil change from the modern Emirate cities. In addition to visiting oriental bazaars and hyper-modern shopping complexes or touring the most famous construction projects currently being completed in the region, **excursions into the desert** woo the traveller. These can be easily organized on site. For example, any hotel rents off-road vehicles. The roads are in excellent condition and make travelling a real joy.

Visiting the Emirates

A **desert safari** should be part of any stay in Dubai and the Emirates. Several organizers offered them (half days approximately 250 AED). They will pick you up at your hotel in the afternoon. Soon after, the off-road vehicle leaves the pavement and drives through the desert. High sand dunes are climbed at a rapid pace. After sunset, the party reaches a » **Bedouin camp**« where a buffet is set up. After an extensive meal, various musical performances, belly dancing and camel rides, visitors are brought back to the hotel. For a really special desert experience, a multi-day stay in the **Al-Maha luxury resort** at the edge of the Hajar mountains (▶MARCO POLO Insight, page 215) is recommended. Finally, **boat tours** along the coast or in the lagoons show the country from a new, unfamiliar perspective. Whether it is a three-hour dinner cruise or full-day fishing trip, an exciting and diverting time is assured.

Desert safaris and dinner cruises

Since the distances between the seven emirates are not great and the roads are excellent, Dubai is handy as a fixed base; from there, one can undertake day trips and excursions comfortably. However, one can plan for an overnight stay on an outing to Muscat in Oman, which is the recommended option for tours of Al Ain or Liwa.

Excursions...

Public transportation is scarce, but there is a bus line from Dubai to Abu Dhabi, Al Ain and Muscat and also from Abu Dhabi to Al Ain. Fast and inexpensive shared taxis travel between the capital cities of the emirates. However, your trip will not start until the vehicle has collected its full complement of 7 or 8 passengers, and then things get very crowded. The inexpensive and numerous taxis are suitable for shorter distances in the areas around Dubai, Sharjah and Ajman. The best solution is a rental car: they are inexpensive, gas is cheap, the roads are excellent and signage is extremely good. The major rental companies are well represented, which is useful in case of an emergency, but smaller local firms also give good deals and are very helpful.

... with shared taxis and rental cars

Tour 1 ## Dubai by Metro

Length of the tour: 50km/31mi
Tour duration: 1 day, including various sightseeing points

Whether in a hire car or a taxi, driving on Dubai's roads can be a rather stressful experience due to heavy traffic and a proliferation of roadworks. The Metro, which opened in 2009, is a far more relaxing prospect.

Four metres / thirteen feet high
The Dubai Metro was designed as a sky train, running for long stretches on viaducts high above the streets of the metropolis. It is thus a great way to tour the city. Air-conditioned stations in futuristic glass and steel are equipped with small shops and refreshment stands, cash machines and toilets. Tickets can be purchased at the counter prior to boarding the Mitsubishi trains, each with five carriages. VIPs, local residents and middle class expatriates can travel Gold Class (twice the price), whilst other passengers can use the Silver Class compartments. There are also separate sections for women and children.

Start: Rashidya
The Red Line begins at ❶ **Rashidya station**, south of Dubai International Airport. Trains leave every ten minutes and it is a good idea to avoid rush hour when setting off. The next stations are Terminal 3 and Terminal 1. Not many passengers use these stations to reach the airport, as heavy luggage is not permitted on board the train. Alight at ❷ **Deira City Centre**, an older shopping mall with a fine city location. The Park Hyatt Hotel stands here like a palace overlooking the Creek. Wander through the park-like grounds to reach the yachts of the adjacent Dubai Creek Golf & Yacht Club and stop at one of the cafés for a drink at the water's edge.

Under the Creek
Return to Deira City Centre station and continue underground to Union Square - which claims to be the largest underground station

in the world. Get off at the next stop, ❸**Burjuman**, to vist the tradtional district of Bastayika and the Dubai Museum located there.

The Metro runs parallel to Sheikh Zayed Road on this stretch of the journey, affording a breathtaking view of the skyscrapers and tower blocks which line Dubai's most important thoroughfare and business zone. It is tempting to alight at the next two stations, ❹**Dubai World Trade Centre** and **Emirates Towers**. A lot of passengers leave the train when they hear ❺**Burj Khalifa** announced via the tannoy. Attractions abound at the foot of the gigantic structure in this charming district with Arabian flair, including Dubai Lake and the largest mall in the Emirate, enough to entertain visitors for hours.

Heading south now, the ride reaches the ❻**Mall of the Emirates** station, with the Ski Dubai indoor arena as its unmissable landmark. Alpine atmosphere is reflected in the design of the neighbouring Kempinski Hotel. A few stops before the Red Line comes to an end in **Jebel Ali**, there is a chance to see the ❼**Ibn Battuta Mall**, named after and inspired by the great seafarer Ibn Battuta (Famous people).

Along Sheikh Zayed Road

Passing oil fields and drilling rigs, the E 12 highway leads through sandy and scree desert terrain, arriving 46km/28.5mi later at Madinat Zayed, a Bedouin settlement with a large park founded by Sheikh Zayed.

Liwa Oases

Dubai by Metro

Tickets

A single fare without a prepaid card (standard paper ticket) costs between 4 Dh (1 zone, approx. 3km/2mi, valid for 90 minutes) and 8.50 Dh (5 zones, valid for 3 hours). Prepaid tickets (Nol Card) are better value.

The most sensible purchase is a Nol Silver Card for 16 Dh (1 day pass) which is valid for all zones and can be reloaded the following day (14 Dh). Tickets are scanned electronically at the entrance and exit.

Rides with the Nol Gold Card (business class, in a manner of speaking) cost twice as much. Children up to the age of five travel for free.

Some technical detail

Opened in 2009, the Dubai Metro became the fourth underground network in the Middle East (following Haifa in 1959, Cairo in 1987 and Tehran in 1999). The Red Line is 52km/32mi long, 4.7km/2.9mi of which run underground. Riding from one end of the line (Rashidya) to the other (Jebel Ali) takes 66 minutes. The Green Line was opened in 2011, some 24km/15mi in length. 2014 saw the Dubai Tram (p.196) begin to run along its ten kilometres/6 miles of track. Trains are driverless and run on Sat–Wed 6am–midnight, Thursday until 2am, Friday only from 10am; further information p.198 and www.rta.ae (Metro) and www.alsufouhtram.com (Dubai Tram).

Tour 2 From Dubai to Al Ain

Length of the tour: 180km/110mi
Tour duration: 1 day

The outing to the oasis settlement of Al Ain, which is part of the emirate of Abu Dhabi, leads to a wealthy city which nevertheless has a marked traditional character. The oasis also has an important cultural history: graves which are thousands of years old in Al Ain prove that the site was already inhabited around 2000 BC.

Leave ❶ ****Dubai** at its south-eastern edge between the end of the Creek and the camel racetrack of Nad Al-Shiba. From there, do not take the Al Ain Road at the Bu Kidra / Country Club Roundabout, which leads directly to Al Ain, but rather the four-lane Ras Al-Khor Road towards **Hatta**. This soon turns into Hatta Road and crosses a scenically charming area of high sand dunes with a reddish shimmer. The metropolis of Dubai keeps spreading further into the desert. Finally the last houses and settlements are left behind, and the rubble and sand desert extends to the right and left of the road. Wire-mesh fences prevent free-ranging camels from crossing the road.

After 30 km/19mi comes the settlement of ❷ **Al-Haba**. At the Haba Roundabout, the road from Dubai meets a freeway that runs from Jebel Ali to Hatta. 8km/5mi further on is the hamlet of ❸ **Quarn Nazwa** where a road crosses the Hatta Road in a north-south direction. Here, a hill looms above the red sand where the remains of shells, starfish and other sea creatures can be found, indicating that this region used to be under water.

After another 7km/4mi, the desert to both sides of the road forms hills of sand. Here there is a gap in the wire-mesh fence that protects the road against stray camels.
Those travelling with off-road vehicles usually drive to the top of one of the Hatta Road Sand Dunes, which are up to 150m/500ft high. At weekends many people can be seen gliding down the dunes by monoski ; dune bashing , i.e. tearing across the dunes in daring manoeuvres, is also popular.

15km/9mi after Qarn Nazwa, at the ❹ **Al-Madam** roundabout, exit right onto the road to Al Ain and cross the southern part of the Al-Madam plains , a flat rubble desert where several wadis of the surrounding mountains end. The rest of the route is dominated by flat

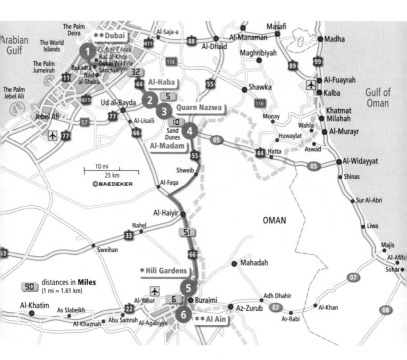

sand and rubble desert occasionally enlivened by bush. Close to Al Ain, dunes reappear to the left and right of the road; huge mountains of sand shimmer in brown and red, and are then interrupted and finally replaced by oasis fields. Date palms and vegetable fields now dominate the scenery. The approximately 200 wells and watering holes in this region form the basis for a rich agricultural community that supplies the emirate of Abu Dhabi.

The ❺***Hili Gardens** archaeological site with an approximately 4700-year-old restored circular grave is located approximately 10km/6mi before Al Ain to the east of the road. Subsequently, the road to Al Ain – called Dubai Road here – crosses part of the Oman oasis of Buraimi, before it reaches the centre of the »Garden City« of ❻**Al Ain**. The climate here is hotter than on the coast, but more bearable since the humidity is significantly lower.

While Al Ain embodies the ideal of a modern oasis, the neighbouring **Buraimi** of Oman still has traditional mud houses and date groves irrigated using the ancient system of canals (▶MARCO POLO Insight, page 228).

Tour 3 # From Abu Dhabi to the Oases of Liwa

Length of the tour: 270km/168mi   **Tour duration:** 1 – 2 days

A road trip from Abu Dhabi to the southern oases of Liwa is a trip into the past, into a time when petroleum dollars did not yet shape the appearance of towns and cities. The ancestors of today's rulers of Abu Dhabi, who founded a settlement on the coast in 1793, came from here. Although the houses of the oases of Liwa were not built until the 1970s and 1980s and are not made from mud, the atmosphere here is much less modern and western.

After leaving ❶***Abu Dhabi City** on the four-lane freeway, follow the road to the south and, at the town of **Mafraq**, exit onto the highway that runs close to the coast towards **Tarif** and **Ruwais**. The well-built road passes numerous offshore islands and oil fields, and runs through the grey salt desert of Sabkha, a barren landscape devoid of life. Shortly after the industrial settlement of ❷**Tarif**, which also has a gas station and several stores, head inland towards the oases of Liwa and Saudi Arabia .

28km/17mi after Tarif, past several oil fields and refineries, comes ❸**Habshan**, where a road branches off to the **Bu Hasa oil field**. It is another 30km/19mi to ❹**Medinat Zayed**, a Be-douin settlement with a large park founded by Sheikh Zayed . After that, the road leads straight through the sand dunes for 80km/50mi; the gantries and to-wers of the oil production facilities are part of the scenery. Finally, one reaches ❺**Mezirah**, the commercial centre of the **oases of Liwa**, 15 small towns that stretch along the edge of the Rub al-Khali , an uninhabited sand desert. They form the largest continuous oasis district of the UAE. The population mainly sustains itself through agriculture. Tomatoes, cabbage and potatoes are the main crops grown in the fields. From Mezirah, the road leads east and west. The remaining oases are strung along this approximately 50km/30mi road, which is paved initially but eventually gives way to a rubble and sand track. Golden and brownish shimmering sand dunes up to 150m/500ft high can be found between the settlements. There are reforestation projects, date palm groves and vegetable fields, all nice-ly fenced in to protect them against the ever-present hungry goats. Here and there palm-frond fences protect against sanding. Most of the houses in the settlements are recent, but there are also occasional Bedouin tent encampments.

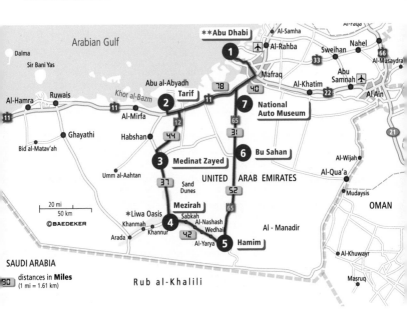

For the return journey, head south-east 64km/40mi along a four-lane road that is hilly in places, passing oases and small settlements to ❻ **Hamim**. Turn left there onto a two-lane country road (E 65) going north, straight as a die through the sandy desert. 80km/50mi further on at ❼ **Bu Sahan** there is a gas station and a café. It is a further 40km/25mi to Sheik Hamad's pyramid-shaped ❽ **National Auto Museum**. A huge model of a Land Rover stands at the front. The car museum displays more than 200 vehicles, including a gigantic copy (scale 4 : 1) of a Dodge Power from 1950, bright red, with 10ft-high wheels and weighing 50 tons. Larger-than-life caravans, giant trucks, brightly coloured luxury limousines and especially Mercedes-Benz: from the »Adenauer Mercedes« to the S-class convertible. The Rainbow Sheikh, as this member of the royal family is called, displays seven S-class limousines in seven garish colours. The car museum has only a few original vintage and classic cars; most of the ones on display are reconstructed, copies or shrill oddities. A cafeteria situated between a huge globe, unusual caravans and a water tower offers refreshment.

❶ daily 7am–5pm, free admission, www.enam.ae

From here the distance to the E 11 highway is 20km/12mi. On reaching it, drive a further 20km/12mi north-east to reach the exit for Abu Dhabi City (30km/19mi).

Tour 4 # From Sharjah to the East Coast

Length of the tour: 320km/200mi
Tour duration: 2 – 3 days

The scenic high point of this trip to the east coast of the UAE is crossing the majestic Hajar Mountains. Those who have enough time should plan for an overnight stay to explore the beauty of this still largely natural region more extensively. There are several hotels in charming locations next to the ocean, for example in Khor Fakkan , a beautiful port and Sharjah exclave on the east coast.

From ❶ ✳✳**Sharjah City** follow the freeway towards Al-Dhaid. Sharjah International Airport, which appears after only 10km/6mi, is worth a side trip. With its three domes, tower and multiple decoration, the airport building looks more like a neo-Islamic mosque then a modern functional building. The airport was built in the late 1970s, when Sharjah was the first emirate to open up to tourism . Sheikh Sultan made a significant contribution to the design; the Emir, who studied in a foreign country and has written several scientific books, is regarded as the intellectual among the government leaders of the UAE.

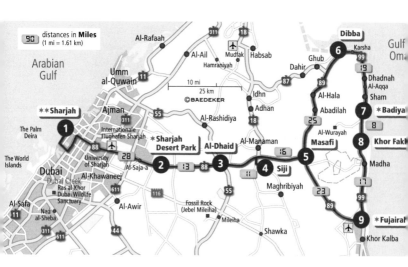

15km/9mi farther on is the ❷***Sharjah Desert Park** with a game reserve, a natural history museum and a herbarium. After another 25km/16mi through sand and rubble desert, sand dunes tower outside the agricultural town of ❸**Al-Dhaid**, a modern and economically prosperous trade centre. New, beautifully decorated residences, an elaborately constructed mosque and a modern souk bear witness to Al-Dhaid's prosperity . Shops and restaurants line the streets. Gardens with fragrant lemon and orange trees, date palms, vegetable fields and sand dunes surround the settlement. In Milheiha, 12km/7mi from here, the bare » **Fossil Rock**« rises above the desert. Here one can discover fossils that are more than 100 million years old (however, taking them away is a punishable offence!).

From Al-Dhaid, another 33km/21mi over god roads takes you to Masafi . 13km/8mi after Al-Dhaid, a road leads to the village of ❹ **Siji** next to the reservoir of the same name, surrounded by a copse of palms; it is a popular destination for an excursion, especially on weekends. Finally, after reaching the foothills of the Hajar Mountains, this tour comes to the long street village of ❺**Masafi**. Masafi is a great place to take a break and saunter through the open-air market, which is among the largest and most colourful markets in the region: farmers sell vegetables, fruit and firewood; Bedouin women squat on the ground hawking essential oils, henna powder, and woven baskets. Goats bleat loudly in the background, and potential buyers inspect carpets and pottery in a leisurely manner.

Masafi is the beginning of the most beautiful landscapes along the route – past canyons that rise steeply, appearing hostile and barren, bathed in glistening light by the sun, with wonderful vistas of green valleys lying far below. There are two alternatives: the northern mountain route that leads to Dibba and the southern route to Fujairah . The best choice is to take one road on the way there, and the other on the way back.

The northern route first passes a bottling factory for mineral water and then reaches the pass after 10km/6mi; just 30km/19mi further on, the picturesque fishing village of ❻**Dibba** lies on the Gulf of Oman at the northern end of the UAE. At the time of prophet Mohammed, Dibba was the capital of Oman . Today, the city is split into three parts that belong to Sharjah, Fujairah and Oman; however, there are no borders and the difference between the Omani part and the areas belonging to the UAE can only be recognized by the more Arabic architectural style in the Omani district.

The trip continues southward along the coastal road, passing the town of **Dhadnah**, which was designed on the drawing board with dozens of identical white row houses: public housing in modern Arabia. 15km/9mi further on is the charming fishing village of **Al-Aqqa**.

Just a few miles south of Al-Aqqa lies ❼*****Badiyah**. Two guard towers, the remains of a Portuguese fort, rise above the oldest mosque in the UAE; two nearby cemeteries date back to the period of islamization in the 7th century and the Portuguese conquest in the 16th century.

Another side trip leads to the **waterfall of Wurayah**. About 5km/3mi before Khor Fakkan , a road branches off to the only waterfall in the UAE that has water all year; it is a very popular destination for outings, as people come here to picnic and bathe in the waterfall's small basin.

Finally, one reaches the port of ❽**Khor Fakkan**, crowned by a palace on top of a hill owned by the family of the Emir of Sharjah. A tree-

Many of the residents of Fujairah emirate live from fishing; these fishermen are in Kalba

lined beachfront street, a souk modelled after the one in Sharjah, many water sports activities, and the Oceanic Hotel invite travellers to take a break.

Another 20km/12mi takes you from Khor Fakkan to ❾**Fujairah**. With its fantastic location between the Hajar Mountains and the ocean as well as its well-kept green spaces, the capital of the emirate with the same name is drawing ever more visitors. South of the city lies **Khor Kalba** with a nature reserve that extends to the border of Oman.

MARCO POLO TIP *Sandy beach* **Insider Tip**

A stopover in Al-Aqqa, 15km/9mi south of Dibba, is well worth it. The beautiful beach and alluring shimmering ocean invite you for a swim. And the sympathetic Sandy Beach Motel with its good, inexpensive terrace restaurant is ideal for taking an extended break, especially for divers (Al-Aqqa, Fujairah, tel. 09 / 2 44 55 55, www.sandybm.com).

From Dubai to Ras al-Khaimah
Tour 5

Length of the tour: 100km/60mi
Tour duration: at least 1 day

For the trip along the west coast of the UAE, a rental car is not essential. The other option is to take one of the affordable shared taxis from one emirate to the next; they wait in specified locations and do not leave until they are full. However, the tour cannot be completed in a day in this case. Not that this is recommended anyway, since there is a lot to see in the smaller emirates of Ajman , Umm al-Quwain and Ras al-Khaimah, which have remained more pristine due to their lack of oil reserves. Umm al-Quwain and Ras al-Khaimah have several hotels that are recommended for an overnight stay.

On departing from ❶**Dubai**, the richest and most modern of the seven emirates is left behind. Thanks to its industry, the only 15km/9mi distant sheikdom of Sharjah is quite wealthy and was able to extensively renovate its historic buildings. The main road between Dubai and Sharjah, the Al-Ittihad Road, turns into the Al-Wahda Road, the main commercial street of the city which runs to the south of the two lagoons. ❷**Sharjah City** has many attractions and outstanding museums – especially in the restored old quarter. Plan at least an entire day for a visit.

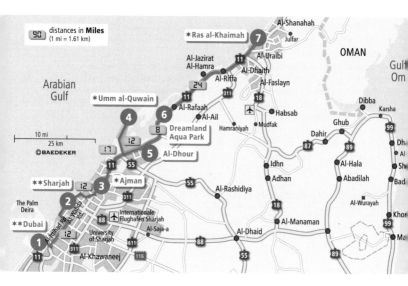

8km/5mi to the north, ❸ ***Ajman**, the capital of the smallest sheik-dom in the UAE, which bears the same name, lies on a peninsula. The commu-nity used to live from fishing and a dhow shipyard; today, industrial districts, a large shipyard and a television station have been added. The fort, erected at the end of the 18th century, protected the emirate in conjunction with the guard towers by the shore and served as the seat of the ruling family for 150 years. It has been converted into a museum and is well worth a visit.

In Ajman the transition from the wealthy emirates like Dubai and Sharjah with a large proportion of foreigners to the poorer emirates, where the locals are still in the majority, is palpable. Life is quieter here, the restaurants are simpler, the locals are more friendly and the buildings are made from coral and adobe instead of concrete and marble. Also noticeable are the forts, which are carefully restored in the northern emirates and thus probably come closer to their original appearance than the perfectly reconstructed forts in Dubai and Shar-jah, which sometimes appear sterile.

The trip north leads 30km/19mi to the emirate of ❹ ***Umm al-Quwain**. The small sheikdom with its 20km/12mi of coastline leads a traditional fishing and agricultural existence. The capital, which has the same name as the emirate, extends along a peninsula 10km/6mi long and only 1km/0.6mi wide, formed by a long estuary. The old quarter, protected by three guard towers and a fort, is located at the northern end. A museum has been established in the renovated fort.

The old port and traditional fish market – which is still very busy – are located on the east side of the old quarter. The large lagoon is ideal for a few hours of bathing.

Outside the city, two other attractions can be found: At the southern end of the peninsula, a side road leads to the ❺**Al-Dhour** archaeological site, and on the coast, about half-way to the emirate of Ras al-Khaimah, the huge ❻*****Dreamland Aqua Park** offers visitors for a day of fun splashing in water.

45km/28mi north of Umm al-Quwain, ❼*****Ras al-Khaimah** is reached. The capital city of the emirate also lies on a peninsula formed by the gulf and a lagoon. In the old quarter, which was built on the northern tip of the peninsula in the 16th century, many decayed houses are made from coral limestone using traditional construction techniques. The 19th-century fort, topped by a splendid wind tower, now houses a museum with archaeological finds, ancient documents, rare coins and a shell collection; the museum is well worth seeing. The busy fish market and the Irani souk are located nearby. A bridge leads across to the modern district of Nakheel, which extends to the foothills of the Hajar Mountains.

> **MARCO POLO TIP** !
>
> *Medieval Arabia*   Insider Tip
>
> Julfar, which used to be a booming port of trade in pre-Islamic times, is located about one kilometre/0.6mi north of Ras al-Khaimah. The »Palace of the Queen of Saba« – which was not built until the 16th century – is located a few kilometres further on at the top of a hill.

From Al Ain to Muscat in Oman
Tour 6

Length of the tour: 365km/225mi
Tour duration: At least 3 days

Up until the 1970s, a trip to Oman was a time-consuming and risky affair. Travelling from the west to the east coast meant crossing the Hajar Mountains . Fields of rubble, occasional Bedouin attacks and a lack of water during the summer months made for a difficult journey. Today, two major highways join the emirates to the east coast. It is still a route of unrivalled scenery: The jagged flanks of the Hajar Mountains gleam majestic and bleak in the sunlight; in some cases, the cliffs rise vertically next to the road, which repeatedly passes deep valleys where date palms thrive.

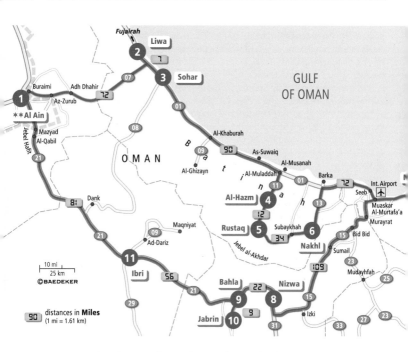

The sultanate of Oman has 500 forts and palaces, many of which have been reconstructed, restored and returned to their former glory. Life here is less hurried than in the neighbouring sheikdoms, and also more »Arab« due to the comparatively low proportion of foreigners. However **Muscat**, the capital of Oman, is a city with a surrounding »Capital Area« that resembles the metropolises of the United Arab Emirates.

From ❶**✶✶Al Ain** head to the neighbouring **Buraimi** and then follow Highway 07 via **Hail** towards Sohar . Almost 120km/75mi further on is ❷**Liwa** on the coastal road between Fujairah and Sohar; the trip continues south along this road for 10km/6mi to the port of ❸**Sohar**. This city is always associated with Sinbad the Sailor , who is said to have lived here in the 8th century. A large white fortress from the 14th century in the city centre provides a panorama view of the city and the ocean. Some of the rooms were converted into a museum about the marine history of the city. A stroll along the new corniche to the busy fish market is also enjoyable.

From Sohar, the coastal road continues through the **plains of Batinah**, a fertile area that supplies the north of Oman with fruit and vegetables. After approximately 120 km/75mi, head inland between **As-Suwaiq** and **Al-Musanah** to tour three Omani forts in the midst of beautiful oases on a 130km/80mi excursion that returns to the coastal road.

25km/16mi after leaving the coastal road, one reaches ❹ **Al-Hazm**, an impressive restored fortress with a working falaj system (►MARCO POLO Insight, page 228) as a special attraction. 20km/12mi further on, the fort of ❺ **Rustaq** towers on a hill above the old quarter. The fortress, which originated in the 7th century and goes back to the 18th century in its present form, has now been perfectly restored. The hot **spring of Ain Al-Kafsah** with its bath houses and the new mosque donated by the sultan also make a visit to this settlement at the foot of the **Jebel Akhdar** (»Green Mountain«) worthwhile. After another 55km/34mi, the monumental fortress of ❻ **Nakhl** towers on a cliff. The hot **spring of Thowarah** in the vicinity of the fort irrigates a green valley, where there are always local families out for a picnic. From drive about 30km/20mi to return to the coastal road.

Via **Barka**, the journey continues to **Seeb** where the international airport of the capital is located; the so-called Capital Area, which stretches for 45km/28mi all the way to ❼ **Muscat**, is just a short distance beyond. The old quarter of Muscat has two Portuguese forts that line a small bay with the sultan's Alam Palace. The ethnological museum of Bait Al-Zubair, with beautiful traditional crafts among other exhibits, is worth a visit. One of the most beautiful hotels on the Arabian peninsula is located south of the city: the Hotel Al-Bustan Palace.

For the return to Al Ain, an alternate route is recommended. The first stop is ❽ **Nizwa**, the former capital of Oman, 175km/110mi south of Muscat, which has a monumental fort with a tower that provides an enchanting view of the blue and gold Great Mosque. At the foot of the fort is a souk with old Omani silver decorations.
Approximately 35 km/22mi west of Nizwa lies ❾ **Bahla**, the centre of Omani pottery, with a city wall of mud bricks that is 12km/7mi long. Although the 17th-century fortress within the wall is a UNESCO World Heritage site, has been undergoing restoration for some years.

Nakhl fortress in front of an impressive backdrop in Oman

The palace of **Jabrin** located 15km/9mi from Bahla, also from the 17th century, has been extensively restored and illustrates the artistic sense of an imam who had the stately rooms exquisitely furnished and decorated.

In **Ibri**, 140km/85mi from Nizwa – the trip leads along a wadi – there is another historic fort with a souk. Al Ain is reached after another 130km/81mi.

Tour 7 To the Fjords of Musandam by boat

Tour duration: At least 1 day, longer with an overnight stay

Early morning mist lies over the ocean and up to the Hajar Mountains rising 2000 metres/6560 feet. A few lonely, old-fashioned dhows crisscross the coastal waters as they return from their nightly fishing expeditions. The Musandam Peninsula, the northernmost part of Oman, divided from the rest of the land by an 80km/50mi wide strip of the UAE, lies between the Arabian Gulf and the Gulf of Oman on the Strait of Hormuz, the only navigable route for ships seeking to enter the Arabian Gulf.

To the Fjords of Musandam by Boat

Tour operators

VIsitors touring the Osmani province of Musandam are required to carry their passports with them (including UAE visa). Tours from Dibba along Musandam's east coast – including transfers from hotels in Dubai, Sharjah, Ras al-Khaimah or Fujairah – can be booked with: Arabia Horizons in Dubai Tel. 04 294 60 60
www.arabiahorizons.com

The Osmani tour operator Khasab Travel & Tours in Khasab offers boat trips from Al-Khasab, with bus transfers from Dubai, Sharjah or Ras al-Khaimah; Dubai/Sharjah to Khasab is a three hour ride (approximately). The company can also arrange hotel accommodation in Khasab.
Khasab Travel & Tours
Al-Khasab, tel 00968 26 73 04 64
www.khasabtours.com
Dubai, tel. 04 266 99 50

WHERE TO STAY/WHERE TO EAT

Al-Khasab - Golden Tulip Resort
£££

approx. 3km/2mi outside Khasab on the road to Ras al-Khaimah *Insider Tip*
Tel. 00968 26 73 07 77
www.goldentulipkhasab.com
The hotel (60 rooms) is located slightly higher up, with lovely views down to the ocean, but no beach.
There is a large swimming pool and a restaurant. Diving expeditions, dhow trips and excursions into the mountains are on offer.

Six Senses Hideaway Zighy Bay
££££

on the east coast of Oman, north of Dibba, 120km/75mi from Dubai.
P.O. Box 212, Dibba
Tel. 00968 26 73 55 55
www.sixsenses.com
A luxury hotel in a wide bay, two hours' drive from Dubai Airport. Spacious villas reflect typical regional style with tasteful decor. Some have direct access to the ocean. Superb cuisine. Water sports activities, excursions and a spa are all available.

The landscape of the sparsely populated peninsula with bays, islands, lagoons, deep fjords (khor) and steep cliffs is something to savour, an experience which can only be gained by boat. A one day cruise usually starts early in the morning with a roughly three hour drive from the UAE, crossing the border into Oman and on to Al Khasab, the provincial capital of Musandam, in the north. This lively harbour town has an old fort which is now a museum. It is from here that the heavy wooden boats known as dhows depart and the adventure, lasting approximately six hours, can begin. Dolphins swim alongside the boats as they pass small fishing settlements. The water is clean and clear, making it easy to spot the colourful fish who live in the fjords – in sharp contrast to the ultramodern Emirate cities where the

Dramatic landscape

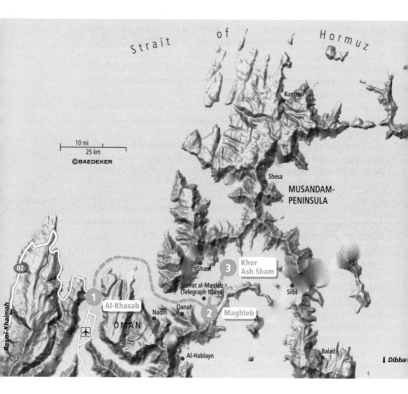

journey began. Cliffs rise up almost vertically, shining in all shades of ochre and brown in the sunlight. Boat passengers are inspired by the tranquility surrounding them.

Through the longest fjord
Maghleb is a small fishing settlement which can be seen from the boat on the offshore island of Jazirat al Maqlab, otherwise known as Telegraph Island as the British established a repeater station there in the mid-19th century.

One of the most popular fjords is Khor Ash Sham, the longest fjord of the peninsula, measuring 17km/10.5mi. Entering the fjord is a thrill in itself, as cliffs rise up sharply on either side, as if one is about to pass through the narrowest of gorges.

Going ashore
If there are plans to go ashore, the boat will drop anchor around lunchtime so that passengers can tuck into some hearty fare. Swimming and snorkelling are also possible (followed by a freshwater shower on board the dhow). Indeed, the special charm of the boat

tour is not the magnificent mountainous landscape as seen from the water, but the time spent on an actual Arab fishing vessel of yesteryear. Comfortable and luxurious it is not, but the earthy atmosphere on board a wooden dhow, clearly designed to be practical more than anything, more than makes up for it, as does the jovial nature of the captain.

In winter months, the water can be really cold and strong winds can add to the chill factor. Nevertheless, wearing the right clothing, which includes a waterproof jacket of some description, will make the trip a particularly memorable one at this time of year, rewarded with splendid impressions created by the sun and shadows, clouds and wind.

Clothing

SIGHTS FROM A TO Z

In spite of rapid development and numerous building projects the seven emirates' old Arabian districts, traditional souks and magnificent landscapes have lost none of their charm.

Abu Dhabi

ABU DHABI

Area: 67,340 sq km/26,000 sq mi
(excluding the islands)
Population: 2.6 million

Emir: Sheikh Khalifa Bin-Zayed
al-Nahyan (since 2004)

Abu Dhabi, the richest of the seven emirates, strives to step out of the shadows of Dubai and become a new tourist magnet on the Arabian Gulf. In recent years, enormous revenues from oil sales have enabled the sheikhdom to establish a modern infrastructure with towering developments and verdant boulevards. Now the capital is energetically sprucing itself up with art, music, motorsport, golf and falconry.

The Emirate of Abu Dhabi covers more than four fifths of the entire UAE. It extends over 400km/250mi from the Qatar Peninsula and the Saudi Arabian border in the west along the Arabian Gulf coastline to Dubai in the north east. The coastal region is dominated by salt flats (sabkhas). The emirate is divided into three regions: the Abu Dhabi Region, the Western Region and the Eastern Region. The majority of the population lives in the city of Abu Dhabi, which serves as the capital of the UAE, the Abu Dhabi Emirate and Abu Dhabi Region, which com-

The Gulf's wealthiest emirate

prises the island of Abu Dhabi and the mainland. The Eastern Region is blessed with extensive groundwater resources and around 200 springs, making it the sheikhdom's most fertile region. Its capital city, Al Ain, situated on the border to Oman, is home to the emirate's university. Numerous oil fields and refineries can be found in the Western Region, the largest of which is located in Ruwais. The district is administered by the city of Beda Zayed, which lies on the road from Tarif to Madinat Zayed. Most of the many offshore sand islands barely rise above the surface as shallow sand banks, but some are important sites for oil extraction, namely Das, Mubarraz, Zirku and Arzanah.

One key factor of the Emirate's economic development is diversification, i.e. the development of additional industries and sources of revenue. The government and private enterprise have been investing in the expansion of the agricultural sector and in the development of a

Traditional mode of transport in front of the Etihad Towers in Abu Dhabi, the financial powerhouse of the UAE

fishing fleet. The sheikhdom's economic focus is on trade and an efficient telecommunications network throughout the entire UAE.

Economy Diversification is a crucial element of the emirate's economic development strategy: exploiting new economic sectors to generate fresh sources of income. Both the government and private industry are investing in agricultural projects and fishing fleets. Further key areas to have been identified are trade and the establishment of an efficient telecommunications network across the UAE.

Tourism Great efforts have been made in recent times to catch up with Dubai in the tourism stakes. Historical buildings may be few and far between, but there are miles of sandy beaches, a wealth of attractive leisure pursuits and no shortage of luxurious hotels, frequented not only by holidaymakers but also business people from the Arabian Peninsula.

✴✴ Abu Dhabi City

 ✴ G 6

Population: 1.14 million

On a peninsula surrounded by the ocean, high-rise buildings glisten in the sun. Wide highways bordered with palm trees and flowers cut through the city centre, two dozen parks and gardens provide a pleasant and revitalizing contrast to dense clusters of buildings. The city of Abu Dhabi may feel like a western metropolis, but conservative tradition still prevails in the UAE capital.

The sheikhdom's eponymous capital stands on a shallow sand island connected to the mainland by three bridges and is surrounded by some 200 islands and islets. Some of them, such as Yas, Lulu and Saadiyat, have been incorporated into the development of the city. Abu Dhabi is the financial hub and administrative centre of the UAE, with aspirations to become a world-renowned cultural capital as well, stepping out of the shadow of the economic metropolis of Dubai – weakened by the global financial crisis. To this end, a new residential settlement is growing on Saadiyat, accompanied by a series of noteworthy museums. On Yas Island, visitors are encouraged to explore Yas Waterworld, »the biggest waterpark in the world«, to play on the ocean view golf course, visit Ferrari World and stay in a five-star hotel. There is also a Formula One racing circuit.

More five-star hotels line Corniche Road, boasting splendid views across the water and of the city skyline. Less expensive accommodation can be found back in the city centre.

HISTORY

Even if first impressions suggest that this is a young city, Abu Dhabi can look back on thousands of years of history. Archaeological finds confirm that the region's first settlement dates back 5,000 years. In the 1950s, Danish archaeologists discovered the ruins of a large settlement on the small island of Umm al-Nar, situated 15km/9mi south of the city centre. The people of the so-called **Umm al-Nar culture** probably lived from fishing and hunting. Based on the remains of large fish found only in the open sea, it seems likely that the inhabitants were able to build large vessels for deep sea fishing; indeed, shipbuilding appears to have been a highly advanced skill. Besides numerous fragments of foundation walls, the excavations also uncovered circular tombs which had been built as towers. These tomb towers reached heights of up to 8m/26ft with a diameter of up to 15m/49ft. Gold and silver jewellery, pearls and drinking vessels made of soft soapstone are proof of the early settlers' advanced cultural development. They are also an indication of early Arab trade. Ceramic vessels painted red and decorated with black geometrical motifs bear a striking resemblance to jars discovered in Mesopotamia, dating from the same period. Archaeologists conclude that commercial relations existed between the two areas.

First settlement

The history of Abu Dhabi's second colonization, however, began much later. The **Bedouin tribe of the Bani Yas**, to which today's ruling families of Abu Dhabi and Dubai also belong, has produced the region's most powerful families since the mid-18th century. It was largely thanks to their unity that the attacks of the orthodox Wahhabi, from what is now Saudi Arabia, could be successfully repelled. In 1761, members of the Bedouin family al-Nahyan from the Liwa Oasis found a freshwater spring on a shallow sand island on the Arabian Gulf coast and founded a settlement there. The Bedouins saw one of the many gazelles who lived on the island drinking from a water hole and named their new home Abu Dhabi, »Father of the Gazelle«. In 1793 more Nahyan family members left Liwa in 1793 to settle in both Al Ain and Abu Dhabi. Qasr Al-Hosn (fort) stands on the site of the spring today.

Second colonization in the 18th century

By the 1950s, the settlement still only consisted of the Al-Hosn Fort plus a small number of mud houses and palm huts, the population amounting to a mere 5,000. Inhabitants lived primarily from agriculture (Al Ain), fishing and pearl diving (MARCO POLO Insight p.276), although the significance of the latter faded in the 1930s with the emergence of pearl farming and artificial pearls. Abu Dhabi could only be reached on foot when the tide was out. There was no electricity and no sewage system. Illiteracy rates stood at over 70%.

Oil exploration
By the end of the 1930s, with the once thriving pearl industry now in decline, the ruler Sheikh Shakhbout granted concessions to British companies to drill for oil and produce petroleum. From 1962, the offshore and desert oil reserves of the Emirate of Abu Dhabi were tapped by foreign firms, leading to the generation of enormous wealth within the next twenty years. Abu Dhabi owns an estimated ten percent of the world's oil reserves – at an average production volume of two million barrels per day, the emirate could supply oil for another 100 years.

Rich metropolis
Abu Dhabi is one of the richest cities in the world. In 1971 it was thus named **capital of the newly created United Arab Emirates**. Magnificent buildings – many built in recent years with futuristic designs – shape the cityscape. While many buildings reflect neo-Islamic style, echoing traditional Arabic architecture with arches and turrets, little remains to suggest the origins of the old Arab settlements. The wide roads of Abu Dhabi, stretching for miles in straight lines, bear far more resemblance to cities of the western world.

Monuments and memorials
Like many countries on the Arabian Peninsula, Abu Dhabi cherishes its monuments and memorials, many of which line the Corniche or have been placed at the centre of roundabouts. Enormous coffee cups and coffee pots are symbols of Arabian hospitality. Besides representations of deer and falcons, imitations of European cultural heritage and famous sites are also popular.

Residential areas
Residential neighbourhoods extend for miles to the south and onto the mainland. Stretches of desert are forever being reclaimed and transformed into urban space. Close to the centre, a largely immigrant workforce from India and Pakistan resides in older, more basic high-rise buildings. Further out, on the fringes of the city, capacious villas sit in lush, verdant surroundings. Pedestrians are seldom seen here. As in America, everybody drives everywhere. The sidestreets of the northern centre harbour a myriad of simple restaurants run by Indians, Lebanese, Pakistanis and Chinese.

WHAT TO SEE IN ABU DHABI CITY

*Corniche
Abu Dhabi's landmark is the 7km/4mi waterfront. Bordered by two luxury hotels, the Sheraton to the east and Hilton to the west, and flanked by street lanterns shaped like traditional fortified towers, it is a popular place among citizens who meet here to take a stroll after their day's work. Colossal arches and monuments, illuminated at night in all the colours of the rainbow, the image of the late leader in the form of a mosaic – the modes of artistic expression are many and

Abu Dhabi City

INFORMATION
Abu Dhabi Tourism
Tourism Campus, Khalifa Park
Abu Dhabi, tel. 02 444 04 44
www.visitabudhabi.ae

SIGHTSEEING
A double-decker bus operated by Big Bus
Tours runs daily from 9am to 5pm to the
sights of the city. It starts every half-hour
from Marina Mall and covers 17 stops
where passengers can hop on and off,
including the Sheikh Zayed Mosque, Emirates Palace, Heritage Village and Iranian
Market. The whole tour takes 2 and a
half hours. Tickets are valid for 24 hours
(200 Dh, 100 Dh for children, 500 Dh for
families. For further information: tel. 800
24 42 87, www.bigbustours.com).
A helicopter tour over Saadiyat Island
and Yas Island, taking in Ferrari World
and the Formula 1 racetrack, the Emirates Palace hotel and Sheikh Zayed
Mosque, shows off the city's architectural wonders. 10, 20 or 30 minute trips
are available, 100–255 € per perso,
www.falconaviation.ae

SHOPPING
Gold and jewellery can be found in the
Gold Centre (alongside the Madinat
Zayed Shopping Centre) in East Road.
Modern ceramics, some with Arabic motifs and decoration, are on sale at Abu
Dhabi Pottery in the Al-Rumarthy Building (Khalidiya Park Street).
The Marina Shopping Mall on the Breakwater peninsula is chic and glamorous,
with more reasonably priced items on
the lower floor. The cafés and restaurant
terraces boast fine views of the Corniche
skyline (Sat–Wed 10am–10pm, Thu, Fri
2pm to 11pm; www.marinamall.ae).

The most traditional shopping mall is the
Abu Dhabi Mall in the Tourist Club Area
alongside the Beach Rotana Hotel. Four
levels offer (almost) all manner of consumer goods, as well as regular supermarket fare (Sat–Wed 10am–10pm, Thu until 11pm, Fri 3.30pm–11pm; www.
abudhabi-mall.com).

WHERE TO EAT
❶ *Al-Dhafra* £££   *Insider Tip*
Dhow Harbour, Al-Mina
(by the fish market)
Tel. 02 673 22 66
www.aldhafra.net
Daily 8.30pm–10.30pm
Dinner cruise with fish and steak specials
on a dhow that sails along the Corniche
with a view of the city skyline.

❷ *Cantina Laredo* ££
Khalidiyah Mall, 1st floor
King Khaid Bin Abdel Aziz Street
Tel. 02 635 48 77
Delicious guacamole followed by Mexican cuisine with a gentle nod to the
Western palate.

❸ *Café Firenze* ££
Sheikh Hamdan Bldg
Tarek Bin-Ziad Street, on the corner of
Al-Nasr Street
www.cafefirenzeua.com
Tel. 02 633 10 80
On the veranda overlooking a park and
inside the prettily decorated restaurant,
international dishes and fresh pizza are
served; try the spinach cannelloni.

❹ *Chinoy Haven Chinese* *Insider*   *Tip*
Restaurant ££
Al Ain Palace Hotel
Corniche Road East

Abu Dhabi

AR RAS AL-AKHDAR

MARINA MALL

Al-Dana Ladies' Beach

Heritage Village

Breakwater

The Breakwater

Abu Dhabi Theatre

New Presidential Diwan

Emirates Palace

Arabian G

Hilton Hotel

Corniche Road West

1st Street

High Court

Khubeirah Street

6th Street

AL-KHUBEIRAH

Children's Garden

Khalidiyah

AL-KHALIDIYAH

Zayed the

Water Tower

Khalidiyah Park

Ministries

Zayed Street

Al Khaleej Al Arabi Street

Khalid M.

AL-BATEEN

Al-Bateen Municipal Centre

Sultan Bin

Al-Manhal

Street

Khalifa Bin Shakhbut

Bus Station

Al Khaleej Al Arabi Street

Municipal Market

Banunah Street

Palace

Sultan Mosque

Bateen

Street

Khor al-Bateen

Palace

Sultan Bin Zayed Street

Al-Khaleej Al-Arabi Street

Dalma

Street

Bateen Palace

Hideriyyat

Palace

Street

Mohammed Bin-Khalifa Street

Sultan Bin- Zayed

Al-Khaleej Al-Arabi Street

Mush Pala

N

0.25 mi

©BAEDEKER

Race Tra Golf Cour

Where to eat
1. Al-Dhafra
2. Cantina Laredo
3. Café Firenze
4. Chinoy Haven
5. Havana Café
6. Abu Shakra
7. New City Palace

Lulu Island

Iranian
Souk

Mina Hurr/ Free Port

Fish
Market

Dhow Harbour

City Police
Station

CORNICHE
Corniche Road West

Formal
Park

Heritage
Park

Corniche Road West

Ittihad
Square

Mina Road (3rd Street)

Istiqlal St.

Sheikh Khalifa
Mosque

Khalid Bin-Al-Waleed St.

Sheikh Khalifa Bin-Zayed

AL-MARK

Lulu St.

Lulu Street

Al-Nasr Street

AZIYAH

Street

Umm Al-Nar St.

Saadiyat

Fort
Al-Hosn

Sheikh Hamdan Bin-Mohammed Street

Cultural
Foundation

Hazza Bin-Zayed
Mosque

t Street

Grand
Mosque

Zayed the Second Street (Electra Street)

Al-Salam Street

Etisalat

Medinat
Zayed
Shopping
Centre

MEDINAT
ZAYED

9th Street

ABU DHABI
MALL

10th Street

ANHAL

Bani Yas Street

As Suwa
Island

East Road

Sheikh Zayed Tunnel

anhal
ce

Al-Manhal Street

Al-Falah Street

Bus
Station

(9th St.)

Sudani Social and
Cultural Club

AL-TABBIYAH

East Road

AL-DHAFRAH

Sudan   Street

Al-Wahdah
Sports and
Cultural Club

Hazaa Bin-Zayed Street

AL-
WDAH

Bus
Terminal

Al-Salam Street

(11th Street)

Sheikh Rashid Bin-Saeed Al-Maktoum Street

AL-WAHDAH

Khor al-Baghal

AL-
KARAMAH

Defence   Street

MUSSALA
EL EID

Prayer
Yard

Airport Rd.

Mohammed Bin-

Khalifa Street

East Road

Khalifa Street

Eastern Ring Road

Sea Palace Road

Mushrif
Khalifa
Gardens

National
Theatre

eik Zayed Airport / Flughafen
Mosque Women's Association

Yas Island,
Khalifa Park

Sea Palace

Sea Palace

Where to stay
1 Emirates Palace
2 Jumeirah at Etihad Towers
3 St. Regis
4 Shangri-La
5 Al Ain Palace Hotel
6 Dana Hotel
7 Mina Hotel

Tel. 02 679 47 77
www.alainpalacehotel.com
The former Mandarin offers Chinese cuisine such as stir-fried vegetable and meat dishes with ginger and garlic; king prawns and the fiery hot and spicy soups are recommended.

❺ *Havana Café* £
Breakwater
(opposite Marina Mall)
Tel. 02 681 00 44
Modern and stylish hotspot for the young Arab hipster crowd at the west end of the Corniche. The large outdoor terrace offers a spectacular view of the Abu Dhabi skyline.

❻ *Abu Sharka* £
Istiqlal Street
(opposite Europcar)
Tel. 02 631 34 00
Egyptian cuisine with tasty vegetable soups; Arab snack bar with exquisite houmous (made from chickpeas).

❼ *New City Palace* £
Khalifa Street
Tel. 02 626 27 62
This three-storey Chinese restaurant also serves Indian meals and a variety of fish specialities.

WHERE TO STAY
❶ *Emirates Palace* ££££
Corniche Road West
Tel. 02 690 90 00
www.emiratespalace.com
The exterior resembles a palace from an Al Dhaid fairytale, whilst marble and gold leaf are testament to the exquisite splendour of the interior. A large troop of staff tends to every guest's wish in the huge hotel comprising 320 rooms, 92 suites and extensive grounds.

❷ *Jumeirah at Etihad Towers* ££££
West Corniche Road
Ras al-Akhdar
Tel. 02 644 60 00
www.jumeirah.com
Opened in late 2011, the hotel is close to the beach, not far from the Emirates Palace and the new Ruler's Palace in one of the five futuristic Etihad Towers. A seductive mix of minimalist and Neo-Baroque interiors is aligned with the vision of a modern, open-minded Arabia. Enjoy the British teatime tradition of high tea, quite literally, in the Observation Tower on the 72nd floor, the highest point in the emirate at present. Scott's, the seafood restaurant, is somewhat closer to the sea, with views of the white beach and the iconic Etihad Towers.

❸ *St. Regis* ££££
Saadiyat Island
Tel. 02 403 65 77
www.starwoodhotels.com
Abu Dhabi's newest 6-star hotel, the height of luxury in typical St. Regis style, living in classic opulence amongst works of art and tropical gardens. The location is suitably excellent on Saadiyat Island, the new museum island. Whether residents are on the beach or by the pool, attentive staff will spoil them with ice-cooled drinks. In the evenings, award-winning chefs are responsible for the menus in several restaurants. Alternatively, guests can opt for contemporary-styled bistro fare.

❹ *Shangri-La* ££££
Between the Bridges, Qaryat Al Beri
Tel. 02 509 88 88
www.shangri-la.com
Insider Tip
Located on the lagoon opposite the city with a fantastic view of the

Great Mosque. Each of the 214 rooms has a balcony or terrace.

❺ *Al Ain Palace Hotel* £££
Corniche Road East
Tel. 02 679 47 77
www.alainpalacehotel.com
Traditional hotel with 120 rooms, a large inner courtyard, pool, good restaurants and diverse evening entertainment.

❻ *Dana Hotel* £££
Tourist Club Area
Al-Ferdous Street
Tel. 02 645 60 00
www.aldiarhotels.com

All 112 rooms come with a kitchenette, so this hotel is ideal for self-catering. Pizza Corner, the Wild West Club, a coffee shop and a rooftop restaurant on the 16th floor complete the package.

❼ *Mina Hotel* ££
Mina Road
(on the corner of Salam Street)
Tel. 02 678 10 00
www.aldiarhotels.com
Situated close to the Corniche, all 106 rooms of this city hotel are equipped with a small kitchenette. Includes a business centre and beach club. Abu Dhabi (map p.154/155)

varied. Fountains, symbols of life in the desert, adorn not only many of the roundabouts along the city's highways, they also feature as highlights of the Corniche.

Parks
Abu Dhabi is proud of its 40 gardens and parks, complete with fountains, walking trails and often with a children's playground. Besides the large parks along the Corniche there are smaller, green oases all over town. Located next to the Women's Higher College of Technology on 32nd Street, the Khalidiya Children's Garden is only accessible to women and children.

Al-Raha Beach
Those who don't have access to a hotel beach or beach club will appreciate the facilities of the Al-Raha Beach (Channel Road), located on the road from Abu Dhabi to Dubai. It provides sun loungers, sun shades and a cafeteria.

Breakwater
One of Abu Dhabi's most attractive spots is the Breakwater, close to Lulu Island, rising out of the water at the western end of the Corniche. The many tall palm trees along the man-made peninsula, built from white sand and debris of demolished buildings, conjure up a **tropical beach atmosphere**. A wide boulevard leads through an arcade where portraits of the rulers from the individual emirates are displayed, out to the spit and the Marina Mall, Havana Café (p.156), dhow restaurants and Heritage Village. This open-air museum offers insights into the culture of old Bedouin tribes and information about the simple fishing huts which stood on the 7km/4mi long promenade as recently as 60 years ago. Workshops inside a souk present the an-

Wandering along the beach in Abu Dhabi

cient Arabian crafts of weaving, woodwork and metalwork. Camel rides and falconry demonstrations are also on offer. A nostalgic photo opportunity is to be found in the form of an ox-drawn well and »falaj« irrigation channel (▶MARCO POLO Insight, p.230), whilst a museum and large restaurant round off the facilities.

❶ Mon–Thu, Sat 9am–5pm, Fri 3.30pm–9pm, admission free of charge

Central Market

Designed by Sir Norman Foster, Central Market stands on the site of the old souk, combining the World Trade Center (www.wtcad.ae), a shopping mall, hotel and the beautiful Souk at Central Market. The impressive facade references the Mashrabiya tradition of Arabic design. Inside, the full splendour of the building is revealed step by step in a masterful synthesis of old Arab souk architecture and hyper-modernism. Oriental and Indian craftwork par excellence can be found among the various shops in the Souk at Central Market.

❶ Al-Markaziyah, Sun–Thu 10am–10pm, Fri, Sat until 11pm

With an entrance like an old Arab drawbridge, fountains and flights of steps like a French chateau, the palace hotel – 800m/2,625ft in length! – is crowned by 114 domes, the largest with a diameter of 42m/138ft. Opened in 2005, the Emirates Palace located at the west end of the Corniche impresses through its incredible size and opulence, a symbol and catalyst of Abu Dhabi's glittering entry into first-class tourism. After finding a space in the underground car park, perhaps alongside the hotel's own fleet of white Rolls Royces, guests take the lift to the foyer and saunter through halls adorned with gold leaf. A 1.3km/almost mile-long beach belongs to the hotel estate.

Emirates Palace

Opposite the Emirates Palace, the five Etihad Towers reach skywards (p.148), veritable landmarks of Abu Dhabi city. Ranging from 234m/767ft to 305m/1000ft in height, they house illustrious companies, luxurious apartments and the small »Avenue at Etihad Towers« boutique shopping complex. The vast foyer of the »Jumeirah at Etihad Towers« hotel is well worth a look, featuring lofty windows which look out to the ocean. A minimalist fountain stands amidst the lounge furniture (▶p.156).

Etihad Towers

Built in 1793, the **first fort of the Nahyan family** was the ruling dynasty's seat of government and residence for almost two hundred years. This vast construction on Sheikh Zayed the First Street, on the corner of Airport Road, was erected at the spot where the legendary freshwater spring was once discovered. The clay-built fort was ultimately torn down when the oil boom arrived. In the year 1982, however, renewed interest in architectural heritage led to the palace's reconstruction, following the original plans. Nevertheless, the fort's straight walls and gleaming white paint lend it a much newer visage, earning the palace its »White Fort« nickname. Some sections can be visited, as a number of rooms have been turned into a museum. Elsewhere in the fort, parts of the state archives are stored. Two inner courtyards and the exterior grounds are covered with luxuriant greenery and laid out with walkways. During restoration, a cultural centre containing a library, exhibition space and rooms for events was added. Here in the Cultural Foundation the emirate's antique books and Qur'an collections are also kept. A free brochure available in the cultural centre has information on all current events.

* Qasr Al-Hosn

> ! **MARCO POLO TIP**
>
> *Fantastic views*   Insider Tip
>
> The terrace of the Havana café commands the finest view of the Abu Dhabi skyline. The modern café with its high-class design is situated at the beginning of the Breakwater peninsula, and is a rendezvous for the stylish young crowd in Abu Dhabi. On Fridays and Saturdays it already gets busy in the morning, when local families meet for breakfast (▶p.156).

Qasr Al-Hosn: periodically closed for renovation work at present

Cultural Foundation: Zayed 1st Street/Al Nasr Street,

❶ Sun–Thu 8am–10pm, Fri 5pm–8pm, Sat 9am–1pm, 5pm–8pm, Tel. 621 53 00, www.tcaabudhabi.ae; admission free

Capital Gate   On Arabian Gulf Street, close to the Zayed Sports City, all eyes are drawn to the 160m/525ft high Capital Gate which stands at an 18 degrees angle. Abu Dhabi's version of the Leaning Tower of Pisa is home to prestigious businesses, apartments and a Hyatt Hotel (www.capitalgate.ae).

* Sheikh Zayed Grand Mosque   The Sheikh Zayed Grand Mosque, the **key place of worship in Abu Dhabi**, rises up at the crossroads of Sheikh Rashid Bin-Saeed Al-Maktoum Street (Airport Road) and Sheikh Zayed the First Street, across from the Cultural Foundation.

Named after Sheikh Zayed bin Sultan al-Nahyan, who died in 2004 (▶p.65), the new Grand Mosque was erected on the south of the peninsula and completed in 2008. Covering an area of 22,000 sq m/240,000 sq ft, this is **the largest mosque in the UAE**, capable of accommodating 10,000 worshippers. Built in Neo-Islamic style, it

Sheikh Zayed Mosque, the largest in the UAE

features a host of wonderfully ornate domes – three enormous domes and 79 smaller ones – and four minarets, numerous outbuildings and arcades. What is probably the largest carpet in the world covers the floor inside, hand-made in Iran by 1200 weavers, 5600 sq m/60,000 sq ft in size and weighing 47 tons. Above, the gigantic chandelier is also the world's largest, crafted in Germany using over two million Swarovski crystals (p.32).

❶ Rashid al-Maktoum Road South, www.szgmc.ae; guided tours (all religious denominations) Sun–Thu 10am, 11am, 5pm and 7pm, Sat 10am, 11am, 2pm, 5pm and 7.30pm; additional free viewing for non-Muslims: daily except Friday, 9am–10am; prayer times: Sat–Thu 9am–10pm, Fri 4.30pm–11pm

Beyond the area of government departments in the west end of the city lies the harbour of Al-Bateen. Traditional Arab dhows are still built here, although they are now powered by diesel engines. A visit to the dhow yard allows a peek at the boat builders at work. Some older boats, in need of restoration, are grounded on the beach, while others bob about on the water. This area also has a number of restaurants, some of which are converted dhows. It is a great place to enjoy the view of old Abu Dhabi and watch the hustle and bustle of the harbour.

Al-Bateen

The Zayed Centre, also known as Baba Zayed's House, is located in a sidestreet off Bainouah Street in the district of Al Bateen. This museum is dedicated to the life of Sheikh Zayed, who died in 2004. Amongst the artefacts on display are three of his cars, his hunting rifle, historical photographs and gifts from foreign delegations.

Zayed Centre

❶ Al Bateen, off Bainouah Street, Sun–Thu 9am–5pm, viewing by appointment, tel. 02 665 95 55, www.torath.ae

At the Women's Handicraft Centre, 5km/3mi south of the centre, visitors are invited to witness demonstrations of textile weaving, basket making and other handicrafts by local women. There is also a jewellery exhibition and the souvenir shop sells blankets, textiles, perfumed oils, ceramics and other products.

Women's Handicraft Centre

❶ Karama Street, off Airport Road, Al-Mushrif, Sun–Thu 8am–3pm, Tel 02 447 66 45, admission free

The Madinat Zayed Shopping Centre in the district of Madinat Zayed (East Street, 4th Street) has taken in many little shops from the souks that were sacrificed to the modernization of the city centre. Cheap cosmetics, clothes and electronic goods can be found here. Next to this shopping centre is the new **Gold Centre**, which houses many stores selling gold and jewellery. On the top floor, the enormous Japanese shop Daiso purveys inexpensive wares, some quite original.

Madinat Zayed Shopping Centre

Falcons

The falcon is the national emblem of the United Arab Emirates. Along with the camel and the horse, this proud bird of prey is one of the favourite animals in Arab tradition (▶MARCO POLO Insight p.164).

These hunting birds were already being bred on the Arabian Peninsula in the millennium before Christ; today it is mainly the European falcon that is trained for hunting from a very young age. A peregrine falcon is able to swoop at a speed of 100m/109yd per second, but such exertions quickly take their toll after a few minutes. Hence 23 hours a day are spent just resting and digesting.

Falconry

Hunting with trained falcons, something which the European aristocracy have also practiced since the Middle Ages, is, in fact, a great art, and is furthermore a very exclusive hobby: talented, female young birds can fetch up to 200,000 dirham (approx. 40,000 Euro) – they are better hunters than the males. Elaborate training takes many months, with the ultimate goal being to teach the bird to hunt in the wild and to bring its prey (steppe birds, sometimes even desert hare) back to the owner. The first step in training is for bird and owner to gain each other's trust. The falcon spends weeks and months in the constant vicinity of its new owner and trainer. A black leather hood, the burqa, is put over the bird's head as soon as the animal becomes agitated. Eventually the birds are taught to lift off from the owner's arm to catch dummy prey on command. Every time the animal returns the dummy to its owner, it is given a reward.

Training in the Ddesert

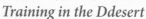

The next step is flying in the wild, where the falcon is trained to catch pigeons. Training is successfully completed if the falcon spots and catches prey in the desert and brings it back. If an animal floats in the air for too long without spotting any prey, the owner will simply wave some dummy prey. The bird of prey returns to receive its reward of food. The bird's head is covered with the burqa and then placed on a 50cm/20in-high perch (wakir) which is artistically uphols-

Abu Dhabi Falcon Clinic: Dr. Margit Gabriele Müller on her rounds

tered with cloth. A foot chain tethers the animal in its place.

Falcon Clinic

Parasites, broken wings, lung disease – even falcons can fall ill. In Abu Dhabi, close to the airport, there is a special falcon hospital which treats between 4,000 and 5,000 of these precious animals every year. Treatment at the clinic, run by a German vet for over a decade, is free for local residents. Examinations, x-rays and operations are carried out around the clock, as the team running this clinic came to understand that »if there's one thing that Arabs can't stand, it's a closed falcon clinic.«

A visitor centre attached to the clinic explains all aspects of falcons and falconry in more detail. The Falcon Hospital has become one of the emirate's most important attractions. Take a tour of the clinic (and see the falcons).

Seihan Road 3km/2mi off the bridge, www.falconhospital.com; tours Sat 10am, Sun–Thu 10am and 2pm, register online or call tel. 02 575 51 55, 170 Dh per person, children up to 9 years of age 60 Dh.

Hunting from the Air

Falconry probably originated in Central Asia. In the Arabic world, it remains a crucial element of culture and tradition to this day. Even if it is prohibited in the emirates – hunting excursions move on to Pakistan or Uzbekistan. Falconry came to Europe with the Crusades; the emperor Frederick II was one of its most fervent proponents.

▶ **Keen eyes**
A kestrel can recognize points 2cm to 3cm/roughly an inch apart from a distance of 250m/820ft.

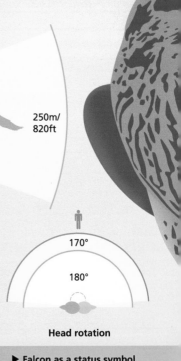

100m/328ft

250m/820ft

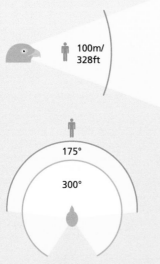

175°

300°

Field of vision

170°

180°

Head rotation

▶ **Region of origin**
of trained falcons

Price (in £)

AMERICA
GERMANY
ARCTIC ZONE

between
12,000 & **35,000**

Top of the range
65,000

▶ **Falcon as a status symbol**
Flacons are more than just a status symbol, they are part of the family. The number of them in captivity underlines their importance.

Germany
about 300

UAE
about 6000

falcon as predator
erent breeds of falcon are trained for different type of prey –
ale birds are preferred, as they have more stamina.

on training
lure is the most important piece of
ning equipment. It hangs on an
rox. 2m/6.5ft long cord which the
oner swings around in the air
signal to the bird to return.

The Hunt
A falcon flies high to hunt.
It grabs hold of its prey or hits it
on the ground.

Swooping steeply,
a falcon can reach
speeds of up to
200kmh/124mph.

Houbara Bustard,
traditional prey

▶ **The falconer's equipment**

Falconry glove
Protection of
the falconer

Lure
Training

Falconry bag
Contains feed

Hood / burqa
Quieting the falcon

Falcon transmitter
to locate the falcon

©BAEDEKER

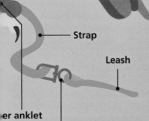

Strap

Leash

er anklet

Hinge

▶ **Falcon Hospital in Abu Dhabi**
The only falcon clinic in the entire world is run
by German veterinary surgeon Margit Müller.

Opened	1999
Cost of treatment	approx. 400 Dirham ≈ 80 €
Patients (per annum)	4600
Patients (daily, during hunting season)	60
Capacity	approx. 80 – 100 Falcons

Persian Souk Persian souks exist in every emirate. Here, the market can be found at the Free Port (Mina Hurr) where dhows bring in goods from Iran. A long row of small – and very small – shops sell everything from rugs to electrical and household goods, anything can be sold cheaply. Behind the souk, the fish market is a hive of activity in the early morning and late afternoon. Various restaurants are situated in an adjacent complex.

Dhow Harbour Traditional boats load and unload their cargo at the quay, lending Dhow Harbour a wonderfully atmospheric quality.

Khalifa Park On the Eastern Ring Road (8th Street) near the old city airport lies a new, modern leisure and recreation park with canals and abras (water taxis), fountains and pools, an aquarium, a theatre seating 3,200, the **Maritime Museum** and a mosque. A miniature train runs between the attractions.
❶ Sun–Thu 3pm–10pm, Fri, Sat 11am–11pm, admission 3 Dh

Maqta Tower Leaving the main island over the Al-Maqta Bridge, the Maqta Tower comes into view atop a small island. The three-storey defence tower was erected in the 19th century on the ruins of a Portuguese watch-tower. It was used to guard the island, which at that time could only be reached from the mainland at low tide. Near the Maqta Tower on the landward side, the Maqta Fort now houses a tourist information office.
❶ Sat–Thu 8am–noon, 2pm–5pm; tel. 02 444 04 44

Saadiyat Island The 27sq km/ 10.4 sq m island of Saadiyat is connected to the main-land by a multilane bridge. Not only has a new urban district for 160,000 people been created here, with apartments, holiday resorts, a marina and nature park, but a new cultural district has also been developed with museums and a concert hall. Abu Dhabi harbours ambitions of becoming the cultural centre of the Arabian Gulf. The American Frank Gehry is planning to open a branch of the New York Guggenheim, Frenchman Jean Nouvel an offshoot of the Louvre, Japan's Tadao Ando a maritime museum and the Iranian-born arch-itecht Zaha Hadid a performing arts centre. Norman Foster is design-ing the Zayed National Museum.
The fine sands of **Saadiyat Beach**, 9km/5.5mi in length are bordered by the Saadiyat Golf Club, the Monte Carlo Beach Club and two lux-ury hotels, the Park Hyatt and St. Regis. The beach along the north-west coast features a beach club and is freely accessible. The Saadiyat Beach Conservation Area, belonging to the Park Hyatt, has been es-tablished to protect the rare hawksbill sea turtles who gather on the moonlit beaches between April and July to deposit their eggs.
The **UAE Pavilion**, resplendent in red gold steel, was designed by Norman Foster for the World Expo 2010 in Shanghai. Its form echoes

Yas Marina Circuit: spectacular Formula 1 track

seven sand dunes, the symbol of the Emirates. Changing exhibitions are staged inside. Models of the future city and art exhibitions can be seen in Manarat al-Saadiyat.

Yas Island covers an area of 25 sq km/10sq mi en route to Dubai on the E10. The »pleasure island« is reached from Corniche via Saadiyat Island. Back in 2009, the UAE's first **Formula 1 race circuit** was inaugurated, winding its way between two wings of the five star Yas Viceroy hotel. The Abu Dhabi Grand Prix has been staged here ever since, plus smaller racing events. Within sight of the track, **Ferrari World** offers high velocity thrills. The Ferrari theme park features what is believed to be the world's fastest rollercoaster, accelerating up to 240kmh/150mph in just five seconds (www.ferrariworldabudhabi.com, p.92). Luxury hotels, Yas Marina (www.cnmarinas.com) and a golf course (www.yaslinks) have all sprung up alongside the Yas Waterworld waterpark.

❶ www.yasisland.ae

Yas Island

The Al-Wathba Camel Race Track is situated 45km/28mi east of Abu Dhabi City on the road to Al Ain. Camel races take place from October to April on Thursdays and Fridays between 8am and 2pm (free admission).

Al-Wathba Camel Race Track

To the west of the airport lies the Masdar future project (www.masdar.ae) designed by Foster & Partners, comprising the zero carbon eco project Masdar City and the Masdar Institute of Science & Tech-

Masdar

nology. Water supply in the car-free city comes from solar-powered desalination plants, waste is recycled, transportation is provided by driverless podcars underground (Personal Rapid Transit). Many more projects are in development, with completion set for 2020, but there is already plenty to see on a visit of Masdar City.

❶ Masdar City, bus 170, daily 8.30am–10pm, admission free, www.masdarcity.ae

Sir Bani Yas Island Situated on a peninsula about 240km/150mi west of Abu Dhabi City, at **Jebel Dhanna**, »Danat Resort« is a comfortable beach hotel (109 rooms, tel. 02 801 22 22, www.danathotels.com). From Jebel Dhanna the island of Sir Bani Yas, 8km/5mi off the coast and 87 sq km/34 sq mi in size, can be reached. Oryx antelopes, giraffes and cheetahs are among the 18,000 animals which roam **Arabia's largest nature reserve**, some on open terrain, others in generously proportioned enclosures. Accommodation is available at the exclusive Desert Islands Resort.

❶ 64 rooms, tel. 02 801 54 00, www.anantara.com

** Al Ain

K 6

Population: 472,000

The »garden city« of Al Ain, a 200 sq km/77 sq mi oasis with around 200 springs and fountains, is located in the desert at the foot of the Hajar Mountains, 160km/99mi east of Abu Dhabi. The city which emerged here during the oil boom not only supplies the emirate with agricultural products but has also become a cultural centre with the country's largest university.

Green city Al Ain and Abu Dhabi are connected by one almost continuous, multilane road, the borders of which are covered with greenery. As the **birthplace of Sheikh Zayed**, Al Ain is held in high esteem. The city has an international airport with direct flights to other Gulf States. About 15km/9mi south of the city, Jebel Hafeet rises 1,350m/4,429ft above the flat, rocky landscape. The green city is traversed by endless wide streets lined with palm trees and oleander bushes, brightly lit at night. Every square and inner courtyard is planted with grass, flowers or shrubbery. The large administrative buildings in modern Islamic style are surrounded by gardens and parks; futuristic-looking mosques reflect the city's wealth. Road signs are usually in both Arabic and English.

The area of what is now the border region between Oman, Saudi Arabia and the United Arab Emirates has been settled for 5,000 years. Hundreds of stone tombs from 3000 to 2700 BC have been discovered in Qarn Bint-Saud, 15km/9mi north of Al Ain on the slopes of Hafeet Mountain , a foothill of the Hajar Mountains. The grave findings suggest trade relations with Mesopotamia. In Hili, 10km/6mi north of Al Ain, tourists can visit the reconstructed foundation walls of a 3,000 year old settlement. Due to its generous water resources, the settlement was used as a hub for caravans for many centuries. Most of Al Ain's history is unknown. At the end of the 18th century, the Al Nahyan family, which at that time still lived in the Liwa Oasis further south, occupied parts of the oases in the Al Ain region. In the 19th century, the Nahyan shared the oases with the Sultan of Oman. In 1866, Saudi Wahhabi conquered the Buraimi Oasis, as it was known, but lost it again to the Sultan of Oman three years later. In 1949, Saudi Arabia raised a claim to the Buraimi Oasis and eventually reconquered it in 1952 with support from Omani fundamentalists who wanted to overthrow Oman's Sultan Taimur for bringing a non-Islamic oil company from overseas into the country. Three years later, the Sultan, supported by British troops, recaptured the oasis region. Sheikh Zayed was governor of Al Ain Province until 1966, when the Sultanates of Oman and Abu Dhabi agreed upon the course of the border between Al Ain and Buraimi. In 1974, Saudi Arabia finally renounced its claims and accepted the border south of the oases. In 2000, a treaty was drawn up to protect the line of the border. In 2011 Al Ain was granted World Heritage status by UNESCO as a cultural and natural site. The traditional Falaj irrigation system, Al Ain's cultural attractions, the tombs of the Hili Oasis and Jebel Hafeet all contributed to the nomination.

History

MARCO POLO TIP

! *Above the desert in a balloon* Insider Tip

The most impressive way to view city of Al Ain and the surrounding red sand dunes is from a hot-air balloon (start 5.30am from Abu Dhabi city, 1 and a half hour ride to Al Ain, then take to the air; back at the hotel 5 hours later; Sept–May, 180 € per person; www.balllooning.ae

WHAT TO SEE IN AL AIN

The fort, also called »Sultan Fort« or »Al-Hosn«, can be found on Zayed bin Sultan Street. The mighty fortification was built in 1910 by Sheikh Sultan Bin Zayed al Nahyan, grandfather of the current emir. Opened in 1971, the **Al Ain National Museum** is is one of the oldest museums of the young state. Now housed in a new building, it includes an ethnographical section depicting life in the desert

*Al-Sharqi Fort

Al Ain

INFORMATION
Tourist information
Ali Bin Abi Taleb Street
Tel. 03 764 20 00
www.visitabudhabi.ae
Sun–Thu 8am–4pm

WHERE TO EAT
❶ *The Wok* £££
Danat Resort
Al Niyadat Street
Tel. 03 704 60 00, closed Sat
The specialities of this hotel restaurant
with a view of the pool are wok and Asi-
an fish dishes.

❷ *Bukhara* ££
Town Square Shopping Centre
Khalifa Bin Zayed Street
Tel. 03 766 00 59
www.bukhararestaurant.com
Indian mid-range restaurant with chapa-
tis, north Indian lamb curry and a fine
selection of vegetarian dishes.

❸ *Golden Fork* £
Khalifa Street
Tel. 03 766 03 36
www.goldenforkgroup.com
Fast-food restaurant with mostly Filipino
and Chinese cuisine. Take-away dishes
available.

WHERE TO STAY
❶ *Hilton* £££
Zayed Bin Sultan Street
(Hilton Road)
Sarooj, tel. 03 768 66 66
www.hilton.de/alain; 220 rooms
Guests are accommodated in the mo-
dern main building or in individual cha-
lets and small villas in the spacious hotel

park. Tennis court, a squash court and a
9-hole golf course.

❷ *Danat Resort* £££
Al Niyadat Street
Tel. 03 704 60 00
www.danathotels.com
200 rooms
This hotel boasts two pools, floodlit tennis courts, two squash halls, a riding sta-
ble and golf driving range with a simula-
tor.

❸ *Al Ain Rotana* £££
Sheikh Zayed Bin Sultan Street
Tel. 03 754 51 11
www.rotana.com
198 designer rooms and suites.
The spacious pool area and outdoors
section of the (buffet) restaurant feature
attractive arcades.

❹ *City Seasons* ££
Sheikh Khalifa Bin Zayed Street
Tel. 03 755 02 20
www.cityseasonsalain.com
77 rooms
The rooms in warm golden and brown
tones are characterized by opulence and
classic style (plus tea and coffee-making
facilities). In addition to a professional
business centre and an excellent health
club with sauna and gym there is an outdoor pool, a restaurant and coffee shop.

❹ *Mercure Grand Jebel Hafeet* ££
Jebel Hafeet Road
Tel. 03 783 88 88
www.mercure.com
124 rooms
15km/9mi south of the city, this mid-

range hotel stands like a modern castle on Jebel Hafeet at a height of 915m/3,000ft. As the only hotel on Al Ain's local mountain, it boasts a unique panoramic view of Al Ain and the surrounding desert. Enjoy the outdoor pool during the day and when the sun sets, gaze down at the twinkling ocean of lights in the city and along the desert highways below. It almost feels like watching the stars from a different planet.

Al-Massa Resthouse £

Municipality R/A, Al Jimi Baldiya Street, corner of Silmi Street
Tel. 03 762 88 84
www.uaealainhotels.com/almassa

The architecture of this modern, comfortable hotel is traditionally Arabian, whilst its 62 rooms correspond to western standards.

❺ One to One Hotel & Resort £–££

Haaza Ibn Sultan Street
(15km/9mi south of Al Ain)
Tel. 03 701 44 44
www.onetoonehotels.com
Quietly situated at the foot of Jebel Hafeet is the Ain Al Faydah spring, where locals come to relax by an artificial lake. The new four-star hotel promises days of relaxation among the locals; nicely appointed rooms in modern Arabian style.

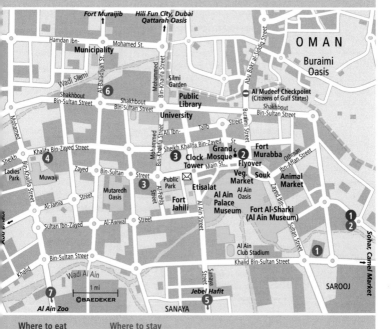

Al Ain

Fort Muraijib
Hili Fun City, Dubai
Qattarah Oasis
Hamdan Ibn-
Mohamed St.
Municipality
Wadi Slemi
Shakhbout Bin-Sultan Street
Mohammed Bin-Khalifa Street
Al-Baladiyah St.
Shakhbout Bin-Sultan Street
Silmi Garden
Public Library
University
Ali Ibn-
Talib
Mohamed
Khalifa Bin-Zayed Street
Ladies' Park
Muwaiji
Zayed
Bin-Sultan
Street
Sheikh
Al-Jamia
Sultan Ibn-Zayed
Mutaredh Oasis
Al-Fahla Street
Al-Awwal
Street
Street
Public Park
Fort Jahili
Clock Tower
Sheikh Khalifa Bin-Zayed
St.
Grand Mosque
Main St.
Etisalat
Veg. Market
Al Ain Palace Museum
Al Ain Oasis
Al Ain Oasis
Fort Murabba
Flyover
Souk
Animal Market
Fort Al-Sharki (Al Ain Museum)
Othman Ibn-Affan Street
Zayed Street
Sultan Street
Abu Bakr al-Siddiq Street
Buraimi Street
Street
Shakhbout Bin-Sultan Street
Al Mudeef Checkpoint (Citizens of Gulf States)
O M A N
Buraimi Oasis
Al Ain Club Stadium
Khalid Bin-Sultan Street
Sanaya Street
Bin-Sultan Street
Wadi Al Ain
Khalid
1 mi
©BAEDEKER
Al Ain Zoo
SANAYA
Jebel Hafit
SAROOJ
Sohar, Camel Market

Where to eat		Where to stay			
❶	The Wok	❶	Hilton	❹ City Seasons	❼ One to One
❷	Bukhara	❷	Danat Resort	❺ Mercure	Hotel & Resort
❸	Golden Fork	❸	Al Ain Rotana	❻ Al-Massa Resthouse	

Al Jahili Fort: the founder of the UAE was born here

before the »Oil Age«. Life-size puppets or models reconstruct the everyday life of Bedouins, pearl divers and fishermen. The archaeological section exhibits Bronze and Iron Age finds from Hili and Jebel Hafeet. A gate next to the museum provides access to Al Ain Oasis, the heart of the old oasis now known as Central Public Gardens. Paved pathways within the walls offer views of palm groves and falaj channels, leading on to the historic Obaid Bin Ali al Nasseri Mosque.

Museum: Sat–Thu 9am–7.30pm, Fri from 3pm, closed Mon; admission 3 Dh

Al Jahili Fort   Built in 1898, Al Jahili Fort is a striking mud brick construction with two imposing round towers. The revered founder of the state, Zayed Bin Sultan, was born here. The extensive fortress site with several gates has an unusual, tapering three-storey tower, a further small fort and a palatial residence. This building, the former emir's residence, has been authentically reconstructed using only traditional building materials – mud bricks made by hand, air-dried and plastered with a mixture of mud and straw.

❶ Tue–Sun and Sat 9am–5pm, Fri 3pm–5pm, admission 3 Dh

Camel Market   The last camel market in the UAE is open all week on Mezyad Road (500m/550yd past the Bawadi Mall and behind a Carrefour supermarket, approximately 10km/6mi southeast of the centre). Merchants sell single-humped Arabian dromedaries. The biggest selection of animals on sale tends to be at weekends (Thursdays to Saturdays), when potential buyers from Abu Dhabi and other emirates arrive in their pickup trucks to scrutinize the livestock – in a relaxed and friendly market atmosphere. The prices are comparatively low; there are no high-class racing camels or breeding mares here, just animals that are valued for their milk and meat.

❶ Daily 7am–5pm, admission free

Souk

On the side of Zayed Bin Sultan Street opposite the public park, the historic souk unfolds in a mix of oriental colours and Asian scents. Household goods are also on sale in the substantially modernized market.

Al Ain Palace Museum

The former home of Sheikh Zayed (p.65), built in 1937, has been extended and converted to a museum. Items and documents associated with the former president and his family are on display. The inner courts, mosaics, calligraphic ornamentation and carved doors convey an impression of the architecture and decorative art typical of the period before the oil boom.

❶ Sanaya Road; Tue–Sun 9am–7.30pm, Fri only 3pm–8pm, admission free

> **! MARCO POLO TIP** 🌐
>
> *Animal market*   Insider Tip
>
> Also called the Livestock Market, the Animal Market is located opposite Al-Sharqi Fort and offers visitors a good chance to snap pictures: goats, sheep, chickens, sometimes calves are brought here early in the morning to wait for their new owners in a roped off enclosure (daily 7am – noon).

Muraijib Fort

On Al-Jimi Street in the Qattarah district – close to the crossroads of Khalid bin Al-Waleed Street and Al Baladiya Street, 4km/2.5mi northwest of the city centre – stands the city's oldest fort, built in 1830 by Sheikh Shakhbut bin Diab al Nahyan. The fort seen here today is a replica. Its fortified roof and surrounding walls are crowned with battlements.

❶ Sat–Thu 9am–4pm, Fri 3pm–6pm, admission 1 Dh Animal matters: Animal Market

Ladies' Park

Men and boys from the age of 10 upwards are not allowed into Ladies' Park, also known as Basra Park. Women meet here to chat with friends while their children are happily entertained at the playground. Zayed The First Street, admission free

Silmi Garden

Silmi Garden, northwest of the city centre on Sheikh Zayed the First Road, is popular with families going for an evening stroll amongst the most beautiful tropical trees and flowers. In the evening, the park walls are bathed in colourful lights.

Tears of The Gods

There is an old Arabic saying: »The smoke of incense reaches heaven as does no other smoke«. For thousands of years, frankincense from Southern Arabia has been one of the most precious substances in the world.

Pliny the Elder described how Emperor Nero burned a full year's supply of frankincense at the funeral of his wife Poppaea. In the tomb of the Egyptian pharaoh Tutankhamun, a small piece of frankincense was found, highly valued in the process of embalming. Frankincense was almost as valuable as gold in former times. The New Testament relates how the Three Kings brought gifts of gold, myrrh and frankincense to Bethlehem.

A World of Fragrances and Scents

Fragrances are still extremely important in the UAE today. Souk alleys are rich in aromas and the scent of incense sticks. Sandalwood, myrrh and musk extract are boiled with frankincense in rosewater then left to cool, hardening into a resin. Frankincense is one of the most commonly used ingre-

Frankincense was almost as valuable as gold and has been known in Arabic culture for thousands of years.

dients in perfume manufacture on the Gulf, a craft steeped in tradition.

Expensive Panacea

Frankincense, the resin from the Boswellia sacra tree, which grows to a height of two to three metres (6 to 10 feet) was known in Arabic culture thousands of years ago. It was used to heal sickness and to mask unpleasant smells. It was also implemented in making cosmetics. There was only one drawback to frankincense: the high price. In ancient times, the resin known as »tears of the Gods« was worth its weight in gold. Harvesting the sought-after substance was bound up in numerous rituals and the practice was restricted to a particular caste.

Incense Road

One of the most important caravan routes for incense ran from Shaba (Yemen) to Marib (also in Yemen), then parallel to the Red Sea coast via Petra (Jordan), capital of the Nabataeans, to the Mediterranean harbour of Gaza (Palestine). The most expensive resin comes from the region which is now Southern

Resin is extacted from the Boswellia tree to make frankincense. An incense burner (below, left) makes a pretty souvenir.

Oman. The trees which grow here produce a resin which is shiny and white and particularly aromatic. Price and quality are determined by the colour. As a general rule, the lighter it is, the more it will cost. The resin is burned on specially crafted earthenware burners, or sometimes on metal ones. The fragrant, rising vapours welcome guests all over the UAE and Oman.

AROUND AL AIN

** Hili
Archaeo-
logical
Gardens

Abu Dhabi's most prominent excavation site is located at the heart of a large park. In the 1960s, Danish archaeologists discovered numerous remains of settlements and overground circular tombs, which confirmed the theory that this region was already inhabited more than 5,000 years ago. Located some 10km/6mi north of Al Ain on the way to Dubai, the Hili Archaeological Gardens can be accessed from Ardh Al Jaw Street near the Dubai Highway, through a large iron gate decorated with flowers. The most significant find is the Great Hili Tomb. Made of smooth stone blocks, the tomb has a diameter of 8m/26ft and is 2.5m/8ft high. Its date of origin is estimated at 2700 BC. The two engraved tomb entrances are remarkable, displaying the shapes of humans and oryx antelopes, clearly identifiable by their two long horns. Based on the burial objects, some of which are exhibited at the Museum of Al Ain, the tomb is attributed to the Umm al-Nar culture between 3000 and 2000 BC. After visiting the circular tombs, allow time for a stroll through the park, which is particularly lively on Thursdays and Fridays when numerous families come here to host picnics on the extensive lawns. A restaurant offers simple meals and refreshments.

❶ Sat–Thu 4pm–8pm, Fri 10am–8pm, admission 1 Dh

Hili Fun City

The 85ha/210 acres amusement park Hili Fun City, often referred to as the »Disneyland of the Middle East«, on Ardh Al Jaw Street (in the direction of Dubai), provides year-round entertainment for the entire family, including a fun fair with a rollercoaster, botanical garden, mini train tour and boat rides as well as cafés and restaurants. Directly next to Hili Fun City is the extremely popular **Al Ain Ice Rink.**

Hili Fun City: Mon–Thu 4pm–10pm, Wednesdays women only, Fri, Sat noon–10pm, admission Mon, Tue 55 Dh, Wed–Sat 60 Dh (incl. attractions), children up to 89cm/under 3ft free; www.hilifuncity.ae

Al Ain Ice Rink: Sat–Thu 4pm–10pm, Fri from 10am, admission 10 Dh, ice skates 20 Dh

Al Ain Zoo

The Al Ain Zoo is situated south of the city, at the end of Zayed Al Awwal Street. Over one thousand mammals from Arabia, Africa and India live here. The zoo is dedicated to the breeding of rare species, a role in which it has been successful in the cases of the endangered Arabian oryx antelope, the desert leopard and a rare fox species. Furthermore, the zoo houses reptiles and almost 2,000 birds, whilst the aquarium gives an insight into the diversity of fish in the Arabian Gulf. Playgrounds and a miniature train that rides from enclosure to enclosure provide extra entertainment for children

❶ Daily 9am–8pm, admission 20 Dh, children aged 10 or younger 10 Dh; www.awpr.ae

The Al Wathba Camel Race Track is located at the west end of the city, on the road to Abu Dhabi. The season runs from October to March, with camel races taking place on Friday and Saturday mornings (admission is free).

Camel Race Track

The Hili Border crossing from Al Ai nto Buraimi **takes visitors into Omani territory**. An »exit fee« of 25 Dh is payable. The first Omani frontier posts are located some 40km/25mi beyond the city, in the direction of Sohar and 27km/17mi towards Ibri. Those wishing to spend the night in Buraimi will need an Omani visa (200 Dh; it can be collected in Wadi Jizzi, 40km/25mi away). A stroll through the old oasis with its vegetable gardens, palm tree groves, water channels and mud houses is particularly pleasant. The historical **Al-Khandaq Fort** in the centre of Buraimi was built in around 1780 by the local tribe of Al-Bu Shami. The compound is bordered by four defence towers and a wide moat.
Sat–Thu 8am–6pm, Fri 8am–noon and 4pm–6pm, admission free

Buraimi

During archaeological excavation work on the island of Umm al-Nar the former Governor of Al Ain, Sheikh Zayed, noticed a resemblance to hills in Jebel Hafeet. Examination of approximately 100 tombs so far has brought to light objects from the end of the third millennium BC. The sites cannot be visited, but numerous finds, including fine copper works, are on display at the museum of Al Ain.

Jebel Hafeet Tombs

Jebel Hafeet, a popular destination in summer

Ain al-Faydah Arabs and expatriates alike enjoy a relaxing weekend on Haza Bin-Sultan Street at the foot of the Hafeet Mountain. Sourced from the Ain al-Faydah lake, the hot spring of Ain Al-Faydah, the »beneficial spring«, is found here. Locals also call the spring Ain Abu Sukhna or »Father of Warmth«. The area around the lake has been developed into a spa region with a hotel, bungalows and playgrounds, as well as sports and leisure facilities. Sadly, the once picturesque lake has lost some of its charm as it is now bordered by a large concrete basin.

Jebel Hafeet A winding road 15km/9mi long leads up Jebel Hafeet. After 10km/6mi at a height of 915m/3,000ft the impressive architecture of the modern Mercure Hotel comes into view (p.170). At km 14 there is a palace of the Nahyan family, and just beyond it the summit at 1200m/3937ft, where refreshments are available in the Top of Hafeet Mountain Café, accompanied by wonderful views.

At the foot of Jebel Hafeet, the **Wadi Adventure waterpark** invites visitors to go kayaking and rafting or to try out the 3m/10ft surf waves; a pleasant waterpark with activities for all the family.

❶ Sun–Thu 11am–8pm, Fri, Sat from 10am, admission 50 Dh, children 25 Dh, family ticket 100 Dh, kayak 150 Dh, raft 100 Dh, www.wadiadventure.ae

Mahdah Mahdah, situated in Oman around 30km/18.6mi from Al Ain, is an oasis town with a fortress-like mosque – date of origin unknown. Today, there is little to remind visitors of Mahdah's past as an important caravan hub.

The ancient houses made of mud and palm leaves are in ruins, as are the two forts in the historic town centre. The citizens of Mahdah were moved to new houses; according to Sultan Qaboos' ambitious plans, every citizen of Oman should live in a modern house with running water and electricity.

Liwa Oasis

✦ E-G 9/10

Population: 45,000

There have been Bedouin settlements along this 50km/31mi stretch of oases amongst date trees and surrounded by high sand dunes for about 300 years. Today, the largest of the 15 towns and villages, arranged in a wide arc along the oasis, is the newly founded town of Mezairaa. The rich supply of groundwater makes it possible to maintain numerous gardens and fields.

The Liwa Oasis

DAY TRIPS
Many Abu Dhabi hotels offer day trips to Liwa in all-terrain vehicles, including excursions into the sandy desert. (approx. 600 Dh per person).

WHERE TO EAT
Suhail ££££
at the Qasr Al Sarab Hotel
Tel. 02 886 20 88
High quality Arab and international food, matched by a superb view over the desert and wadi from the roof garden.

Green Liwa Oasis ££
in the Liwa Hotel
Tel. 02 882 20 00
International and Arab cuisine; a view onto sand dunes and gardens.

Liwa Resthouse £
Mezairaa, behind the police station
Tel. 02 882 20 75
The restaurant of this small hotel serves simple Arabic dishes.

WHERE TO STAY
Qasr Al Sarab ££££
Qasr Al Sarab Road, Hamim
Tel. 02 886 20 88

www.anantara.com
For lasting memories: built in Arabian Bedouin style, this resort stand in the desert 12km/7.5mi east of Hamim and is undoubtedly the emirate's most romantic and evocative hotel (p.106). The suites are at once luxurious and rustic (from 42 sq m/452 sq ft), the outdoor terraced areas are grandiose. Not forgetting the Anantara Spa and an excellent excursion centre which organizes off-road tours, horse riding and camel safaris.

Liwa Hotel £££
Mezairaa
Tel. 02 882 20 00
www.almarfapearlhotels.com
Comfortable accommodation in the sandy desert: this hotel (66 rooms including three 3-bedroom villas) is located on a hill surrounded by green parks; includes a large pool and tennis courts.

Liwa Resthouse £
Mezairaa
on the hill behind the police station
Tel. 02 882 20 75
19 rooms, 2 suites
This simple hotel includes a pool and offers multiple sports facilities, including sand skiing.

The Liwa Oasis, **one of the largest oasis system**s on the Arabian Peninsula, is located on the edge of the Rub al-Khali desert known as the »Empty Quarter«. The world's largest sandy desert covers a broad area of Saudi Arabia and reaches as far as Oman. In the heat of summer, predominantly locals leave the coastal region to enjoy the less humid and climatically more pleasant town of Liwa. New, as a rule simply constructed houses line the sandy trails; wire mesh fences are designed to keep freely roaming goats from grazing their way through the laboriously tended oasis region. Small shops sell food and textiles while restaurants, which seem more like snack bars, offer basic meals.

On the edge of the Empty Quarter

Rub al-Khali –The Empty Quarter

Natural desert regions cover at least 30% of the earth's surface. Most deserts are slowly increasing in size, due to climatic changes and the intervention of man, as forests continue to be chopped down, for example. The biggest desert in the world is the Sahara in North Africa. It spans eleven countries and is almost as large as Europe, covering 9 millon sq mi/3.5million sq mi.

▶ The sandy desert – Rub al-Khali
Rub al-Khali is the largest sandy desert in the world, covering almost the entire southern third of the Arabian Peninsula.

Coverage	Saudi Arabia, Yemen, Oman, United Arab Emira
Area	800,000 sq km/308,000 sq
Length/breadth	approx. 1000km/620
Precipitation	less than 50mm/2in per annu

©BAEDEKER

▶ How sand dunes are created
Desert sand piles up to form dunes. In Rub al-Khali they can reach up as high as 300m/984ft.

Barchan

The wind blows for longer periods from one direction, driving the sand quicker at the ends than in the middle.

Longitudinal or seif dune

Longitudinal or s dunes are conside taller and run pa to the wind direc

Transverse dune

The dunes run at a perpendicular angle to the wind and are divided from each other by deep furrows.

Star dunes

If the wind direc keeps changing, star-shaped dune formed. Their po seldom changes.

Deserts of the world

- Desert climate
- Savanna climate
- Tundra climate
- Ice climate

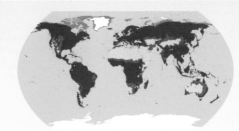

Types of desert

Geologists distinguish between gravel desert and scree desert (serir), stone or rock desert (hamada), sandy or dunes desert (erg), salt pan desert (sebka) and marl or clay desert (takyr).

de Uyuni salt flat

Country	Bolivia
Area	11,000 sq km/4247 sq mi
Length/breadth	110km/68mi x 140km/87mi
Precipitation (per annum)	150mm/6in

Gobi Desert

The Gobi is characterized by gigantic sand dunes, growing as tall as 400m/1312ft. The landscape also features barren steppes, mountain ranges and salt lakes.

Country	Central Asia
Area	1,200,000 sq km/463322 sq mi
Length/breadth	2000km/1242mi x 800km/500mi
Precipitation (p.a.)	30mm/1.2in to 200mm/8in

Desert is alive

The desert may appear barren and empty, but many species of flora and fauna have perfectly adapted their organisms to the desert climate.

History The founding fathers of Abu Dhabi and Dubai came from the Liwa oases which were colonized by the Bedouin tribe, the Bani Yas, in the early 18th century. They lived in simple barasti huts made of palm leaves. Sedentariness bred political differences among tribe members. In 1793, the Al Nahyan family left the tribe to settle in the coastal region further north, leading to the foundation of Abu Dhabi. In 1833, another branch of the Bani Yas, under the leadership of Sheikh Maktoum, left the oases and founded another settlement north of Abu Dhabi: Dubai. For Europeans, the region south of the pirate coast remained unknown territory for a long time. In 1948, British colonial officer Wilfred Thesiger (▶Famous People) became the first European to reach the oases with his camel caravan. His report is one of the great works of travel literature (▶p.303).

Camel trek on the edge of Rub al-Khali

The settlement of Madinat Zayed is lined with inviting cafés and restaurants. Beyond them, 150m/164yd-high sand dunes rise up on
both sides of the street. Every now and again, free-roaming camels
wander up to the fence which keeps them off the street.

Madinat Zayed

The main oasis town is Mezairaa, from which a tarmacked road leads
east and west, connecting the individual villages. Odd trails leading
north and south are poorly signposted and hence better avoided by
visitors who are unfamiliar with the region.

Mezairaa

Between Mezairaa and Hamim, the impressive Fort Attab is well
worth a visit. The headquarters of the Bani Yas with three mighty
round towers has been restored and is open to the public.

Fort Attab

Ajman

AJMAN

Area: 250 sq km/96.5 sq mi
Population: 263,000

Emir: Sheikh Humaid Bin-Rashid
al- Nuaimi (since 1981)

Tourism is still in its infancy in Ajman. With a new luxury hotel resort, however, the emirate is now trying to catch up. After all, the sheikhdom's wide, sandy Ajman beach is one of the UAE's most beautiful coastal stretches.

The smallest of the seven emirates, situated between Sharjah and Umm al-Quwain on an inlet of the Arabian Gulf, is completely surrounded by Sharjah on the landside. Ajman has two remote exclaves used for agriculture: the oasis settlement of Manama, approximately 60km/37mi to the east and Masfut, approximately 160km/99mi to the southeast, close to the border with Oman in the Hajar Mountains, which is known, amongst other things, for its marble quarries; The emirate has also begun exploiting its copper and iron resources.

Surrounded by Sharjah

As no oil has yet been found in Ajman, it is **one of the poorer regions in the UAE** and has depended on financial support from Abu Dhabi for the last four decades. This has enabled Ajman to build a thriving shipyard, a television station and steelworks, the Arab Heavy Industries Company. Living expenses here are among the lowest in the UAE, hence more and more foreign workers decide to live in Ajman and commute to work in the other sheikhdoms. Part of the population still lives on fishing, e.g. sardines, which are dried and sold as fertilizer to agricultural businesses.

Ajman's history is virtually identical to that of Sharjah. Under Sheikh Rashid Bin-Humaid al-Nuaimi, the first ruler of Ajman, who reigned between 1820 and 1838, the emirate separated from Sharjah in 1820. In the same year, Sheikh Rashid was one of the seven emirs to sign the first peace agreement, the General Treaty, with the British.

History

Ajman is the smallest of the seven emirates and is a peaceful rather than hectic place. The old fort now houses the Ajman Museum.

✱ Ajman City

✦ J 3

Population: 250,000

While there are still some old buildings in the northern part of the city, the modern and largely characterless buildings beyond the lagoon and in the southern fringe areas of Ajman reveal a fast-growing 21st-century Arabic city.

Ajman, the **capital of the emirate** which shares its name, is situated between the Arabian Gulf and the Khor Ajman estuary which cuts inland in the north. Small shops line the streets of the city centre, as well as several banks, bureaux de change and simple restaurants serving Arabic cuisine. A stroll through the Old Souk is a great way of becoming familiar with the hustle and bustle of everyday life; here, the haggling over prices lasts from early morning until long after dark. Except during lunchtime that is, when the city streets seem entirely deserted.

Ajman City

SOUKS

The Old Souk on the east side of the marina mainly sells foods such as meat, fish, spices, fruit and vegetables. The separate fish souk has a particularly varied selection. At the Iranian Souk near the marina, merchants offer imported household goods, especially plastic goods in all shapes, sizes and colours. The Gold Souk on Omar Bin al-Khatab Street, somewhat oversized for Ajman, primarily attracts a more local crowd. Ajman City Centre is a new, modern souk with numerous shops and several restaurants, actually located outside the city on the road to Ras al-Khaimah.

BEACHES

The wide and sandy beach between Sharjah and Ajman is little frequented, but also lacks proper infrastructure. The beach on the west coast of the peninsula is less appealing and often quite dirty; it is only cleaned at Coral Beach and in front of the Ajman Beach Hotel. Note: the currents at Ajman beaches can be dangerous.

WHERE TO EAT

❶ *Hai Tao* £££
at the Kempinski Hotel
Tel. 06 714 55 55
Closed on Tuesdays
Fine Szechuan and Cantonese cuisine

❷ *Falcon* ££
Ajman Marina
Tel. 06 742 33 44
Enjoy Arabic specialities in a pleasant atmosphere

❸ *India House* ££ Insider Tip
Sheikh Hamid Bin-Abdul Aziz Street
(next to Choithram)
Tel. 06 744 24 97
www.indiahouseajman.com

WHAT TO SEE IN AJMAN CITY

The city's most prominent site is situated on the east side of Central Square: the Ajman Museum is housed in an 18th-century fort, the oldest monument of the city. The marvellously restored building once served as residence to Sheikh Rashid al-Nuaimi, the current ruler's father, who died in 1981. Two watchtowers secured the coast and the Khor Ajman; wind towers provided cooler conditions during hot summer days (►p.272).

*Ajman Museum

The museum hosts an interesting archaeological exhibition; among them are Bronze Age burial objects and a replica of a 5,000-year old burial site as discovered in the emirate. The finds confirm that Ajman was also colonized at a very early stage. Like the museum in Dubai, life-size figures portray everyday scenes from the past. On the ground floor the exhibition rooms, arranged around the large inner courtyard, include a traditional bakery, a tailor, a barber and herbal healer, as well as a replica of an old Arab coffee house. A Qur'an school and an old police station can be seen on the first floor, which is also an

Guests come here for the vegetarian food, such as exotic vegetables from the tandoori oven.

❹ *Ajman City Centre* £
Tel. 06 743 28 88
The food court of the Ajman City Centre is ideal for a quick snack in between exploring the sights.

❺ *Al-Masa Café* £
Corniche
Tel. 06 747 41 63
Arabic snacks in a shisha café

WHERE TO STAY
❶ *Ajman Kempinski Hotel & Resort* £££
Ajman Corniche
Tel. 06 714 55 55
www.ajmankempinski.com
Directly located on a beautiful, wide private beach, the Ajman Kempinski offers plenty of sports facilities, including water sports, tennis and squash. Ideal for fami-

lies (there is a kids club on site). All 189 rooms and suites come with an ocean view. The hotel houses eleven restaurants and bars.

❷ *Ajman Beach Hotel* ££
Al-Khaleej Road
(Ajman Corniche)
Tel. 06 742 33 33
www.ajmanbeachhotel.com
The hotel is situated approx. 20km/12.5mi from Dubai airport. Its 65 rooms are comfortable; the beach is covered with bright, white sand. Daily shuttle bus service to Dubai.

❸ *Al-Waha* £
Sheikh Hamid Bin-Abdul Aziz Street
(near Kuwaiti Hospital)
P.O. Box 28 69
Tel. 06 742 43 33
A Simple hotel, centrally located. All 233 rooms equipped with bathroom and air-conditioning.

Ajman

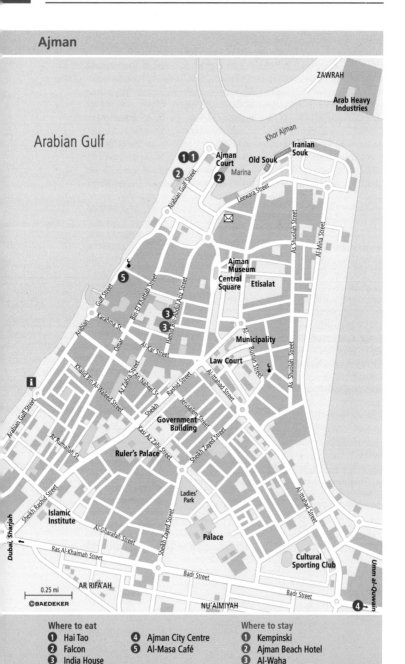

ZAWRAH

Arab Heavy Industries

Arabian Gulf

Khor Ajman

Iranian Souk

Ajman Court

Old Souk

Marina

Arabian Gulf Street

Leewara Street

As Shuolah Street

Al-Mina Street

Ajman Museum

Central Square

Etisalat

Gulf Street

Bin El Khattab Street

Hamid Bin Abdul Aziz Street

Karahma St.

Arabian

Omar

Al-Kar Street

Municipality

Al-Bustan Street

As Shuolah Street

Law Court

Al-Ittahad Street

Khalid Bin Al-Wafeed Street

Az Zahra Street

An Nafeel St.

Rashid Street

Jerusalem Street

Sheikh

Government Building

Kasr Az Zahr Street

Sheikh Zayed Street

Ruler's Palace

Ar Rumailah St.

Ladies' Park

Islamic Institute

Sheikh Rashid Street

Arabian Gulf Street

Al-Gharafah Street

Sheikh Zayed Street

Palace

Al-Ittahad Street

Cultural Sporting Club

Dubai, Sharjah

Ras Al-Khaimah Street

Badr Street

Badr Street

Umm al-Quwain

AR RIFA'AH

NU'AIMIYAH

0.25 mi

©BAEDEKER

Where to eat
1. Hai Tao
2. Falcon
3. India House
4. Ajman City Centre
5. Al-Masa Café

Where to stay
1. Kempinski
2. Ajman Beach Hotel
3. Al-Waha

ideal place to take a closer look at the **wind tower** which is still in use. This affords an insight into the simple, yet effective, construction of the traditional air-conditioning system which Persian merchants introduced in the 19th century.

Sat–Thu 9am–1pm and 4pm–7pm, Fri 4pm to 7pm; admission 5 Dh

The former palace of Sheikh Humaid Bin-Rashid al-Nuaimi on Sheikh Rashid Street, where the Emir resided long after his inauguration in 1981, can only be admired from outside. Sheikh Humaid now lives in a new palace on the northern Arabian Gulf Street across from the Ajman Beach Hotel. The palace, built in neo-Islamic style, has a large dome and four watchtowers, and is surrounded by well-kept lawns and enormous date trees. Photography is prohibited.

Ruler's Palace

The harbour, with its fully laden dhows, water taxis (abras) and fishing boats, is situated at the northern end of Arabian Gulf Street. The hustle and bustle on the piers and on the water can be best observed from a nearby coffee house or restaurant.

Ajman Marina

The dhow yard opens a window on the past. The traditional wooden ships are still built using time-honoured techniques, although shipbuilders have also begun using fibreglass as a building material. Ships at different stages of completion – still built without any design plans – can always be found in the yard. Authentically detailed model dhows, crafted by yard workers in their free time, are sometimes sold at the shipyard, making attractive souvenirs to take back home.

*Dhow yard

Dubai

DUBAI

Area: 3,885 sq km/1,500 sq mi	**Emir:** Sheikh Mohammed Bin-Rashid
Population: 2.3 million	al-Maktoum (since 2006)

Dubai is the tourist epicentre of the United Arab Emirates, with an unparalleled number of luxurious hotels and better shopping facilities than anywhere else. The choice of restaurants, serving both Arabic and international cuisine, is enormous; a seemingly endless row of hotels lines Jumeirah beach.

The Emirate of Dubai, situated between Sharjah in the north and Abu Dhabi in the south is the second largest emirate of the UAE, with 70km/44mi of coastline and an interior stretching 80km/50mi inland. The emirate owns three exclaves in the other sheikhdoms, the largest of which is Hatta. The emirate's eponymous capital lies on both sides of Dubai Creek (Al-Khor), which is between 200 and 800 metres (219–875 yards) wide, an inlet (Khor in Arabic) stretching 12km/7.5mi into the sheikhdom.

Economy

Dubai is **the most important trade centre** in the United Arab Emirates, including the country's most significant harbours Jebel Ali and Port Rashid. Port Rashid can accommodate four cruise liners at the same time, thereby adding to the emirate's growing importance as a cruise destination. Home to over 7,000 companies, Jebel Ali is by far the largest industrial site on the Arabian Gulf. With the Dubai World Trade Centre and more than 40 conventions per year, the emirate has also become the number one trade fair location for the Middle East. Dubai's most recent coup is underway: in order to create new sources of income besides petroleum, the free-trade zone »Internet City«, an »Arabian Silicon Valley« as it were, has been established 20km/12.5mi outside the city.

HISTORY

First settlement

Dubai was colonized as early as the 2nd millennium BC. Finds in Qusais, 13km/8mi northeast of Dubai, lead to the assumption that, even at this early stage, the region now covered by the emirate was an influential centre of trade. Around 500 BC, people settled in Jumeirah, where they constructed quite elaborate complexes of buildings.

Burj Khalifa, a dream come true of endless growth

Among the finds are the remains of one structure which was most likely used as a palace, as well as walls of a 20-room caravanserai. During the Umayyad Period (661–750), Dubai served as a resting post for caravans en route from Oman to Mesopotamia.

The founding of Dubai

Recent Islamic history of the Dubai sheikhdom begins in 1833, when the Bedouin tribe, the Bani Yas, left the Liwa Oasis for the coast under the leadership of Sheikh Maktoum Bin-Butti al-Blofas and settled at Dubai Creek. In the early 20th century, more and more Persian merchants chose Dubai as their new place of residence and built spacious, multi-storey residences from coral limestone.

Commercial metropolis on the Arabian Gulf

During the first half of the 20th century, Dubai evolved into an commercial metropolis on the Arabian Gulf. In 1935, the Deira Souk already included more than 300 vendors. This level of growth was matched by Dubai's increasingly significant role as a transport hub: close to the city, **Dubai International Airport** came into operation in 1971 and became the largest airport on the Arabian Peninsula, at least until completion of the Al-Maktoum International Airport which is currently under construction near Jebel Ali. In the year 2000, the opening of the Burj Al Arab luxury hotel (▶MARCO POLO Insight p.218), definitively attracted international attention. The dawn of the 21st century witnessed a turbulent phase of development. Dubai was not immune to the world financial crisis. The World

Dubai: sun loungers against a backdrop of skyscrapers

artificial island project faced insolvency in 2009 and construction work on the 828m/2716ft high Burj Dubai faltered until Abu Dhabi stepped in with an injection of funds. This led to the renaming of the building as Burj Khalifa when it was inaugurated in 2010. The adjacent Dubai Mall is the world's second-largest shopping complex. An artificial palm-shaped island, The Palm Jumeirah, extends 4.5km/3mi into the sea, with a high-level monorail connecting the city to the Hotel Atlantis and its Aquaventure waterpark. By the sea to the south of the city, a district called Dubai Marina was built, with stunning high-rise buildings and skyscrapers around an elongated yacht harbour. Construction of another artificial island, The Palm Jebel Ali, began here in 2002 but the project was abandoned in 2009. Dubailand is being built to the east of the city, the artificial archipelago Deira Island is emerging to the north, whilst The World venture drags on in fits and starts. Dubai will host the World Expo in 2020.

✶✶ Dubai City

— ✦ J 4

Population: 2.28 million

A glittering metropolis, state-of-the-art shopping malls, oriental charm in the old town, artificial islands, fine sandy beaches, sunshine all year round, people from 120 nations: Dubai is a multifaceted city.

Building work is going on all over Dubai. To make space for new, hypermodern projects, buildings from the 1970s and 1980s are torn down or artificial islands created. The city is not only the most important city of the seven emirates in terms of tourism, but is also the commercial and economic centre of the Middle East, the hub for trade, finance and services.

The cityscape is predominantly western and decidedly green, thanks to an underground irrigation system. Not only the median strips of city highways blossom with date palms and bougainvilleas, roses and oleander bushes. Splendid residential palaces of the local upper class lie hidden behind high walls.

The traditional lifeline of the city is **Dubai Creek**, 12km/7.5mi long, 200 and 800 metres (219–875 yards) wide. The inlet splits the historic heart of the city into two halves: **Deira** on the eastern bank and **Bur Dubai** to the west. Rows of heavy laden dhows, often five deep, line the quay wall on the Deira side at all hours – the large freighters dock at Port Rashid near the city or at the commercial harbour of Port Jebel Ali.

Overview

Beyond Port Rashid in the west of the city, lies **Jumeirah Beach** which stretches some 20km/12.5mi to the new Dubai Marina. White sand, turquoise blue water and luxurious hotels constitute the ultimate tourist domain. Of the various artificial peninsulae planned off the coast, only Palm Jumeirah has come to fruition. The World project has run into difficulties, whilst Palm Deira, conceived on a much larger scale, has been considerably trimmed down (p.220). Along Sheikh Zayed Road to the south, in the shadow of the Burj Khalifa skyscraper, lies the burgeoning hypermodern city centre of Dubai Downtown. The industrial district, free trade zone and the new commercial harbour of Port Jebel Ali all lie immediately to the west of Dubai Marina.

Transport Simple, diesel-powered wooden boats (abras) sail across the creek between Deira and Bur Dubai. Air-conditioned waterbuses ferry passengers up and down the creek. Heading away from the city, several bridges span the creek (and more are in the planning stages). Close to the mouth of the estuary, the Al-Shindagha Tunnel and a pedestrian tunnel cross underneath.

The **Metro** came into operation in 2009 (p.198). A ride in the air-conditioned carriages, which travel as high as 6m/20ft along a viaduct, is both quick and cheap, offering a fine overview of the city. The Red Line runs from the airport through the city centre, then southwest along Sheikh Zayed Road to Port Jebel Ali. The Green Line connects residential and industrial districts on both sides of Dubai Creek. The Dubai Tram thus far runs between Jumeirah Beach, Dubai Marina and Al Sufouh (with connections to the Metro and the monorail which goes to the Palm Jumeirah palm island; p.196). Several bus routes run between Dubai and Sharjah (p.262; Dubai stop: Baniyas Square, in Sharjah: Al Wahda Road). The first section of Al-Maktoum International Airport, a new international airport near Jebel Ali, was opened in 2011.

> **!** MARCO POLO TIP
>
> *Along the Creek by waterbus* **Insider Tip**
>
> The air-conditioned waterbuses can carry up to 36 passengers on four lines across and along the Creek (fare: 4 Dh). A wonderful harbour tour from Shindagha to Creek Park is just the ticket for tourists, costing 25 Dh.

WHAT TO SEE IN DEIRA

Deira Deira stands on the eastern bank of the creek, part of the historic centre of the city. Its heart is the Al-Ras headland (Al-Ras = head), home to the richly colourful Deira Souk which consists of the Gold Souk, one of the emirate's main attractions, and streets purveying foodstuffs, textiles and household goods. This area and the bank of the creek are best navigated on foot. East of the entrance to the creek, a second artificial island is emerging in the gulf: Palm Deira was originally designed to be 49 sq km/19 sq mi, or eight times larger than Palm Jumeirah. Not only did the financial crisis shrink the project to just 15 sq km/6 sq mi, Deira Island will no longer take the shape of a palm (www.nakheel.com). A number of luxury hotels and modern towers of steel and glass line Bani Yas Road which follows the creek on the south side of Deira. The postmodern Municipality Building (city hall) strikes an imposing figure, an open, square construction cased in light marble which stands over a round, red granite building. A giant globe fountain complements the ensemble. Immediately in front of the city hall, a sculpture of a dromedary with a chess board on its back commemorates the 1986 World Chess Olympiad in Dubai. The Etisalat Telecommunications Corporation's skyscraper is a real eye-catcher with a gigantic golf ball antenna on the roof. Opposite Dubai International Airport (DXB), the famous Dubai Creek Golf & Yacht Club is right alongside the creek.

The souk began in the 19th century on the Al Ras headland at the mouth of the creek. By 1910 it was the largest souk on the Gulf coast. It is bordered by Al Sabkha Road to the east, Al Khor Street to the north and the creek to the west. Inside, the souk is divided into different sections. Two restored wind towers right next to Deira Old Souk Abra Station mark the entrance to the **Spice Souk**. The narrow alleyways are packed with sacks and bowls filled with herbs and spices from the Middle East and Asia. Enchanting aromas of paprika, curry, cumin, coriander, cardamom, turmeric, ginger, cloves, chilli peppers and dried fish. Hand-crafted pottery in which incense resins are burned might be a purchase worth considering.

Deira Old Souk

Textiles can be found in the Naif Souk, south of the street of the same name. Fruit, vegetables, meat and fish are sold at the northeast end of the creek, for example in a large hall beyond Al Khaleej Road, east of the Al Shindagha Tunnel.

Naif Souk

❶ Sat–Thu 10am–1pm, 4pm–10pm, Fri from 4pm; Metro: Baniyas Square

The Gold Souk, one of Dubai's most popular attractions, is adjacent to the Spice Souk and can be reached via the Gold Souk Bus Station or the Hyatt Regency Hotel. 300 tons of gold are imported annually from the UAE, roughly 10 to 15 per cent of global production, most of which ends up in Dubai's Gold Souk and the New Gold Building. Dubai is, in this respect as well, quite a gold mine. Over 300 shops line both sides of the covered street. As soon as the sun sets, limousines with tinted windows stop at both ends of the pedestrian zone and Arab women from neighbouring states and emirates, dressed in

**Gold Souk

Around Dubai

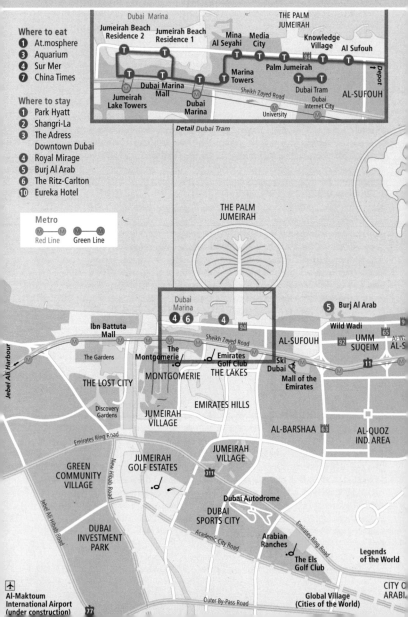

Where to eat
1 At.mosphere
3 Aquarium
4 Sur Mer
7 China Times

Where to stay
1 Park Hyatt
2 Shangri-La
3 The Adress Downtown Dubai
4 Royal Mirage
5 Burj Al Arab
6 The Ritz-Carlton
10 Eureka Hotel

Metro
Red Line   Green Line

Detail Dubai Tram

Dubai Marina
THE PALM JUMEIRAH
Jumeirah Beach Residence 2
Jumeirah Beach Residence 1
Mina Al Seyahi
Media City
Knowledge Village
Al Sufouh
Marina Towers
Palm Jumeirah
Dubai Marina Mall
Jumeirah Lake Towers
Dubai Marina
Sheikh Zayed Road
Dubai Tram
Dubai Internet City
AL-SUFOUH
Depot
University

THE PALM JUMEIRAH

Dubai Marina
4 6   4
94
Ibn Battuta Mall
Sheikh Zayed Road
AL-SUFOUH
5 Burj Al Arab
Wild Wadi
UMM SUQEIM
9
The Gardens
The Montgomerie
Emirates Golf Club
Ski Dubai
Mall of the Emirates
92
11
AL-S
THE LOST CITY
MONTGOMERIE
THE LAKES
Discovery Gardens
EMIRATES HILLS
AL-BARSHAA
35
AL-QUOZ IND. AREA
Emirates Ring Road
JUMEIRAH VILLAGE
JUMEIRAH VILLAGE
GREEN COMMUNITY VILLAGE
JUMEIRAH GOLF ESTATES
311
Jebel Ali Harbour
New Hibab Road
Dubai Autodrome
Jebel Ali Hibab Road
DUBAI INVESTMENT PARK
DUBAI SPORTS CITY
Academic City Road
Arabian Ranches
The Els Golf Club
Emirates Ring Road
Legends of the World
CITY O ARABI
Al-Maktoum International Airport (under construction)
77
Outer By-Pass Road
Global Village (Cities of the World)

Arabian Gulf

THE WORLD
(under construction)

DEIRA ISLAND
(under construction)

N

3 mi

5 km

©BAEDEKER

Port
Rashid

see map
Dubai • Downtown

Jumeirah
Mosque

7

BUR
DUBAI

DEIRA

Al-Khaleej Road

Jumeirah Rd

Burjuman

Union Square

JUMEIRAH

Safa Park

2

BASTAKIYA

Al-Rasheed Road

10

SHARJAH

Sheikh Zayed Road

Maktoum
Bridge

Burj
Khalifa

1

Dubai World
Trade Centre

3

Al-Ittihad Road

Sharjah-Stadt

11

-QUOZ

DOWNTOWN
DUBAI

44

Dubai – Al Ain Rd

Dubai Health
Care City

66

Creek

1

AL-NAHDA

Dubai Camel
Race Course

11

Al Garhoud
Bridge

Dubai
International Airport

AL-QUSAIS

Dubai

Dubai
Festival City

Dubai
Opera House

Al-Badia
Golf Club

Four Seasons
Golf Club

MUHAISNAH

Nad Al-Sheba
Golf Club

44

411

91

Etisalat

L-MARQADH

Meydan City
Racecourse

Ras Al Khor Road

89

Emirates Ring Road

66

Al-Rashidiya

AL-RASHIDIYA

DUBAILAND
der construction)

311

AL-MIZHAR

Dubai – Al Ain Road

NADD AL-SHIBA

AL-WARQAA

MUSHRIF
PARK

Academic City Road

WARSAN

Dubai City

INFORMATION

Government of Dubai Department of Tourism and Commerce Marketing

Al Fattan Plaza, Airport Road, Deira
Dubai
Tel. 04 282 11 11
Sun–Thu 8am–2pm
www.dubaitourism.co.ae
There are also tourist information kiosks
in the larger shopping malls.

TRANSPORT

Simple, diesel-powered wooden boats
(abras) run back and forth across the
creek between the districts of Deira (in
the east) and Bur Dubai (in the west)
from 6am to midnight. There are 6 designated ferry stops; 1 trip costs 1 Dh
(have the exact change ready).
A more comfortable way to travel is one
of the air-conditioned waterbuses which
follow three routes between Al Shindagha station at Sheikh Saeed House
and Al Seef station opposite the Etisalat
building; single journey 2 Dh, return 4
Dh.
The fully automated Metro operates
Sat–Wed from 6am to midnight, Thu
until 2am, Fri 10am–2am, with trains
every 6 to 8 minutes (▶map p.196).

The Dubai Tram service opened in November 2014 (tram, map p.196).
For information on local transport in Dubai and for buses to Hatta, Ai Ain, Sharjah, Abu Dhabi city and to the other emirates: Roads & Transport Authority (RTA),
tel. 800 90 90 (toll-free) and www.rta.ae.
Prices: single tickets or day passes are
available from self-service machines.
Alternatively, the so-called Nol Card is a
rechargeable card which calculates fares
according to length of journey. Prices:
single trip in 1 zone: 2.50 Dh; day pass
14 Dh.

SHOPPING

The extravagant range of souks and
malls in the shopping paradise of Dubai
can quickly eat into visitors' holiday budgets (▶p.105). Nevertheless, a visit to
Dubai would not be complete without
exploring at least one of these consumer
temples. A few tips and addresses worth
noting: Antiques, including silverware
from Yemen and Oman, can be found at
the Souk Al Bahar (opposite Dubai Mall)
and Souk Khan Murjan in Wafi City.
»Book World« in the Dubai Mall boasts
the greatest selection of books (in the
UAE). Ceramics with Arabic designs, an-
tiquarian and lead glazing wares are
among the specialities of The Courtyard
on Sheikh Zayed Road. In Bastakiya, the
Majlis Gallery and XVA Gallery (with two
patios and restaurant) present regional
contemporary art and crafts.
The best known shopping complexes are
the Mall of the Emirates in the south of
the city, the Wafi Mall, Dubai Mall and
Deira City Centre.

The Dubai Mall
▶p.226

Ibn Battuta Mall
Sheikh Zayed Road, Jebel Ali (between 5th and 6th Interchange)
Metro: Ibn Battuta; www.ibnbattuta-mall.com, Sun–Wed 10am–midnight, Thu–Sat until 1am
The design of the mall is inspired by the voyages of 14th-century seafarer and adventurer Ibn Battuta (famous people); shop amongst Andalusian patios, see the Egyptian sphinx. China, India and Persia also extend invitations; 250 shops, restaurants and food courts.

Mercato Mall
Jumeirah Road, Jumeirah II
Metro: Burj Khalifa; www.mercatoshoppingmall.com, daily 10am–10pm
The Bella Italia exterior hints at the marvels inside: Florentine Renaissance palazzi, Venetian bridges and historic fountains adorn this relatively small mall. Among its 120 shops are Next, Laura Ashley, Mango and a Spinneys supermarket. European expatriates living in Jumeirah meet at the cafés under the glass dome.

Wafi Mall
▶p.213

Mall of the Emirates
Sheikh Zayed Road, 4th Interchange
Metro: Mall of the Emirates
www.malloftheemirates.com, Sun–Wed 10am–10pm, Thu–Sun until midnight
One of the biggest shopping temples in the world, complemented by the twin attractions of a Kempinski Hotel in chalet style and the spectacular »Ski Dubai«.
More than 450 shops (notably the elegant British department store Harvey Nichols) are gathered here, including the Emporio Armani Boutique and neighbouring Armani Caffè – with exclusively Italian staff – where the fashion-conscious linger. Free shuttle bus service to selected hotels.

Al Ghurair Centre
Corner of Al Riqqa Road, Omar Ibn Al Khattab Road, Deira, at the Gold Souk
Metro: Al Riqqa
www.alghuraircentre.com, Sat–Thu 10am–10pm, Fri 2pm–10pm
Over 200 shops and restaurants, including French Connection, Guess, Esprit, various cosmetics and sports retailers.

Deira City Centre
Al Garhoud Road, Deira (opposite Dubai Creek Golf & Yacht Club) Metro: Deira City Centre
www.deiracitycentre.com, Sun–Wed 10am–10pm, Thu–Sat until midnight
Dubai's favourite consumer temple with an impressive array of mid-range and deluxe offerings. Approximately 370 stores plus cafés, restaurants and a (self-service) food court.

Insider Tip

Hamarain Centre
Abu Baker Al Siddique Road, next to the Marriott Hotel
Metro: Abu Baker Al Siddique
www.hamaraincentre.com, Sat–Thu 10am–10pm, Fri 2pm–10pm
75 shops including top fashion brands, leather goods, handicrafts, electronics, jewellery, cosmetics and international cuisine in ten restaurants.

CITY TOURS
Two open-top double-decker bus routes run from Wafi City and Deira City Centre to the most prominent sights of Dubai (The Big Bus, tel. 04 340 77 09, www.bigbustours.com, May–Sept daily 3pm–8pm, Oct–April daily 9am–5pm; fares:

adults 220 Dh, children 100 Dh, families
540 Dh).

❶, ❶, etc. see map p.196 (Greater
Dubai) or map p.206 (Dubai Old Town)

WHERE TO EAT
❶ *At.mosphere* ££££
Burj Khalifa
1 Emaar Boulevard, Downtown Dubai
122nd floor
Metro: Burj Khalifa
Tel. 04 888 38 28 (be sure to book as
early as possible in advance)
www.atmosphereburjkhalifa.com
The highest restaurant in the world in
the tallest building in the world – with
similarly lofty prices. Arabic and international dishes. A lift shoots up
442m/1450ft in just 58 seconds to reach
classically styled, yet modern restaurants
with mahogany walls and café au lait limestone floors: »Lounge« serves finger
food and the like, »Grill« specializes in
international and Arabic steaks.

❷ *Al-Dawar* ££££
Hyatt Regency Hotel
Corniche Road, Deira
Tel. 04 204 09 12 34
www.dubairegency.hyatt.com
This revolving restaurant on the 25th floor
of the Hyatt Regency Hotel offers a large
buffet with international specialities.

❸ *Aquarium* ££££
Dubai Creek Golf & Yacht Club, Deira
Tel. 04 295 60 007
www.dubaigolf.com
Exquisite fish restaurant in the
35m/115ft-high clubhouse; elegant, exclusive atmosphere.

❹ *Sur Mer* £££
Meydan Beach Club, JBR Walk

Dubai Marina
Tel. 04 433 37 77
www.meydanbeach.com
Admission Sun–Thu 250 Dh (incl. 100
Dh food & drink voucher), Fri–Sat 495
Dh (incl. 250 Dh voucher)
Favoured meeting place for Dubai socie-
ty; international cuisine served in a chic
beach club.

❺ *Danial* £££
Twin Towers, 3rd floor
Baniyas Road
(next to the Radisson Blue Hotel)
Tel. 04 227 76 69
www.danialrestaurant.com
Fine Iranian cuisine. Try the kebab special for two or more people. Fish dishes
and one inexpensive daily dish are also
served.

❻ *Bayt al Wakeel* ££ Insider Tip
Souk al Kabeer
(Bur Dubai)
Tel. 04 353 05 30
This trading house, built in 1935, stands
at an abra landing stage on the creek;
Arabic and Western cuisine.

❼ *China Times* £
Jumeirah Plaza Centre
Jumeirah Beach Road
Tel. 04 344 29 30
A Chinese restaurant with an extensive
menu and delicious dishes. Ideal for fa-
milies with children.

❽ *Food Court* £ Insider Tip
Twin Towers
Baniyas Road
(next to the Radisson Blue Hotel)
The most beautiful food court in town is
situated on the 3rd floor of the shopping complex by the creek. Choose between the air-conditioned hall and the

large balcony with a great view of the activities on the water.

❾ *Apple* £
Twin Towers
Baniyas Road
(next to the Radisson Blue Hotel)
Tel. 04 227 77 41
www.applecaferestaurant.net
Romantic restaurant on the third floor of the shopping complex, with decent Arabic fish dishes. Excellent balcony view of the creek. Shisha available.

WHERE TO STAY
❶ *Park Hyatt* ££££
Dubai Creek Golf & Yacht Club
Al-Garhoud
Tel. 04 602 12 34
www.dubai.park.hyatt.com
Situated on the Creek. 225 large and luxurious rooms with balconies looking onto the golf course, yacht club or Dubai Creek. Tennis courts, spa and gym, several excellent restaurants.

❷ *Shangri-La* ££££
Sheikh Zayed Road
(corner of Al Safa Street)
Tel. 04 343 88 88
www.shangri-la.com
302 rooms
Metro: Financial Centre
The hotel stands on Sheikh Zayed Road, close to the new district of Downtown Dubai. The very name which Malaysian founder Robert Kuok chose for his hotel chain conjures up images of paradise, as described in James Hilton's novel Lost Horizon. A copy of the book lies in each of this wonderfully luxurious resort's 302 rooms in warm, earthy tones. Some of the city's finest restaurants, a delightful spa and opulent pool layout are all

designed to pamper guests around the clock.

❸ *The Address Downtown Dubai* ££££
Emaar Boulevard
Downtown Dubai
Tel. 04 436 88 88
www.theaddress.com, 196 rooms
The design hotel opposite Burj Khalifa near the Dubai Mall is 306m/1004ft high, with stunning views from the Neos Bar on the 63rd floor.

❹ *Royal Mirage* ££££
Al Mina Al Seyahi Street
Jumeirah Beach
Tel. 04 399 99 99
www.oneandonlyresorts.com/one-and-only-royal-mirage-dubai
253 rooms
The hotel with its domes, over a thousand palm trees, marble halls and Moroccan antiques, seems to have been lifted directly from the pages of an oriental fairytale. The spacious lobby features golden frescoes and a ceiling decorated with lights, crowned by a large dome. As the name suggests, the hotel is owned by the royal family.

❺ Burj Al Arab ££££
Jumeirah Beach
Tel. 04 364 75 55
www.burj-al-arab.com
Built on an artificial island, the Burj Al Arab reaches skywards like the bulging sail of a dhow. The 180m/590ft-high lobby is a cathedral of light and gold. Fountains spray water 50m/164ft into the air. The hotel has its own helicopter landing pad. Breathtaking views from the Skyview Bar on the 27th floor, with the coast and sea visible through panoramic glazing.

❻ The Ritz-Carlton ££££
JBR Walk, Jumeirah Beach
Dubai Marina
Tel. 04 399 40 00
www.ritzcarlton.com
138 rooms and suites
At this luxury hotel, situated 25km/15.5mi south of the city centre on Jumeirah Beach, guests are looked after by as many as 350 employees. Equipped with several restaurants, bars, a cigar room, a beach club, three pools, a kids' pool and club, a 300m/328yd stretch of private beach, tennis and squash courts and a fitness room, this hotel provides a mixture of European luxury and oriental flair.

❼ Radisson Blu £££
476 Baniyas Road, Deira
Tel. 04 222 71 71
www.radissonblu.com
301 rooms
This hotel encompasses a shopping arcade with fashion and antique stores, as well as several restaurants, of which the »Fishmarket« is not only the most beautiful, but also has rather an unusual concept: diners take a shopping basket and wander along an enormous counter laden with fresh fish, shellfish and vegetables. The choice of food is then prepared as requested while guests enjoy the view of the scintillatingly illuminated creek and Bur Dubai after sunset.

❽ Marco Polo ££
Al-Mateena Street
Tel. 042 72 00 00
www.marcopolohotel.net
126 rooms
The hotel is situated close to the Al Ghurair shopping mall. Includes a French, Indian and Tex-Mex restaurant, an English pub, a nightclub and discotheque.

❾ Riviera ££
Dubai Creek Corniche
Tel. 042 22 21 31
www.rivierahotel-dubai.com
109 rooms
The hotel, with its marvellous view of the creek, is located next to the Twin Towers complex. It has a simple but good restaurant, serving Arab as well as Thai and Japanese cuisine.

❿ Eureka Hotel £
Al Rigga Road, Deira
Tel. 042 95 44 66
www.eurekahotel.ae
Mid-range hotel with 96 small en suite rooms. Fitness centre, a little rooftop pool and an Indian restaurant.

⓫ Ahmedia Heritage Guesthouse ££–£££
Al-Ras Road
Al-Ras, Deira
www.heritagedubaihotels.com
Tel. 042 25 00 85
Close to the Ahmadiya School and the gold and spice souks, this small hotel in traditional Arab style has 15 spacious rooms and a pleasant restaurant.

black, climb out and disappear immediately into the glittering jewellery shops. Gold is sold according to the current value by weight (1 troy ounce of gold = 31 g) and purity (24 carat = 100% gold, 18 carat 75%, 14 carat 58% and 10 carat 42% gold). Bargaining over the price is customary, with discounts often possible, especially for those who buy several pieces at once. With larger purchases, customers receive small gold gifts as a complimentary bonus (opening hours as in Deira Old Souk, p.195).

Dubai Municipality Museum stands at the entrance to the Spice Souk in what was a trading house in the 1950s. From 1957 to 1964, the upper floor housed the city's municipal offices. The balcony affords lovely views of the creek and souk.

Dubai Municipality Museum

❶ Baniyas Road, Sun–Thu 8am–3pm, admission free

Contrast to modern shopping malls: Deira Old Souk

Abras, simple wooden boats, travel back and forth across the creek between the districts of Bur Dubai and Deira

Women's Museum At the edge of the Gold Souk, the small, yet vibrant Women's Museum in a 1950s house is dedicated to the many hidden or invisible women of the region, spiritual or artistic, some as wives and quiet advisors who had great influence on important men. Listen to the powerful voice of a famous woman long since dead who recorded her poems on tape. There are no photographs of her, however, as it was uncommon to take pictures of women at the time when she was alive. To round off the tour, enjoy a tea with cake and dates.

❶ Bait Al Banat, Sikka 28; Sat–Thu 10am–7pm, admission 20 Dh, www.womensmuseumae.com; Metro: Al Ras

The first school in Dubai, housed in a traditional clay building, was founded in 1912. It is located on a side street off Al-Ahmadiya Street, not far from the Souk. The current ruler Sheikh Mohammed Bin-Rashid Al-Maktoum was a pupil here. Commissioned by the successful merchant Sheikh Mohammed Bin-Ahmad Bin-Dalmouk, the school consists of twelve classrooms surrounding an inner courtyard. Initially, only adult men were educated here; later, in 1926, boys were also accepted, but no girls. Following meticulous restoration works, Al-Ahmadiya was reopened as a museum in 2002. Even the Qur'an inscriptions decorating the tall walls of the cool classrooms have been restored.

Al-Ahmadiya School

❶ Sat–Thu 8.30am–8pm, Fri 2.30pm–4.30pm, admission free; Metro Al Ras

Next to the Al-Ahmadiya School stands a traditional, two-storied house which was built in 1890 and progressively enlarged to its present size of 935 sq m/10,000 sq ft by its various owners, one of whom was a wealthy pearl trader. It has now been elaborately restored and turned into **a museum** to convey an insight into family life in early Dubai. All of the rooms lead off a courtyard graced with a fountain; it is worth visiting the reception and meeting rooms (majlis), verandas, living quarters, storerooms and the kitchen.

Heritage House

❶ Sat–Thu 8am–8pm, Fri 2.30pm– 8pm, admission free; Metro Al Ras

Sheikh Saeed was builder of the Naif Fort, a defensive fortification near the Naif Roundabout, designed to protect the Deira side from incursions. The building, which was built only in the 1930s, consists of an enormous tower overlooking the Creek, and other long, expansive sections. Today it houses a police station.

Naif Fort

❶ Metro: Baniyas Square

One of the three watchtowers which guarded the old district of Deira in the 19th century has been reconstructed. Erected in 1870, it stands in a small park on Naif Road at the Burj Nahar Roundabout. Originally built of clay and shell limestone, the round tower with a diameter of around 10m/33ft has two tiny windows at the top, surrounded by numerous narrow loopholes and bays. The roof of the tower is encircled by small battlements.

Burj Nahar

❶ Metro: Union Square

Situated on the eastern shore of Dubai Creek, close to the airport, this 18-hole golf course stretches over 80 hectares/200 acres and has quickly evolved into a venue for highly remunerated championships. Only constant underground irrigation and the care of hundreds of foreign workers allow the course to retain the lush green grass on the arid desert ground. Even for non-golfers, a visit to this immaculately maintained facility is worthwhile. The clubhouse boasts an extraor-

Dubai Creek Golf & Yacht Club

Dubai • Downtown

Where to eat
1. At.mosphere*
2. Al-Dawar
3. Aquarium*
4. Sur Mer*
5. Danial
6. Bayt al-Wakeel
7. China Times*
8. Food Court
9. Apple

Where to stay
1. Park Hyatt*
2. Shangri-La*
3. The Address Downtown Dubai*
4. Royal Mirage*
5. Burj Al Arab*
6. The Ritz-Carlton*
7. Radisson Blu
8. Marco Polo
9. Riviera
10. Eureka Hotel*
11. Ahmedia Heritage House

Outside*
see map
Around Dubai

Map labels:
- Deira Fish, Meat & Vegetable Market
- Station
- Women's Museum
- YA
- Palm Deira
- Green Line
- 103 Road
- Galleria Centre
- Al-Khaleej Road
- Al-Khoor Street
- Al-Daghaya Street
- Al-Sabkha Road
- AYAL NASIR
- SABKHA
- Naif Road
- Naif Souq
- Deira Street
- Al-Wasl Souq
- Al-Burj Street
- AL-MURAR
- Naif Road
- rlton Square
- Deira Tower
- Baniyas Sq.
- Al-Nakhal Street
- NAIF
- Al-Maktoum Street
- Twin Towers
- AL-RIQQA
- Hospital
- Al-Maktoum Hospital
- Memorial Plaza
- icipality uilding
- Union Square
- Union Square
- Umer Ibn Al-Khattab Road
- Fish Roundabout
- AL-MUTEENA
- Al-Muteena Street
- Salah Al-Din Rd.
- Etisalat
- Al-Ghurair City

dinary architectural design: its 35m/115ft roof construction is shaped like the sails of a traditional dhow (p.117). The chrome and glass building houses swimming pools, fitness rooms and a café/restaurant. The no less spectacular clubhouse of the marina, which is designed like the upper deck of a luxury liner, is a short walk away from the golf clubhouse.

❶ Metro: Deira City Cenre; www.dubaigolf.com

WHAT TO SEE IN BUR DUBAI

Bur Dubai   Bur Dubai, located on the southwest side of Dubai Creek, is the city's oldest district. The most pleasant way to arrive there is by water taxi (abra) from Deira. **Bastakiya** is here, a neighbourhood with the last few remaining historic houses and wind towers (▶MARCO POLO Insight p.272) and the old souks. Standing on **Shindagha peninsula** at the tip of Bur Dubai, it feels as if the oil boom era has returned. And yet just a few steps from the abras landing stage, it is possible to disappear into the bustling throng of the souk. Aromas of incense, curry and coriander waft through the air. Two reconstructed Bedouin villages with narrow alley and coral stone houses, Heritage Village and Diving Village, offer insights into daily life in Dubai at the beginning of the 20th century.

Bait Al-Wakeel   Bait Al-Wakeel, close to Bur Dubai Abra Station, was constructed in 1934 by the former ruler Sheikh Rashid Bin-Saeed Al-Maktoum as the first office and administrative building outside the palace. Today, it also houses a restaurant with Arab and international dishes and a terrace overlooking the busy boat traffic on the Creek (Metro: Al-Fahidi).

Old Bur Dubai Souk   Adjacent, to the right, the Old Bur Dubai Souk is a traditional souk arcade which was completely restored in 2002. The somewhat younger Deira Old Souk stands on the opposite bank of the Creek (p.195) and sells textiles, arts and crafts, ceramics and spices.

Al-Fahidi Fort and **Dubai Museum   At the heart of the old town centre, Al-Fahidi Fort is the emirate's oldest fortification, serving as a monitoring station and observation post. Built in 1787 with mud bricks and coral stone blocks around a large courtyard, the complex is over 40m/45yd long and 33m/36yd wide. The square northwest tower, in which cattle and gunpowder were stored, was erected in 1799. In the 20th century, the fort was used as a police station and prison.

Thorough restoration work commenced in 1971. Today the fort is home to the National Museum. Enter through the nail-studded wooden gate, taken from Sheikh Saeed's house in Shindagha, flanked

An old dhow in »dry dock« in front of Dubai Museum

by two cannon. Boats which were in use until the mid-20th century are on display in the courtyard. Note also a traditional barasti hut made of palm leaves and branches with a wind tower on the roof. Take the spiral staircase down to the museum basement, where life-size figures re-enact scenes of life and work in old Dubai, enhanced by atmospheric light and sound effects: scenes at the harbour, for example, pearl divers, traders weighing and checking the pearls, a 1960s souk, boys reading suras from the holy book to the rhythm of their teacher's stick in a Qur'an school. Other rooms are dedicated to Bedouin life: sparkling stars shining above their white tents; men sitting around an open fire, listening intently to the tales of a storyteller. Other themes include astronomy and the desert by night. The archaeology section displays tomb finds from Hatta and Al-Qusais dating back 3500 years.

❶ Sat–Thu 8.30am–7.30pm, Fri 2.30pm–9pm, admission 3 Dh; Metro: Al-Fahidi

New Diwan

Across from the museum stands the administration building of the Emir of Dubai, known as New Diwan, however it is not open to the public. The entrance is flanked by two massive wind towers. Built in

1990, the traditional-style construction includes hundreds of arches decorating the many windows, arcades and hallways. The wrought-iron bars lend the building a very special charm.

*Grand Mosque

The Grand Mosque of Dubai is directly opposite the fort, its 70m/230ft-high minaret tower visible from a distance. No less impressive are the nine large and 45 smaller colourful, lead-glazed domes, built between 1996–1998. The original Grand Mosque, which stood here in 1900, served as the architectural inspiration for the newer building. As the emirate's most prominent Islamic place of worship, the Grand Mosque can accommodate 1,200 believers. Non-Muslims are not allowed to enter.

**Bastakiya

Bastakiya takes its name from the town of Bastak in southern Iran, a reminder of the Iranian merchant families who settled here. They

Bastakiya, the oldest district in Dubai

built mostly two storey houses here in coral and shell limestone, the larger homes richly adorned with carved wooden doors and window screens. The two reception rooms (majlis) had separate entrances, one for the man of the house and one for his wife or wives. One or more wind towers on the rooftop channelled cooler air into the living quarters below. Many families left the cramped district of Bastakiya in the mid-1970s and the buildings fell into disrepair. Numerous houses were torn down, but those which remained were lovingly restored. Today, some of them are occupied by hotels, restaurants, cafés, galleries, shops, museums and offices.

❶ Metro: Al-Fahidi

MARCO POLO TIP

! *Art and handicrafts*   Insider Tip

Art, unusual design objects and furnishings, Omani basketry and more traditional handicrafts can all be found in the Majlis Gallery, next to the Al-Fahidi Roundabout. The splendid, historic merchant's house accommodating the gallery merits a visit on its own, affording insights into its construction and giving an impression of how people used to live before the beginning of the oil era (www.themajlisgallery.com; Sat–Thu 10am–6pm; Metro: Al-Fahidi).

The Sheikh Mohammed Centre for Cultural Understanding on the edge of Bastakiya, towards the creek, organizes guided walks through Bastakiya. On Mondays and Wednesdays at 10am it serves a traditional breakfast (50 Dh) and on Sundays and Thursdays at 1pm a traditional lunch (60 Dh, advance booking essential for both).

Sheikh Mohammed Centre

❶ Historic Building, Al Seef Road, Metro: Al-Fahidi; Tel. 04 353 66 66, www.cultures.ae; Sun–Thu 9am–6pm, Sat until 1pm

To find out more about life in Dubai before oil was discovered, visit the two small museum villages on the Al Shindagha headland at the mouth of the creek. At the **Diving Village** with low, palm-leaf houses in old Arabian style, visitors can cast themselves back into a 19th-century fishing and pearl diving community. The dhows on display, including the models still being built in the Gulf today, evoke memories of Dubai's centuries-old seafaring tradition.

Museum villages in the Shindagha district

It is just a short walk from Diving Village to Heritage Village (Al-Tourath). In this recreated traditional souk, arts and crafts are exhibited and offered for sale, while potters and weavers can be watched at work. The small stands of the village market sell almond and date sweets, served with tea from small handleless cups. Events are staged regularly during the winter months, such as folk dances or a Bedouin wedding.

*Heritage Village

Heritage Village: Sat–Thu 8am–10pm, Fri 8am–11am and 4.30pm–10pm, admission 2 Dh; Metro; Al-Fahidi
Diving Village: opening hours, see Heritage Village, admission free

*Sheikh Saeed House   The residence of Sheikh Saeed al-Maktoum, ruler of Dubai from 1912 until 1958 and grandfather of the current emir, was erected on the Shindagha spit in 1896. Designed in traditional Islamic style, it was completely restored some years ago. The wind towers of the mud-brick palace, elaborate woodcarvings, the balconies and shaded inner courtyard convey an impression of the splendour in which houses were decorated even before the oil boom. Many of the approximately 40 rooms present various exhibitions and collections. The Al-Maktoum wing exhibits some particularly interesting historical black-and-white photographs of the ruling family and figures from the emirates dating back to the first third of the 20th century, as well as rare photographs depicting life in Dubai between 1948 and 1953. The oldest images show the Al-Fahidi Fort, which was built to guard Dubai, and the Al-Ahmadiya School, the emirate's first school. The Coin and Stamps wing presents coins from the emirates and other countries of the Arabian Peninsula, the oldest dating back to the late 18th century. Old stamps marked »Trucial States« are from the 19th century (History p.47/49). The Marine Wing is dedicated to the Arabian Gulf and exhibits photographs of pearl divers and ancient dhows, scale replicas of abras, fishing boats and dhows, as well as old tools for pearl diving (MARCO POLO Insight p.276). Another room is devoted to social, cultural and religious life in the Dubai of the 1950s. There is a beautiful view of the creek from the terrace on the first floor.

MARCO POLO TIP

! *Dubai from the air*

Seawings operates round trips in flying boats along the coast of Dubai. A small Cessna takes off from the Jebel Ali Hotel or from the creek in front of the Park Hyatt Hotel and flies over the Dubai Marina, Palm Jumeirah, Burj Al Arab, The World and the city (40 mins, 1395 Dh; Seawings, Club Joumana, Jebel Ali Hotel, tel. 04 883 29 99, www.seawings.ae).

❶ Sat–Thu 8.30am–8pm, Fri 3pm–8pm, admission 2 Dh; Metro: Al Ghubaiba

Sheikh Juma al-Maktoum House   Close by stands the palace of Sheikh Saeed Al-Maktoum's brother, originally built in 1928. Known as the House of Traditional Architecture, the building was constructed according to old drawings.
❶ Sun–Thu 10am–noon, 3pm–5pm, admission free

Creekside Park   This well-kept park in the south of the Bur Dubai side of the creek, between Al-Maktoum Bridge and Al-Garhoud Bridge, was one of the Maktoum family's favourite projects as Dubai's rulers sought to turn the emirate into a green oasis. The development cost approximately 100 million Dh, with planners from all over the world brought in to create an attractive centre for leisure and relaxation with an abundance of trees, luxuriant flowers and lush lawns. An amphitheatre with a capacity for 1,200 spectators hosts theatrical performances and concerts. Creekside Park also has a **children's museum**, with a focus on natural history and science, promoting interactive learning experiences. A **cable car** provides splendid views of activity in the creek from a height of 25–30m/82–99ft.

❶ Daily 8am–11pm, Fridays women only. Admission 5 Dh; cable car 25 Dh per person, 30 minute ride; Metro: Healthcare City

At the southern end of Creekside Park, there is a water park with gigantic slides, wave riding and surfing. Special attractions include water tornados, a water vapour show and a water cinema, where films are projected onto the water's surface. There are also numerous restaurants, snack stands, bars and live music.

❶ Daily 10am–midnight, admission 40 Dh, Splashland 10am–8pm, admission 125 Dh, www.wonderlanduae.com; Metro: Healthcare City

*Wonder-Land Theme & Water Park

The Al-Boom Tourist Village, designed in traditional Arabic style, is another leisure park to the south of WonderLand Park. Exhibitions and representations of Dubai culture can be enjoyed here. There are several restaurants and, in the evenings, dinner cruises on the creek for around 200 Dh.

❶ Daily 9am–1pm, www.alboom.ae; admission free

Al-Boom Tourist Village

A few streets west of Creekside Park, the architecturally ambitious Al-Wafi Shopping Mall contains more than 300 shops. Outside, replicas of Egyptian statues catch the eye, whilst porticos and atria dominate the interior. Beneath the glass roof of a huge pyramid, designer fashion, children's clothes and shoes from the US and Europe compete for shoppers' attention. A stroll through the mall numbers among the most popular leisure activities for locals. The high-tech games hall on the third floor is a magnet for young people. The attractions of Wafi City, apart from the shopping mall, are the **Souk Khan Murjan** in the style of a 14th-century souk with 150 shops selling antiques, art and crafts, the Raffles Hotel and a complex known as The Pyramids, with a spa and gym and several restaurants.

❶ Oud Metha Road, off Sheikh Zayed Road, Metro: Healthcare City; Sat–Wed 10am–10pm, Thu, Fri until midnight, www.wafi.com

Al-Wafi Shopping Mall

The Karama Shopping Area is situated right in the middle of the residential area of Al-Karama, in the district of Bur Dubai. Its countless little shops are particularly popular among foreign visitors and guest workers. A vast array of textiles, sporting goods, bags and shoes can be found here – although fake merchandise is rife amongst the famous brands and designer goods. The district makes a rather shabby impression and shoppers may be accosted in front of the stores – an uncommon occurrence in Dubai. Please note: it is a crime to import counterfeit goods into the EU.

Al-Karama

WHAT TO SEE IN JUMEIRAH (▸map p.196/197)

First choice for holiday-makers

First choice for sun-seeking holidaymakers is Jumeirah Beach, which stretches west for miles from Port Rashid. Unsurprisingly, this is where the elite hotels, most famous shopping streets and promenade can be found – beach does not necessarily have to mean bathing beach. The hotels here have their own private beaches (non-guests can purchase day memberships for the hotel beach clubs). One beach that is open to the public is **Jumeirah Beach Park**. Slightly inland, on a level with Jumeirah Beach Park, meanwhile, Safa Park may not be beach life as such, but is a wonderful spot to relax in beautifully verdant surroundings.

Jumeirah Beach Park: daily 8am–11pm, Mon women only, admission 5 Dh;
Safa Park: daily 8am–10pm, Thu, Fri until 11pm, admission 3 Dh

*Jumeirah Mosque

Impossible to miss, Dubai's most impressive mosque sits enthroned on Jumeirah Beach Road, west of Port Rashid. Based on the medieval Fatimid style of the Egyptian caliphs, it is an outstanding example of modern Islamic architecture: two minarets tower over a majestic dome; high archways accentuate the main entrance, above which hang three heavy iron chandeliers. European stonemasons were hired for the filigree designs on sandstone surfaces. The numerous diamond-patterned stone window grilles have an impressive effect. The ivory-coloured place of worship, where even members of the ruling family gather for Friday prayer, is encircled by spacious lawns. Non-Muslims can access the mosque as part of a guided tour organized by the Sheikh Mohammed Centre for Cultural Understanding (p.211).

Meeting point: in front of the mosque; Metro: Emirates Towers. Registration begins at 9.45am, admission 10 Dh, duration 75 minutes. Men must wear long trousers, women can collect headscarves and abayas at the entrance. Information: www.cultures.ae

*The World

The World is an archipelago comprising 253 islands and islets, 3km/2mi to 8km/5mi off the coast in the Arabian Gulf. Seen from an aircraft flying overhead, the islands look like a map of the world. To create the group of islands, covering an area of 9 x 7 km/5.5 x 4.5 mi, some 320 million cubic metres of sand and limestone were deposited on 34 million tons of rock foundations and surrounded by an artificial reef 27km/17mi long. The individual islands, 2.5 hectares/6 acres to 10 hectares/25 acres in size, represent continents or countries and were originally to have been sold for prices between 15 and 50 million US dollars, giving investors the freedom to build according to their own designs. The global financial crisis has delayed any number

»The World« archipelago in the tomorrowland of architecture

of projects, including hotel developments. The first beach club with restaurant, bar, cabañas (chalets) and pool opened on Lebanon Island: Royal Island Beach Club has its own boat to pick up guests from the Jumeirah Fishing Harbour 1 (every thirty minutes from 10.30am–7pm, daily, tel 050 617 65 07, www.royalislandbeachclub.ae, admission 250 Dh).

Jumeirah Archaeological Site

For some years now, the excavations in Jumeirah which began in 1969 have been open to the public. The oldest finds are remnants of a civilization which settled here in the 5th century. A splendid building complex with stucco and mosaics probably served as the residence of a city official. Another structure, numbering some 20 rooms, is believed to have been a caravanserei. Remains of a souk and other residential buildings have also been discovered. The easiest way to look around the site is with a travel agency tour. Permission to visit can be obtained in the Dubai Museum (p.208). The site can only be inspected in the company of a member of the excavations team. If one is available, the tour can begin.

❶ Between Safa Park and Jumeirah Beach Park, east of al-Maktoum School, Metro: Business Bay; Sun–Thu 9am–2pm, admission free

Al-Sufouh

Al-Sufouh district is situated between Sheikh Zayed Road and Al-Sufouh Road, which runs into Jumeirah Beach Road south of the Burj Al Arab (p.218). Archaeologists estimate the burial sites to be many thousands of years old, dating back to the Umm al-Nar Period (around 2700–2000 BC, History p.45). The discovery of the site was quite sensational, as the round and above-ground communal grave with a diameter of over 6m/20ft is one of the largest of its kind. The grave finds, now exhibited in Dubai Museum, include finely wrought jewellery and ceramic vessels as well as bronze spearheads. Visits only possible with a travel agency tour group.

Umm al-Sheif Majlis

Also known as **Majlis Al-Ghorfat**, the former summer residence of Sheikh Rashid Bin-Saeed al-Maktoum stands in the coastal town of Umm Suqeim. Built in 1954 in traditional fashion using coral stone and plaster, it has now been restored and made accessible to the public. On the ground floor there is a large, open veranda. A storage room is located beneath the stairs. The upper floor consists of a divan or meeting room (majlis) decorated with rugs, lamps, floor cushions, guns and Arabic coffee pots. The summer palace also has a garden with an old irrigation system (falaj).

❶ Jumeirah Beach Road, south of Jumeirah Beach Park, by the »No. 1 Supermarket«; Sat–Thu 9am–8.30pm, Fri 3.30pm–8.30pm, admission 1 Dh; Metro: Business Bay

A visit to Wild Wadi Water Park next to the Jumeirah Beach Hotel, looking across to the spectacular Burj Al Arab luxury hotel, is an unforgettable experience for children. The park's attractions include the »Jumeirah Sceirah«, said to be the biggest, fastest water slide in the world. Figures from Arabian legends and fairytales, such as Sinbad or Scheherazade create a thrilling atmosphere for all visitors. Rides, shops and cafés inside the park provide all-day entertainment.

Wild Wadi Water Park

❶ Daily 10am–6pm or 7pm, admission 275 Dh, children up to 1.10m (3ft 7in) tall 215 Dh, www.jumeirah.com, Metro: First Gulf Bank

Venice in Dubai: the district of Madinat Jumeirah has developed between The Palm Jumeirah and the Burj Al Arab. Five-star hotels, an exquisite Arabian-style souk, fine restaurants, cafés, bars and the Madinat Theatre are all linked by waterways. It looks especially romantic in the evening, when the palm trees along the 4km/2.5mi of canals of Madinat Jumeirah are enchantingly illuminated. Abras ply the waters to take hotel guests and diners to their destinations.

Madinat Jumeirah

❶ www.madinatjumeirah.com; Metro: Mall of the Emirates

Off the coast of Jumeirah, the artificial island of The Palm Jumeirah extends 4.5km/3mi into the sea. For a wonderful view, take an easy ride on the elevated monorail that runs from Gateway Station (with car park) on the mainland to the crown of the »palm« (Crescent). There are two stops along the 4.5km/3mi route (return journey 25 Dh), terminating at Atlantis, a spectacular themed hotel (www.atlantisthepalm.com).The huge pink palace evokes a sunken, submarine world. Non-residents can only access the shopping arcades and Lost Chambers aquarium.

The Palm Jumeirah

The Aquaventure Waterpark which belongs to Atlantis has many attractions, including water chutes that descend from the tip of a pyramid into a pool. On either side of the »trunk« of the palm, Anchor Marina has space for 600 boats. Villas line the 16 »palm fronds«, whilst the trunk is predominantly populated by apartment blocks, several storeys high. Before the financial crisis, these villas and apartments were among the emirate's most coveted real estate on the international market, whereas today prices are considerably

Aquaventure Waterpark

Burj Al Arab – Pure Luxury

The Burj Al Arab hotel is more than just a symbol of economic power, it is also the ultimate Dubai landmark. Reaching 321 metres/ 1,053 feet into the sky, the »Arabian Tower« is the most spectacular – after it was opened in the year 2000, it quickly became the most famous luxury accommodation in the world.

Superlatives in abundance: the tallest hotel in the world (an inaccurate distinction), a monument to luxury, the garden of Allah on Earth – journalists from all over the world could not contain their amazement when they arrived in Dubai for the grand opening of the Burj Al Arab, reporting on the newest symbol of a modern and rich state.

The Hotel's Own Island

Standing on an artificial island created specifically for the purpose, 300m/328yd off Dubai's Jumeirah Beach, the Burj Al Arab rises up into the sky like the sail of an old Arabian dhow. The building is stabilized by 800 concrete pillars driven 40m/131ft deep into the ocean bed. It took more than 3,500 workers to complete the hotel in time for the national holiday on 2 December 1999. According to the owners of the hotel, who include the Emirates national airline – the majority of which belongs to the ruling Al-Maktoum family – the building costs in the region of 1.5 billion Euro are well invested; after all, the Burj Al Arab helps position Dubai as an exclusive city destination and also spreads the fame of the small emirate.

Cathedral of Light and Gold

No expense has been spared: the 180m/591ft atrium lobby is a cathedral of light and gold. Canopies extend from columns covered with 0.001mm of thin gold leaf; a water fountain, omnipresent in the Emirate of Dubai, sends water jets 50m/164ft into the air.

The suites have a minimum size of 170 sq m/203 sq yd and cost approximately 800 Euro per night. The bill for the two 780 sq m/933 sq yd royal suites on the 25th floor comes to approximately 8,500 Euro per night – breakfast not included, but with a personal butler. A total of 1,200 employees look after 202 suites. On each floor, there is one room for the butler and one for a bodyguard.

A private lift takes guests up to a world of superlatives, catering to the tastes of Arab customers used to luxury: the suites are equipped with state-of-the-art communications technology and a revolving four-poster canopy bed, grandiosely decorated in gold and purple. Other rooms also feature gold leaf decoration. A baroque mirror hangs from the ceiling over every double bed. The two levels of the suite are connected by a lift. The bathroom is decorated with mural paintings. Thanks to a sophisticated cooling fan, the mirrors will not steam up. The vase on the floor is illuminated from inside, and the video room is almost as big as a cinema.

Chief designer Khuan Chew called the project a »once in a lifetime« assignment, one which took years of planning and preparatory work. Each room was built according to individually designed colour sketches. Every room was assigned a colour scheme of five shades based on two main colours, to prevent an overload of colour with the chosen materials. The rooms and suites were decorated by the interior designers of KCA International Designers, who used materials from more than three dozen countries. Rare types of marble were bought from shut-down quarries, exotic woods were imported from Sumatra and Java, and blue granite was acquired in Brazil for 1300 Euro per square metre.

The underwater restaurant »Al-Mahara« is accessed via a lift designed to resemble a submarine. Dinner is served in a futuristic-looking dining room, conjuring up memories of science fiction novels by Jules Verne. Huge panes of bulletproof glass reveal the underwater world of the Arabian Gulf. It is a stunning presentation of a marine paradise, with specially designed coral gardens and tropical fish that are fed regularly by hotel staff.

The small Juna Lounge in the mezzanine creates an intimate atmosphere. Cigar fans will appreciate the first-rate selection.

With separate facilities for men and women, the interior design of the »Assawan Spa & Health Club« wellness area on the 18th floor is inspired by the Jordanian royal city of Petra. The rooms are designed in relaxing shades of blue, green and yellow; Moorish mosaics decorate the walls and pillars, and a simple beam ceiling creates a pleasantly unpretentious contrast to the luxury materials.

Even those not staying at the hotel can visit this monument to luxury – they just need to reserve a table in one of the restaurants or the Skyview Bar on the 27th floor. Afternoon tea will cost 465 Dh per person, Friday brunch or dinner from 500 Dh upwards (information: Burj Al Arab, P.O. Box 74147, Dubai, tel. 04 301 76 00, www.burj-al-arab.com).

Artificial Creations

The continental shelf of Dubai reaches far into the ocean, hence the waters off the coast are relatively shallow for a number of miles. This characteristic has proved advantageous to the developers of the Palm Islands. Special ships dredged the ocean bed and built up new islands. One has been completed, several other projects were halted when the financial crisis of 2008 led to a drop in demand.

▶ **United Arab Emirates**
Released from the British protectorate in 1971. An alliance of seven emirates which are largely independe of each other in economic and political terms.

▶ **Dubai's artificial islands**

- ▇ completed
- planned
- ▇ Abandoned project / uncertain

Palm Jumeirah
5.6 sq km/2.15 sq mi
The only one of the Palm Islands project completed to date. Dubai gained 78km/ of additional coastline with the islands, on which over 4000 expensive residentia properties and a series of exclusive hotels have been constructed.

Palm Jebel Ali
Abandoned due to insufficient demand. Land reclamation almost complete.

Jumeirah Islands
2.74 sq km/1 sq mi
Since 2004, more than 50 islands, surrounded by waterfalls, canals and lagoons, wait for luxury villas to be built.

| 4km/2.5mi |

▶ Comparison:
some of the biggest
artificial islands in
the world

**Chek Lap Kok
Airport**
12.5 sq km/4.8 sq mi
Hong Kong (China)

Barro Colorado Island
15 sq km/5.79 sq mi,
Panama

Chubu Airport
4.7 sq km/1.8 sq mi
near Nagoya, Japan

Danube Island
4.9 sq km/
1.89 sq mi
Austria

Bock (near Hiddensee)
3.6 sq km/1.38 sq mi
Germany

©BAEDEKER

*EMIRATE
OF DUBAI*

ection

U.A.E.

Deira Islands
The abandoned Palm Deira project
(49 sq km/18.9 sq mi) is to be replaced
by the 15.3 sq km/5.9 sq mi
Deira Islands.

The World
270 islands in the form of a
world map – land reclamation
prepared, but project uncompleted.

*DUBAI
CITY*

lower (www.palmjumeirah.ae). The Atlantis hotel, meanwhile, has no shortage of guests.

»Lost Chambers« aquarium: admission 100 Dh
»Aquaventure« waterpark: admission 250 Dh

Dubai Marina Buzzing, urban and spectacular: Dubai Marina with the **Jumeirah Beach Residences** is a new district on the southwestern border of Jumeirah. The skyline of hotel and apartment skyscrapers reflects in the water of the vast marina. With towers averaging 150m/500ft in height (the tallest reaching 300m/1000ft), Dubai Marina feels reminiscent of Hong Kong or Manhattan (indeed, architects from the USA drew up the plans). An arts and crafts market is held on the promenade from Wednesday to Saturday. Dubai Marina Walk makes for a relaxing stroll of an evening, the promenade on the water's edge lined by cafés, hotels and boutiques. The sparkling centre of Dubai Marina is the yacht club, where Dubai's young set meet to dine in the restaurant or on the terrace overlooking the water.

❶ Metro: Dubai Marina, www. dubai-marina.com

MARCO ⊕ POLO TIP

! **Palm view** *Insider Tip*

The best view of The Palm Jumeirah with marina, Hotel Atlantis and Aquaventure can be enjoyed from the Observatory, a restaurant on the 52nd floor of the neighbouring Hotel Marriott Dubai Marina, Al-Sufouh Road, Dubai Marina, from 5pm, tel. 04 319 40 00, www.marriott.com; Metro: Dubai Marina.

The Walk at JBR Dubai City was not built with pedestrians in mind. There are, however, little oases which can make it worthwhile to leave the car parked in the garage. One of them is JBR Walk, named after Jumeirah Beach Residences, a luxury residential complex. The 1.7km/1 mile walk starts at the Ritz Carlton Hotel, built in the style of a Mediterranean palace and set in a tropical park which leads along the coast. Although it is not actually closed to vehicles, the atmosphere to the left and right of the road is, by Dubai standards, almost leisurely. Street cafés, boutiques and restaurants with terraces that look out to sea make nice places to take a break and relax. In the hot summer months, fans on the boardwalks spray a cooling ice mist on passers-by among palms and flowering shrubs.

❶ Metro: Dubai Marina

SHEIKH ZAYED ROAD – DUBAI'S BUSINESS DISTRICT (▶Map p.196/197)

Burj Khalifa No matter which way you look at Dubai, the city's newest landmark and the **tallest building in the world**, designed by the American architect Adrian Smith, always occupies centre stage. It also marks the centre of the city's new business district, designed from scratch, Downtown Dubai (p.226).

The tapering Burj Khalifa shoots like a rocket 828m/2,716ft up to the sky at the beginning of Sheikh Zayed Road. Prior to its opening in 2010, the building was known as Burj Dubai, but was renamed as a consequence of the financial crisis, subsequently bearing the name of its sponsor Sheikh Khalifa Bin-Zayed al-Nahyan, the ruler of Abu Dhabi.

57 lifts give access to 162 storeys. Part of this three billion dollar tower (1st to 8th floor, 38th and 39th floors) is occupied by the 160 suites and 144 residences of the Armani Hotel Dubai. In January 2011, the At.mosphere restaurant opened on the 122nd floor. The **viewing platform At The Top** on the 124th floor, at a height of 442m/1450ft, opened in 2010. To get there, visitors take a moving walkway from Dubai Mall to the Burj Khalifa and ascend at 10m/33ft per second in a two-storey lift that takes just one minute. The 360° viewing platform is glazed to wall height and also has an open balcony. Saudi Arabia has already signed a construction contract for a 1000m/3280ft tower, the so-called Kingdom Tower, which will dwarf the Burj Khalifa – if it is completed.

❶ Financial Centre Road, off Sheikh Zayed Road, 1st Interchange, www.burjkhalifa.ae, Metro: Dubai Mall/Burj Khalifa

Observation Deck: tickets on the ground floor of Dubai Mall next to the entrance to At the Top, Sheikh Zayed Road, Downtown Dubai, daily 8.30am–1am; admission 125 Dh or 400 Dh (immediate entry). Tickets can be booked in advance online, www.burjkhalifa.ae

Burj Khalifa is the centre of the new city district Downtown Dubai, designed for work and living, commerce and shopping. Entertainment is also on the agenda: a man-made lake features the 150m/490ft-high **Dubai Fountain**, where, from 6pm in the evening, a 5-minute light and sound show takes place every half hour. Jets of water dance to the sound of classical and Arab music, illuminated by thousands of lights. The Address Downtown Dubai luxury hotel boasts superb design in the lobby, whilst the nearby hotel The Palace brings back the opulence of a historic sheikh's residence.

Downtown Dubai

Close to Burj Khalifa lies the **world's second-largest shopping mall**, the Dubai Mall. Visitors are attracted by some 1200 shops and boutiques, including a gigantic bookshop, the Dubai Aquarium, the Dubai Ice Rink, a gold souk and 120 cafés and restaurants. The likes of H & M, Zara, Banana Republic, Gap and Levi's are joined by exclusive Arab fashions (First Lady), designer labels (Moschino, Blumarine, Ferre) and department stores (Marks & Spencer, Debenhams). Thanks to its spectacular display of art, the Dubai Mall is more than a place to shop, it is worth a tour on its own merit – not to

Dubai Mall

High Altitude Euphoria

The tower of superlatives was inaugurated in January 2010 and is the world's tallest structure with the highest floors in use. Architect Adrian Smith found inspiration in the three flowers heads of the Hymenocallis, a desert flower brought from Central America and cultivated in the emirates.

Burj Khalifa –
architectural desert flower

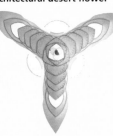

▶ **The Burj Khalifa in numbers**

11 300 steps

189 floors

57 lifts

Built from **2004 – 2010**

Costs approx.
1 Billion €
(1.5 Billion US-$)

Area **517.240 sqm/
5.5 million sq ft**

330,000 m³
of cement

22 million hours
of labour

1044 residential
apartments

Building sway up to
1.5 m/5ft

Approx. **18 Million KWh**
per year

▶ **Still the tallest**

**300m/
984ft**

**443m/
1453ft**

**540m/
1771ft**

**553m/
1814ft**

**828m/
2716ft**

**1000m/
3280ft**

Eiffel Tower	**Empire State Building**	**Ostankino Tower**	**CN Tower**	**Burj Khalifa**	**Kingdom Tow** (construction be in January 201
Paris France	New York USA	Moscow Russia	Toronto Canada	Dubai UAE	Jeddah Saudi Arabia

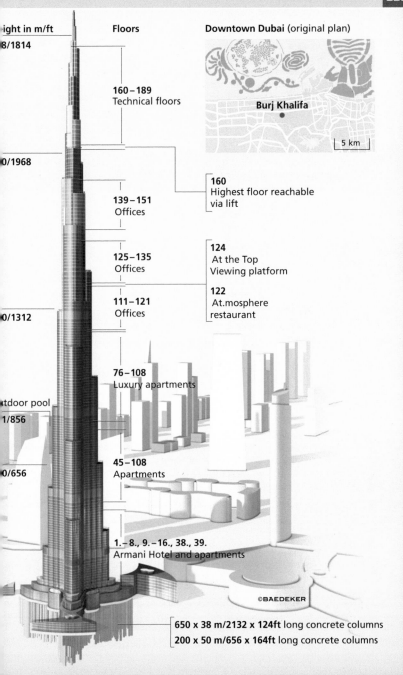

225

ight in m/ft

8/1814

0/1968

0/1312

tdoor pool
1/856

0/656

Floors

160–189
Technical floors

139–151
Offices

125–135
Offices

111–121
Offices

76–108
Luxury apartments

45–108
Apartments

1.–8., 9.–16., 38., 39.
Armani Hotel and apartments

Downtown Dubai (original plan)

Burj Khalifa

5 km

160
Highest floor reachable
via lift

124
At the Top
Viewing platform

122
At.mosphere
restaurant

©BAEDEKER

650 x 38 m/2132 x 124ft long concrete columns
200 x 50 m/656 x 164ft long concrete columns

mention the Dubai Aquarium, the largest aquarium in the world, which is also here. Opposite the mall, the **Souk al-Bahar** houses 100 boutiques for Arab crafts, carpets, jewellery and art.

From the ground floor of the Dubai Mall a window measuring 33x8m/108x26ft opens onto the **Dubai Aquarium and Underwater Zoo**, where 33,000 marine animals swim. A tunnel provides more views of the underwater world.

Dubai Mall: Financial Centre Road, from Sheikh Zayed Road, 1st Interchange, Metro: Burj Khalifa/Dubai Mall, a travelator walkway (800m/2600ft) connects to the mall, www.thedubaimall.com; Sun–Wed 10am–10pm, Thu–Sat until midnight

Dubai Aquarium & Underwater Zoo: www.thedubaiaquarium.com; admission to tunnel and underwater zoo 70 Dh

Downtown Dubai, the newest district in Dubai City

At the heart of the new district of Meydan City, southeast of Downtown Dubai, is the racetrack (www.meydan.ae), replacing the Nad al
Sheba Racecourse which had seen better days. Every year between
January and March, its 1.6km/1mile-long grandstand fills up with
dignities of the Arab world and international guests for the Dubai
World Cup (p.84). It is possible to take a tour through the world-famous Meydan stables to admire the thoroughbreds at close quarters.
Completing the portfolio, , the Meydan Hotel is a five-star establishment befitting what is probably the biggest and most elaborate racecourse in the world.

Meydan City

Opened in 1979 in the presence of Queen Elizabeth II, the Trade
Centre consolidated the emirate's reputation as a major Arabian economic power. It is still one of the most prestigious business addresses in all of Dubai. Around 200 companies reside in the 39 floors of
the Dubai World Trade Centre; its tower is one of the city's landmarks
and was its highest building before the completion of the luxurious
Burj Al Arab hotel (MARCO POLO Insight p.218).
❶ Trade Centre Road, on the corner of 2nd Zabeel Road;
Metro: Trade Centre

Dubai World Trade Centre

Skiing in the desert. The venue for desert skiing is the 85m/280ft-
high indoor arena attached to the Mall of the Emirates (p.98). The
winter wonderland of artificial snow and Alpine illusions is a sight to
behold. A chair lift takes skiers to five slopes of varying levels of dif-
ficulty. There is a 90m/100yd-long quarterpipe for snowboarders, a
valley where children have fun with plastic tubes, and everyone
meets to drink hot chocolate at the cosy mid-station ski chalet called
Café Avalanche.
❶ Mall of the Emirates, Sheikh Zayed Road, 4th Interchange, Metro: Mall of
the Emirates, tel. 04 409 41 00, www.theplaymania.com; Sun–Wed
10am–11pm, Sat from 9am, Thu 10am–midnight, Fri from 9am, admission
200 Dh for 2 hours, children 170 Dh, all day pass 300 Dh incl. equipment

Ski Dubai

About 20km/12.5mi south of the city centre, the 18-hole course
Emirates Golf Club hosts international championships. The clubhouse, built and arranged like a group of Bedouin tents, is world famous. One of these concrete tents is owned by the ruler of Dubai.
❶ Metro: Nakheel; www.dubaigolf.com

Emirates Golf Club

OUTSIDE THE CENTRE

North of Dubai, on the border with Sharjah, the calm waters of this
beach club are ideal for families, particularly those with small children. Open to the public, the park is open to the public and equipped

Al-Mamzar Beach Park

MARCO ● POLO INSIGHT

? *Did you know*

that each of Dubai's six golf courses needs between 3.5 million and 7.5 million litres (925000–1.9 million US gallons) of water every day? An 18-hole golf course thus uses a minimum of 335 × 4.5 million litres per year, as overcast or rainy days when irrigation is unnecessary are few and far between.

with changing rooms, showers, a large swimming pool and open-air restaurant. It all adds up to a relaxing day at the beach.

Al-Mamzar Lagoon, Al-Khaleej Road, Hamriya, daily 8am–10pm, Wednesdays reserved for women and children; admission 5 Dh, per car 30 Dh

Approximately 13km/8mi northeast of Dubai lie the excavations of **Al-Qusais**, an extensive ancient burial site. The graves date back to around 2000–500 BC. Burial objects include spearheads and axes made of bronze for men, and make-up utensils for women. Visits are only possible as part of an organized travel agency tour.

Mushrif Park   To the southeast, beyond Emirates Road, this recreational park is popular among locals and guest workers alike. Besides a restaurant, shaded picnic areas and two swimming pools – one for women and one for men – there is also a funfair, an aviary, a skate park and facilities for pony and camel rides. The »**World Village**« is famous for its replica models of sights from around the globe. A miniature railway take visitors to all the attractions.

Daily 8am–11pm, Wed women only, admission 3 Dh, per car 10 Dh

*Khor Dubai   The Emirate of Dubai provides wintering grounds for hundreds of
Wildlife   bird species. The southern end of Dubai Creek in particular has be
Sanctuary   come a preferred habitat for migrating birds, as the shallows on the shores offer plenty of food. Between February and April, and again from September to November, the Khor Dubai Wildlife Sanctuary, a designated area of 6 sq km/2.5 sq mi south of the city, near the end of the Creek, is particularly well-suited to birdwatching. Here the estuary widens to a shallow lake with several small islands, making it a paradise for waders. So far, 88 different bird species have been identified, which can be observed from three hides. The most striking birds are the pink flamingos; Sheikh Mohammed bin Rashid Al Maktoum, ruler of Dubai, provides them with carotene-rich feed to keep their feathers nice and bright. Observation points are located off Ras Al Khor Road (Gurm/Mangrove), in the district of Al Jaddaf (Budhaira/Lagoon) and beyond Oud Metha Road (Fahir/Flamingo).

Sat–Thu 9am–4pm, www.wildlife.ae, admission free; Metro: Creek

Dubailand   Announced several years earlier that it would be be the largest leisure and theme park on the planet, construction of Dubailand finally began in 2008. Southwest of the city, to the east of the E 11 highway and close to the new airport, the site covers more than 140 sq km/55 sq mi. In addition to shopping complexes such as the Mall of Arabia, Disney-style theme parks are planned. There will be an Outlet City for bargain hunters, a Golf City for friends of the fairways, a Motor City for Formula 1 fans, interactive museums on Islamic art, popular art and fine arts, as well as sports and more shopping facilities. In 2009 work came to a stop in the wake of the world financial crisis, as it was impossible to finance further activities by sales of real estate. Work on the project was interrupted when the financial crisis hit in 2009, with a revised completion date set for the end of 2015 (www.dubailand.ae).

Hatta

✦ L 5

Population: 12,000

Hatta oasis and its extensive palm groves are surrounded by sand dunes and the Hajar Mountains. The restored fort is well worth a visit, as are the Hatta Pools, crystal clear rock pools situated in a wadi 17km/10.5mi south of Hatta.

Approximately 100km/61mi southeast of Dubai, the exclave of Hatta stands on Omani territory at the foot of the Hajar Mountains. Once an important trading hub on the route between Oman in the north and the Arabian Gulf, Hatta has, in recent decades, served as **a popular weekend destination** for Dubai citizens who enjoy its moderate climate and particularly charming landscape.

Charming Dubai exclave

The well-made highway (E 44) from Dubai leads to Hatta Road, past neat residential areas and mosques. Follow the signs into Hatta, passing by small cubic houses – state-built accommodation for Bedouin families – and increasingly impressive sand dunes reaching heights of 170m/558ft. At sunrise and sunset they appear to glow in a reddish hue. The terrain between Dubai and Hatta is also ideal for sandskiing and sandboarding. In the early afternoon, whole groups of four-by-fours can be seen driving up the dunes. Travel companies organize »days in the desert« which are sure to meet westerners' expecations of an endless ocean of sand. Just before Hatta, the land levels out and the vast oasis stretches out in front of the Hajar Mountains.

The old village stands on a hill in a date palm grove, guarded by a fort with two watchtowers. The fact that Hatta is a popular destination for weekend getaways means the settlement is increasing in size. The newly built houses feature traditional architectural details such as simple façades and small windows to keep out the heat. Colourful iron gates are decorated with traditional Arabic symbols – coffee

Concrete Rivers

Only a few of the old water channels in the Emirates still exist or have been restored. They are called falaj, Arabic for »to distribute«. They stretch along the edges of wadis and pass through palm groves and gardens.

The layout of the aflaj (plural of falaj) system is rather sophisticated, and the forks and distribution points can be changed by repositioning the stones to direct the flow to other channels and into different gardens. This is also how bathhouses and cattle troughs are supplied with water. The channels have a width and height of up to 20–50cm/8in–1ft 8in, and are made of brick clay and stones fixed with concrete. The shapes can vary; some channels are carved into rock. Approximately 2,500 years ago, Persians introduced this technology to the region of what is now the UAE and Oman.

King Solomon's Water

According to an old legend, it was King Solomon, revered as a prophet, who sought to relieve the misery of the people living in the water-poor regions, ordering his helpers to create a system of stone water channels. There are two classifications of ain-aflaj systems (ain = spring), using either the more common surface channels (ghail-falaj) or underground channels (qanat-falaj). If a spring is located at a higher elevation, a basin is constructed next to the spring. The water flows into the channel and can descend for miles into the villages and nearby fields.

Qanat-falaj

The construction of an underground qanat-falaj is more difficult. Up in the mountains, water is collected from a groundwater spring and carried through a tunnel built within the rock. The stream here must also have a low gradient – otherwise the tunnel would have to be bigger and consequently much harder to build – so the falaj often runs for miles through the mountain. The maintenance work on the falaj is done by a wakil, who accesses the falaj via specially constructed shafts.

Water Master

The wakil is in charge of the water supply and is elected by the village community. His task is to look after this precious resource. He changes the water distribution by repositioning the connections and forks according to a fixed schedule. Depending on the area to be irrigated and according to inherited rights and newly bought shares, the water is channelled for different lengths of time. Today in the UAE, there are hardly any remains of the old water system; this arduous method has been replaced by water desalination plants. In Oman, however, the tradition is still very much alive. Fields across the entire country are watered by functioning and well-maintained aflaj. One system

The ancient canals are used like this too

well worth visiting is near Al Ain, at the oasis of Buraimi, granted World Heritage status by UNESCO in 2011.

Water Register

For centuries, falaj books have documented the exact distribution of water for each channel system, including details about the families living in the drainage area, the size of property and purpose for water access – household, garden or cattle. In a land register, the wakil controls and enters the individual rights, the time of day and duration of water access, as well as its acquisition or sale. Because one channel can supply up to a hundred families with water, his job requires discretion and conscientiousness, which has often successfully prevented disputes

from igniting through the ages. Nevertheless, the history of the Arabian Peninsula is marked by battles over oases and water rights. These disputes have sometimes even resulted in the construction of massive fortifications around and over springs.

There are strict rules about how the precious water may be used. The supply of drinking water has top priority: water is channelled to the local fountain where the village folk extract it, driven by a sense of responsibility for the community. Here, the falaj is often covered with a stone plate to protect the channel and its water from pollution. Then the water is directed to locations for bathing or cleaning, e.g. mosques, followed by the supply for cattle and irrigation of agricultural areas.

Hatta

WHERE TO STAY

Hatta Fort Hotel £££ Insider Tip
Tel. 04 809 93 33
www.jaresortshotels.com
50 comfortable chalets are situated in a garden which is rich in bird life. Amenities include a 9-hole golf course, swimming pools, tennis courts archery and

clay pigeon shooting. Advance bookings are highly recommended, as the hotel is extremely well frequented, especially at weekends!
The Jeema Restaurant mainly serves Arabic cuisine. Those who find the temperatures a little cool here can adjourn to the Gazebo Coffeeshop by the pool.

pots, date palms, dromedaries – illustrating the people's links to their past. Hatta's plans to boost »tourist development« include a souk for handicrafts and souvenirs at the entrance to the settlement, a zoo, a recreational park, a chair lift into the mountains and a tourist information office.

WHAT TO SEE IN AND AROUND HATTA

Hatta Heritage Village

Parts of the 16th-century oasis village had fallen into a state of disrepair from the 16th century, but have now been authentically restored using construction materials which were produced according to traditional techniques: a mixture of sun-dried mud and straw. Missing doors and windows were brought in from neighbouring emirates and other Arabian countries. It was thus possible to reconstruct the old fort along with its pair of imposing watchtowers from the year 1800, the historic mosque, originally built in 1780, and two dozen residential houses.

A stroll among the old houses leads to the falaj channels (▶MARCO POLO Insight p.230) which irrigate the gardens. Narrow alleys weave their way between mud-brick houses and so-called barasti huts made of palm leaves. A small fort stands in the centre and a children's playground has been created up alongside the falaj channels.

An exhibition of traditional pottery and weaving techniques, Bedouin garments and camel equipment complete the museum.

Sat–Thu 8am–8pm, Fri 2pm–8pm, admission free

**Hatta Pools

17km/10.6mi south of Hatta lies one of the most impressive landscapes in the Emirate of Dubai: the Hatta Rock Pools are a group of ravines carrying water all year round. Several travel companies organize half and full-day tours here. The Hatta Fort Hotel also offers tours lasting several hours. However, with a four-by-four and decent maps, tourists can also visit Hatta Pools by themselves.

From the roundabout on the road from Dubai to Hatta, near the Hatta Fort Hotel, turn right and head southeast. At the local police station about 3km/2mi further on there is another small roundabout. Turn south here and pass a school with colourful mural paintings. The road first leads to the small oasis villages of Jeema, known for its mineral water, and Al-Fay; continue then along a dirt road, reaching Hatta Pools after nearly 17km/10.5mi. There are many idyllic picnic spots along the road, in the shade of shady palm trees (the Hatta Fort Hotel is happy to put together picnic boxes). At Hatta Pools, however, natural shade will be sought in vain. Around the pools, numerous well-maintained and restored falaj channels slope down gently (►MARCO POLO Insight p.230) to carry water along the sides of the wadi into the groves and gardens of the surrounding villages.

Fujairah

FUJAIRAH

Area: 1,175 sq km/453.7 sq mi	**Emir:** Sheikh Hamad Bin-Moham-
Population: 202,000	med al-Sharqi (since 1974)

Sandy beaches and palm trees, the impressive backdrop of the Hajar Mountains and the colourful underwater world of the Gulf of Oman. This emirate on the Indian Ocean has much to offer.

The Eastern part of the United Arab Emirates is marked by the impressive panorama of the rugged Hajar Mountains. The mountain range runs south from the northern Musandam Peninsula and has a length of about 80km/50mi in the territory of the UAE and a width up to 30km/19mi. The highest elevations in the UAE measure 1000m/3281ft (compared to 3,000m/9,843ft in Oman), separated by deep, often fertile valleys. Fujairah, the emirate situated on the **Gulf of Oman**, includes three Sharjah exclaves in its territory and is unlike the other sheikhdoms for various reasons. Nature lovers will appreciate the magnificent tours through the spectacular scenery of Fujairah's Hajar Mountains. For many years, interaction between the inhabitants from the east coast and the people from the rest of the country was minimal. It was not until 1976 that a proper tarmacked highway connected Dubai and Fujairah. With the extension of the international airport, previously used mainly for importing and exporting goods, Fujairah is now competing with the other emirates for the favour of foreign tourists. After all, the underwater world of the Gulf of Oman, with coral reefs and rocky beds for snorklers and divers, has far more to offer than the flat, sandy west coast.

Mountains, verdant landscapes and a colourful underwater world.

In Fujairah, neither oil nor gas has yet been discovered; Fujairah's expenditure is ensured only by generous donations from Abu Dhabi. Besides fishing, steady income is provided by poultry and cattle farms, where the majority of the male population is employed. Fujairah's deepwater port, built to the north of Fujairah City in 1981, is the second largest in the UAE and very much on the radar of international trade. The port and a new pipeline will soon ship or deliver up to 70% of Abu Dhabi's daily oil production to the rest of the world – bypassing the Strait of Hormuz, just 40km/25mi wide, whose east bank is controlled by Iran.

Economy

Coffee pot roundabout and mosque in the centre of Fujairah City

History
Finds from an early settlement on the east coast, including ceramic shards and jewellery, date back to the beginning of the Common Era. However, little is known about the early inhabitants of this region. In 632, during the process of Islamization, the Battle of Dibba saw Saudi Arabian Muslims defeat the east coast inhabitants of what is now the UAE; a burial site near Badiyah is evidence of this event.

The Emirate of Fujairah was long coveted by foreign powers. Due to the fact that the coast offered many sheltered harbours and also lay at an intersection of centuries-old seafaring routes, the inhabitants feared invasions from foreign sailors. For protection, they built watchtowers at the harbours of Dibba, Khor Fakkan and Fujairah. In the 16th century, members of the Sharqiyin tribe living in Fujairah suffered repeated attacks by the Portuguese, who ultimately took the harbours and extended the watchtowers, turning them into Portuguese forts. The Dutch took an interest in the east coast in the 17th and 18th centuries, the British in the 19th century. Towards the end of the 19th century, Sheikh Abdullah Bin-Mohammed al-Sharqi succeeded in uniting the continuously feuding tribal families in the common struggle for independence. Fujairah, which was part of Sharjah, declared its independence in 1903, and the locals' resistance against British occupation increased. The conflict culminated in the bombardment of the city of Fujairah on 20 April 1925, during which almost the entire fort was destroyed. It was not until 1952 that the British finally recognized Fujairah as the seventh »Trucial State« (History p.50).

Fujairah City

✦ L 4

Population: 87,400

Wide streets traverse the city of Fujairah in which only a few buildings are more than 50 years old. Distances in the city are short, which makes walking more practical than taking a car. The mosque in the centre of town may only be entered by Muslims.

Fort and palm gardens
The old town to the north of the mosque consists of little more than a few original houses and numerous ruins. The slightly elevated fort, now restored, which stands alongside the palm gardens also belongs to the historic town. In the past, majestic date trees added to the reputation and modest wealth of the city. A long, broad beach dotted with sunshades stretches out at the northern edge of the city. From the Hilton Hotel a new corniche runs south, parallel to the beach.

Fujairah City

INFORMATION
Fujairah Tourism Bureau
Trade Centre, 9th Floor
Hamad Bin-Abdullah Road
Tel. 09 222 95 39
www.fujairahtourism.ae

WHERE TO EAT
❶ *Al-Meshwar* £££
Hamad Bin-Abdullah Road
Tel. 09 223 11 13
The most striking building in town also
houses the best restaurant. On the
ground floor is a café with (shisha) terrace, on the first floor Arabian cuisine.

❷ *Bikers Cafe* ££
Fujairah International Marine Club
Tel. 09 224 46 86
Motorbike lifestyle and specialities of the
emirates, an unusual mixture which
proves particularly popular with local
youngsters. A range of coffee specialties
and a wide variety of exotic juices and
mocktails.

❸ *Pizza Inn* £
Fujairah Trade Centre
Hamad Bin-Abdullah Road
Tel. 09 222 25 57
www.pizzainn-me.com
This pizzeria offers a wide range of pizza
and tasty pasta dishes. Opens at 10am.

WHERE TO STAY
❶ *Hilton* £££
Beach Road
Tel. 09 222 24 11
www.hilton.com/fujairah
On the waterfront north of the Old
Fishing Harbour near the coffee pot
roundabout, a pleasant hotel with 92
rooms, swimming pool, fitness centre,
water skiing facilities and the Breeze beach restaurant. *Insider Tip*

❷ *Al-Diar Siji* ££
Hamad Bin-Abdullah Road
Tel. 09 223 20 00
www.aldiarhotels.com
Central location by the Trade Centre. 90
rooms, a health centre, pool, sauna, tennis court, beach club, cinema and a
bowling alley as well as several restaurants and a discotheque.

❸ *Adagio* ££
Hamad Bin-Abdullah Road
Tel. 09 223 99 11
www.accorhotels.com
Friendly, well-maintained hotel in the
centre with 72 rooms. A hint of luxury
with a feelgood factor for a moderate
price.

WHAT TO SEE IN FUJAIRAH CITY

The old town is a historic mud house settlement situated northwest   Old
of Al-Nakheel Road, 2km/1.25mi from the city centre. By the   Settlement
1980s, most of the houses had been entirely washed away by rain.
Goats lay in the shade of the few surviving foundation walls. In recent years, an effort has been made to reconstruct the few remaining houses.

Fujairah

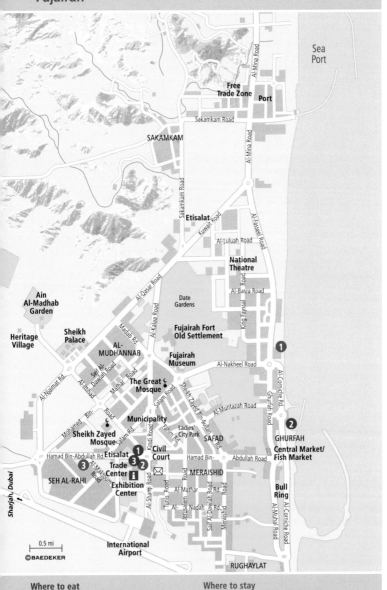

Sea Port

Free Trade Zone
Port

Al-Mina Road

Sakamkam Road

SAKAMKAM

Sakamkam Road

Al-Mina Road

Etisalat

Kuwait Road

Al-Luluah Road

Al-Fasseel Road

National Theatre

King Faysal Road

Al-Basra Road

Ain Al-Madhab Garden

Al-Qasr Road

Date Gardens

Madab Rd.

Al-Kalaa Road

Fujairah Fort Old Settlement

Sheikh Palace

Heritage Village

AL-MUDHANNAB

Sefi Al-Dawlah Road

Fujairah Museum

Al-Nakheel Road

Al-Comiche Rd.

Al-Njaimat Rd.

Al-Ittihad Road

Mathar Road

The Great Mosque

Salam Road

Sheikh Zayed Bin-Sultan Rd.

Al-Muntazah Road

Ghurfah Road

Municipality

Ladies' City Park

Mohamed Bin-Road

Sheikh Zayed Mosque

Salam Rd.

Kindi Rd.

Fahim Rd.

SAFAD

GHURFAH

Central Market/ Fish Market

Etisalat

Civil Court

Hamad Bin-Abdullah Rd.

Hamad Bin-Abdullah Road

Trade Center

SEH AL-RAHI

Al-Maktoum Road

Exhibition Center

MERAISHID

Al-Mathar

Bull Ring

Al-Munai Road

Al-Comiche Road

Tunis Road

Al-Sharei Road

Jerusalem Rd.

Al-Nadah Rd.

Saif Al-Dawlah Rd.

Meraishid Road

Sharjah, Dubai

0.5 mi

©BAEDEKER

International Airport

RUGHAYLAT

Where to eat
❶ Al-Meshwar
❷ Bikers Café
❸ Pizza Inn

Where to stay
❶ Hilton
❷ Al-Diar Siji
❸ Adagio

Today the Old Settlement houses the **Fujairah Museum**. Besides excavation finds from Bithnah and Badiyah – mainly ceramics and jewellery – there is also an ethnographic section displaying household goods, farming tools, traditional garments and weapons.

❶ Mon–Thu 8am–1pm, 4.30pm–6.30pm, Fri 2pm–6pm; admission 5 Dh

The battle scars on Fujairah Fort, built on a hilltop in 1670, have intentionally been left for all to see as a reminder of the city's bombardment in 1925. Standing several storeys high on the Al-Kalla Road, the fort consists of three main sections, a huge round tower and several large halls.

❶ Sat–Thu 9am–5pm, Fri 2pm–5pm; admission 3 Dh

Fujairah Fort

Fujairah's main souk (Central Market) can be found in the city centre on Hamad Bin-Abdullah Road (near the roundabout on the corner of Ghurfah Road). The **fish market** is situated near the Central Market. Noise levels rise when the daily catch is auctioned every morning. Right alongside, numerous vending stalls offer a rich and colourful range of fruit and vegetables.

Central Market, souks

The entire eastern border of the city of Fujairah, approximately one third of its area, is covered by expansive date gardens. The people here also cultivate fruit and vegetable gardens, selling their produce not only at the local markets but also further afield in the neighbouring emirates. The rich water supply enables types of plant or tree to thrive which cannot be found in the other emirates, such as bananas and mangos.

Date Gardens

On the southern corniche, the circular, dusty bullfight arena hosts between ten and fifteen »Arabian bullfights« on Friday afternoons. The Fujairah bulls do not fight human adversaries, but each another. Two mighty Brahmin bulls – originally from India and highly resistant to heat and lack of water – are led into the arena by their owners, held on a rope attached to their horns or through a nose ring. On command, the men let go off the ropes and the heavy beasts charge towards one another, snorting loudly as they push and shove head to head. If neither of the bulls gives way, a referee decides which animal wins. Usually this type of bullfight passes without bloodshed. Should the animals, however, threaten to injure one another, they are separated immediately. There is no prize money; instead the winning bull's value increases – they usually cost between 3,000 and 30,000 Dh – and with it the owner's reputation.

**Bull Ring

❶ Admission free

On the northwestern edge of the city at the end of Al-Ittihad Road, a Heritage Village similar to the ones in Dubai and Abu Dhabi was

Heritage Village

built in 1997. Two cannon flank the entrance to the vast area which covers approx. 6000 sq m/7176 sq yd. Various exhibitions recreate the emirate's recent past: collections of old household goods, ceramic vases and bowls, which are still used by some of the rural population today for storing dates, olive oil or cheese. Fishermen's tools are kept in traditional huts made of palm leaves. A particularly charming spot in the Heritage Village is where it meets the lush, green **Madhab Sulpheric Spring Park** which is irrigated by a sulphurous mineral spring – a very popular spot for walks and picnics.

Heritage Village: Sun–Thu 8am–1pm, 4pm to 6pm, Fri 2pm–6pm; admission free
Madhab Sulpheric Spring Park: Sat–Fri 10am–10pm, admission 4 Dh

AROUND FUJAIRAH CITY

Kalba   The village of Kalba, which belongs to Sharjah, is located some 10km/6mi directly south of Fujairah International Airport on the Gulf of Oman. A wide corniche road runs alongside the white sandy beach from Fujairah City through Kalba and on to Khor Kalba, a

Thrills without bloodshed: bullfight in Fujairah

creek which lies close to the Omani border. A narrow green park with palms, gardens and playgrounds nestles between the beach and the road. Between Kalba and Khor Kalba, the Breeze Grill at the Breeze Motel attracts hungry guests, particularly local families at weekends.

Kalba Old Fort (Al-Hosn) sits on a hill amidst several derelict houses from the old settlement of Kalba on the corniche. Its current form (p.49) dates back to reinforcement work carried out by the Portuguese in the 16th century. The fort is not open to the public. **Kalba Old Fort**

Opposite the fort stands the Bait Sheikh Saeed al-Qassimi residence, built in 1900, and now home to an ethnographic museum. Exhibits include archaeological finds from the area, traditional garments, coins and items of everyday use. **Ethnographic Museum**

❶ Al-Hosn, Sat–Thu 9am–1pm and 5pm–8pm, Fri 5pm–8pm; admission 3 Dh

A few kilometres/miles south of Kalba, the Khor Kalba inlet first turns inland then runs parallel to the coast for 4km/2.5mi inland. A bridge provides access and there are picnic sites on either side of the road. Fishing boats are moored on the lagoon, an ice factory which belongs to the fishermen's cooperative can be seen on land. At its southern end, the inlet becomes a mangrove swamp, the world's northernmost, designated as a nature reserve. The brackish water offers the Khor Kalba mangroves ideal conditions for growth. Nowhere else in the United Arab Emirates can boast such a wealth of plants, birds and marine wildlife. Canoe tours, operated by a nature conservation group, are an excellent opportunity to find out more about the ecosystem. Groups are accompanied by expert rangers and, with a bit of luck, visitors may sight the local dugongs (sea cows) who live in the shallow waters off the coast. ***Khor Kalba Mangrove Reserve Park**

MARCO POLO TIP

! *Sea breeze* Insider Tip

The Breeze Motel (34 rooms, tel. 09 277 88 77, www.breezemotel. com) on the corniche of Kalba may often be booked out at weekends (Thursday to Saturday), but at other times provides low-price family accommodation by the sea with mini-golf and a pool. On the beach opposite, the Breeze Grill serves lamb and fish dishes with a sea view – and a cool breeze.

The old village of Al-Hayl with its historic castle is situated in the wadi of Hayl, 8km/5mi southwest of Fujairah. In the 19th century, this palace-like fort was the main residence of the emirate's ruling family, defending them against attacks from the neighbouring Omani region. Although mainly built from mud, the building is still in good repair. The square, three-storey defence tower is open to visitors. From the battlements on the rooftop there is a fine view of the **Al-Hayl** palace, the surrounding abandoned village and the wadi, which carries water all year round.

❶ Al-Hayl Palace (Al-Hayl Castle) opens when a cruise shop docks at the Fujairah terminal

Qidfa

In 1985, about 15km/9mi north of Fujairah, agricultural workers in a date grove discovered a horseshoe-shaped grave from the Iron Age on the northern edge of Qidfa village. The approximately 3,000 year old grave contained burial objects such as jars, daggers, axes and jewellery, which are now on show at the Fujairah Museum.

*Al-Wurayah

Near Zubarah, 5km/3mi north of Khor Fakkan (p.279), a road branches off from the coastal route and heads southwest towards the **Al-Wurayah waterfall**. Just before that, another turnoff leads to the Wurayah Dam, one of Khor Fakkan's two reservoirs. After approximately 12km/7.5mi, the road ends shortly before the Wurayah waterfall, which supplies a flow of fresh spring water all year round. In 2013, the area was declared a nature reserve under the name **Wadi Wurayah National Park** and closed with immediate effect in order to remove all of the rubbish which had collected here and to erase the colourful graffiti from the rocks. A date for the opening of the park has not yet been announced.

> **!** MARCO ◉ POLO TIP
>
> *Mountain trips* Insider Tip
>
> A trip into the Hajar Mountains is absolutely worthwhile. Alongside remote villages, the tour leads past mineral springs and even a waterfall. These mountain expeditions, however, definitely require a four-by-four vehicle; otherwise it's better to join an organized tour, which can be booked in the hotels.

Badiyah

35km/22mi north of Fujairah, the small town of Badiyah is renowned for its **Thursday Market**, a major agricultural event which attracts people from the entire emirate. Close to Badiyah, tourists can visit a first-rate historical site in terms of art and culture: the **Al-Badiyah Mosque** is the oldest mosque in the UAE. The various estimations of its age range from between 1300 (beginning of Islamization) and 800, but recent investigations suggest a date of around 1446. The squat building, which was most likely named after its sponsor Othman, also called Masjid al-Othmani, has a floor space of only several square yards. The modest, whitewashed mosque is characterized by four low domes, supported by a single pillar. Wooden double doors lead inside. The mosque has been renovated and is back in use. Appropriate clothing is required, but non-Muslims may be denied entry at times. North of the mosque, the ruins of the Badiyah Fort dominate the landscape.

Dibba: a town in three parts

Dibba, 60km/37mi north of Fujairah, is a beautifully situated coastal town with wide, sandy beaches. As a natural harbour, Dibba was an

Al-Hayl fort at the foot of the Hajar Mountains

important trading post in the 7th century. Following the victory of Muslim forces from Saudi Arabia over the inhabitants of the east coast, completing the Islamization of the Arabian Peninsula, the settlement faded into insignificance. Today, picturesque rocky bays and delightful sandy beaches greet tourists. Divers and snorkellers are attracted to an underwater world of coral and rocky riffs, teeming with fish.

Stretching into the distance, the grey-green shimmering mountains of the Musandam Peninsula are a most impressive landmark of the region belonging to Oman and well worth a boat trip or diving expedition. It may not be immediately obvious, but Dibba is split into three parts, a third each for the Emirates of Fujairah and Sharjah and the Sultanate of Oman. On closer inspection, differences in architectural design become apparent: the houses in the Omani district are more traditionally Arabic in style, with colourful iron gates bearing typical emblems such as camels, coffee pots and water pipes. A UAE tourist visa is required to visit the Omani district of Dibba Byah to the north. Passports and visas must be presented at the border, as is also the case if continuing to Zighy Bay and the Six Senses hotel located there.

Musandam Peninsula

Bithnah   Surrounded by date palms in a picturesque valley, Bithnah Fort stands 15km/9mi northwest of Fujairah on the way to Dubai or Sharjah. Built in a small oasis in 1735, the fort guarded the strategic **Wadi Ham** route through the Hajar Mountains. Excavations of the surroundings came up with several indications that the Bithnah Oasis may already been inhabited more than 3,000 years ago. The ceramics and metal items found in a T-shaped communal grave, used from approximately 1300 to 300 BC, document the level of cultural development of settlers in that period. The Museum of Fujairah has a replica of the grave as well as an exhibition of the burial objects discovered inside. The excavation site itself is not publicly accessible.

Musandam   The **Omani enclave of Musandam on the northern tip of the Arabian peninsula is roughly half the size of Majorca, covering an area of approximately 30 x 90 km/20 x 55 mi. Since 2013 it has been necessary to possess a visa for the border region north of Dibba. This can be obtained from a travel agent or tour operator. The population of around 30,000 lives in Khasab or in tiny villages that can only be reached by boat. Main attraction is the dramatically beautiful mountain range which rises up to 2,000m/6,500ft and falls steeply into the shining blue sea. Wadis and inlets reach far inland and into the

Musandam, the Omani enclave, with tall, rugged mountains, concealed bays and inlets reaching deep inland

mountains. The best way to explore this wilderness is to take a local guide. A leisurely alternative is a trip on a dhow that has been converted for leisure tours. With luck, dolphins may be spotted en route. Snorkellers and divers can discover a colourful underwater world of bright shoals of fish and coral forests. Starting points for these tours, which can last for anything up to several days, are Dibba and Khasab (both two to three hours by car from Dubai).

! MARCO POLO TIP

Spectacular view **Insider Tip**

North of the Bithnah Oasis, on the road to Sharjah, the view of the old fort surrounded by date trees is absolutely stunning.

Information: www.khasabtours.com and www.musandamdiving.com; p.142

Ras al-Khaimah

RAS AL-KHAIMAH

Area: 1,625 sq km/627 sq mi	**Emir:** Sheikh Saud Bin-Saqr
Population: 431,000	Bin-Mohammed al-Qasimi (since 2010)

Rugged mountain peaks, green oases and simple fishing settlements: located on the Arabian Gulf, Ras al-Khaimah, or RAK for short, is the northernmost sheikhdom of the United Arab Emirates and the last to become a member of the federation when it joined on 10 February 1972. Like Fujairah, it possesses some of the country's most beautiful landscapes.

Ras al-Khaimah means »top of the tent«. The assumption is that this expression refers to the emirate's steep mountains whose summits resemble the shape of tents – once the home of the nomadic people of Ras al-Khaimah. The emirate has 70km/43mi of coastline and is mountainous, save for a 10km/6mi stretch of coast. It is bordered by the Omani exclave of Musandam, the mountainous peninsula and the Strait of Hormuz. Thanks to the large mountain range and the numerous water sources which originate in the Hajar Mountains, the emirate has the most fertile land in the entire UAE, complete with sprawling palm oases. The plains are used for growing crops and grazing cattle.

Top of the tent

There are no glittering boom towns here, at least not yet. The population still lives from fishing and agriculture, exporting its produce to the other six emirates. Again, due to the large mountain range, it rains here more than in the neighbouring emirates. The first agricultural research station on the Arabian Gulf was set up in 1960 not far from the **capital Digdagga**. Today the oasis supplies the emirates with poultry, eggs, milk and meat, dates, fruit and vegetables.

In Ras al-Khaimah, oil production only began as late as 1984, with the opening of the Saleh field in the Arabian Gulf. Its yield triggered the development of an industrial area north of the capital. Tourism has not played much of a role to date, in spite of the fourth largest sheikhdom in the UAE emirate having largely unspoiled beaches, mountainous hinterlands and authentic Arabic flair. Concerted efforts are being made to improve infrastructure for tourism, in many cases with a laudable emphasis on environmental substainability.

Ras al-Khaimah, the northernmost emirate of the UAE, attracts visitors with its mountains, desert and ocean, all within 30 minutes radius

Mina al-Arab On a 3km/2mi-long coastal strip on the southern edge of Ras al-Khaimah City, the new district of Mina al-Arab is emerging between the beach and the lagoon, partly on land reclaimed from the sea. Covering an area of 2.8 sq km/1 sq mi, Mina al-Arab (»Arab harbour«) is being developed as a holiday resort with hotels, apartments, shopping malls, lagoons and a marina, surrounded by a nature reserve (information: www.minaalarab.net).

Al Marjan Island 25km/16mi south of Ras al-Khaimah City, four man-made coral-shaped islands, all interconnected, are being created off the southwest coast, as in Dubai. They will extend 4.5km/3mi into the sea, providing 2.7 sq km/1 sq mi of land for marinas, shopping malls, hotels and apartments (www.almarjanisland.com).

History The area of what is now Ras al-Khaimah was already colonized in the second millennium BC. During excavations on the slope of the Ghallila Mountains, an oval-shaped grave was found; in Shimal two elongated graves with several side graves. The oldest findings include stone bowls with engraved decorations, bones, fish hooks, stone beads, shell jewellery, ceramics, model ships, bronze arrowheads and spearheads, as well as stone markers – an indication of subterranean graves. Similarly old artefacts were discovered above the hot springs of Khatt, at what might have once been an oasis settlement. The area of the Wadi Qawr is the site of 3,000 year old communal graves as well as remains of two settled villages from the same period.

The harbour town of Julfar, north of Ras al-Khaimah, is of legendary importance, praised centuries ago by the explorers Ibn Battuta (Famous People) and Marco Polo. Founded at the beginning of the Islamic Period, the town is also mentioned in the Qur'an. One of its famous navigators was Ahmed Bin-Majid (Famous People), the »Lion of the Sea«, whose logbooks were long used for navigation by Arab sailors.

At the beginning of the 18th century, the British became increasingly active in the Gulf region, seeking to extend their power. The Qawasim, based in Ras al-Khaimah, were still a thorn in the side of the British, as the Qasimi trading fleet and far-reaching trade relations competed with the interests of the British East India Company. By the end of the 18th century, the Qawasim owned the largest trading fleet of the Indian Ocean, and controlled sea trade on both coasts of the northern Gulf region. In 1819, Major General Sir William Grant Keir conquered the city and the nearby Dhayah Fort. Based on the peace treaty between the British and the rulers of the nine sheikhdoms, signed in 1820, Sheikh Sultan Bin-Saqr al-Qasimi regained Julfar and the other Qasimi harbour towns, but only in exchange for British domination of the Gulf coast. In this way, the »Pirate Coast« became the »Trucial Coast«, otherwise known as the Trucial States.

* Ras al-Khaimah City

K 2

Population: 230,000

Ras al-Khaimah is still a world away from the modern, luxurious metropolis of Dubai (for now). Most of its houses, architecturally simple constructions of one or two storeys, were erected in the 1970s and 1980s. The Old Town still contains a few older buildings in more traditional style.

An estuary (al-Khor) divides the city in two, connected by two bridges and water taxis. To the west, the Old Town of Ras al-Khaimah is the more interesting side for tourists. To the east lies the New Town of Al-Nakheel. Visitors from Dubai, 100km/62mi away, can drive here via multilane highways or catch a plane: the international airport is located 15km/9mi outside the city. A popular destination for tourists is the **Tower Links Golf Course**, an 18-hole course with a hotel and marina, set in a mangrove forest (www.towerlinks.com).

Coastal town on the Musandam Peninsula

Beautiful backdrop: the sweeping beach of the Al-Hamra Fort Hotel, bedecked with palm trees, sets holidaymakers' hearts racing

Ras al-Khaimah City

INFORMATION
RAK Tourism Development Authority
Ras al-Khaimah
Chamber of Commerce Bldg, 5th floor
Al Jazah Road
Tel. 07 233 89 98
www.rasalkhaimahtourism.com
Information for visitors is also available
in the National Museum of Ras al-Khaimah.

WHERE TO EAT
❶ *Shehrazad Tent* £££
Ras al-Khaimah Hotel
Eid Musallah Road
Tel. 072 36 29 99
The best restaurant in the emirate, offering Asian and Arabic specialities.

❷ *Al-Sahari* ££
Sheikh Muhammed Bin-Salem Road
Tel. 072 33 39 66
Reasonably priced, tasty Lebanese dishes. Grilled fish and chicken are the specialities.

❸ *Pizza Inn* £
Sheikh Muhammed Bin-Salem Road
 (next to the post office)
Tel. 072 33 40 40
An »Italian enclave« with Arabic-inspired pizza and pasta dishes.

WHERE TO STAY
❶ *Banyan Tree Al-Wadi* ££££
Wadi al-Khadiya
E311 motorway, exit 119, then 7km/4mi to the south
www.banyantree.com
Banyan Tree is a byword for luxury, Asian-inspired design and the ultimate in nature experiences. The luxurious hotel

is located 20km/12.5mi south of RAK City at the heart of the Wadi Khadiya nature reserve, 100 hectares/247 acres in size. Exquisitely appointed desert villas look like 21st-century bedouin tents; each has its own pool and sun deck, the perfect vantage point from which to observe wild animals drinking at water holes in the reserve. Here and in the beach club villas some 30 minutes away, guests can enjoy the best of both worlds, the desert and the sea. The hotel also has its own falconry (p.109).

❷ *Hilton Al Hamra Beach & Golf Resort* £££
Vienna Street
Tel. 072 44 66 66
www.alhamrabeachandgolfresort.hilton.com
20k/12.5mi south of the city, this hotel is designed like an Arabic fort, complete with wind towers. Many of the 266 rooms have a balcony and a view of the ocean.

❸ *Hilton Hotel* £££
RAK Creek, tel. 07 228 88 88
www.hilton.com
227 rooms
The hotel is situated on the lagoon, a second Hilton right on the beach. Amenities and activities include a gym, water sports, a pool, tennis and fishing trips. A free shuttle bus goes to Dubai and the hotel's beach club.

❹ *Ras al-Khaimah Hotel* ££
Al-Khouzam Road / Eid Musallah Road; Khouzam
Tel. 07 236 29 99
www.rasalkhaimahhotel.net; 93 rooms
The hotel stands on a hill overlooking

the dhow harbour. A wide variety of water sports facilities, a pool, tennis and squash courts, sauna and workout room.

❺ *Bin Majid Beach Resort* ££
Bin Majid Road, tel. 07 244 66 44
www.binmajid.com 125 rooms and chalets
The inexpensively priced chalets **Insider Tip** are directly on the beach. Two restau-

rants, a bar and discotheque, two pools, a private beach, playground and gym.

❻ *Mangrove* ££
Al-Kohr Road
Tel. 07 233 77 33
www.binmajid.com 55 rooms
Located in the centre of the city, the hotel belongs to the Bin Majid group. It has two popular restaurants, cafés and bars. Good value for money.

WHAT TO SEE IN RAS AL-KHAIMAH CITY

Sightseeing focusses on the Old Town, although there are only a few old, traditional houses left and of those remaining, many are empty and awaiting renovation. The emirate's historic fort was built during the Persian occupation between 1736 and 1749. Now, only the square tower to the left of the entrance remains from this time. All other parts of the building having been built in the following centuries, serving as a palace for the ruling al-Qasimi Family – most recently for Sheikh Saqr, who died in 2010. When Sheikh Saqr had a new palace built for himself in 1960, the fort served as police headquarters, then as a prison. Since its renovation in the 1980s, the fort has been home to the National Museum.

Old Town, *Old Fort

The museum features an ethnography department and an archaeology department, with exhibits and finds from Ras al-Khaimah, as well as a natural history department with an extensive collection of shells and numerous fossils. The oldest piece of the archaeological collection, a stone knife, dates back to the third millennium BC. The bulk of the collection comprises finds from the archaeological site of Shimal. Also interesting is the collection of silver coins, which were discovered in 1965 during excavation work on an old well. They have been attributed to the Persian Samanid and Buwayhid tribes and date back to the period between 920 and 981. An additional 124 silver coins were found in 1985, minted under Persian rule between 1010 and 1023 in Sohar, in what is now Oman. Other exhibits include finds from the former harbour town of Julfar, mostly from the 16th and 17th centuries, including bronze coins, Chinese porcelain, jugs from Thailand and ceramics from Vietnam.

*National Museum of Ras al-Khaimah

🄾 10am–5pm daily, except Tue, admission 3 Dh

Pearl Museum RAK Pearls, a company specializing in cultured pearls, opened a pearl museum in 2012. Everything there is to know about the history of pearl diving can be found on the museum's two levels. This was an important branch of trade until the 1930s, when Japanese cultured pearls came to the fore. Pearls of all shapes and sizes are on display

Ras al-Khaimah

0.25 mi

©BAEDEKER

N

MA'RID

Ruler's Palace

Museum and Center of the Navigator

Al Mamourah Road

Al-Hu

Al-Mountasser Road

COMMERCIAL CENTRE

Bin-Majid Road

Oman Road

Al-Araii

Fish Souk

Ferry

Electicity Road

Jezaah Road

Hotel Road

Port Saqr Deep Water Harbour

3

Bin-Dahii Road

Al-Hasiat Road

Oman Road

AL-NAKHEEL

Al-Qawasim Corniche

Al-Sahari Road

Old Fort, National Museum

Vegetable Souk

Bridge Road

Al-Hosn St.

Al-Juwa

Al-Hosn St.

Al-Hosn Garden

OLD TOWN

Indian Islamic Court

2

Al-Khor Road

Al Manar Mall

Industrial Area

Kuwaiti Hospital Road

AL-JUWAIS

Municipality

DAFAN

6

Khor Ras al-Khaimah

Al-Qorm Road

Oman Road

Al-Qawasim Corniche

Muhammed Bin-Salim Road

Dahan Road

3

✉

Al-Qidar Road

King Faisal Rd. Sheih

Court

Pearl Museum

5

2

1

DAHAN

Eid Musallah Road

Eid Prayer Ground

4

1

Khouzam Road

DUWAR AL-QUSIDAT

Industrial Area

Abu Shak Road

Tower Links Golf Club

Khouzam Road

Industrial Area

Ruler's New Palace

Khouzam Road

KHOUZAM

here, along with apparatus, tools and accessories, including diving suits and boats. Excursions to pearl farms are on offer.

Al Qawasim Corniche, by appointment

Tel 09 715 01 98 04 80, www.rakpearls.com

The **Museum and Center of the Navigator Ahmed Bin-Majid** in Mamourah Road, northwest of the Hilton Hotel, displays boats and items connected with the city's seafaring history, recalling the great mariners and cartographers of the 15th century.   Bin-Majid Museum

Al Qawasim Corniche, Sat–Thu 9am–noon and 4pm–6pm, admission free

AROUND RAS AL-KHAIMAH CITY

In 1272, Marco Polo visited the harbour town of Julfar, beyond the lagoon on the northern edge of Ras al-Khaimah, and praised its beauty. Ahmed Bin-Majid (Famous People) was born here in 1432. He was one of the most famous navigators of Arabia and author of 40 works on geography and navigation. He is also believed to be the inventor of the magnetic compass. Toward the end of the 15th century, the Portuguese controlled the region around Julfar; in the early 16th century, building a garrison, a tollhouse and two forts to guard the coastal region. At the beginning of the 17th century, British and Dutch colonialists challenged the Portuguese position and destroyed both of their forts in the year 1633. Situated in the hills above the bay of al-Mataf, this historic site is about 2km/1.2mi long and 300 to 400 metres (328 to 438 yards) wide. In various places, foundation walls of 14th-century residential buildings and streets were uncovered and further dwellings from earlier times exposed beneath those. The foundations of a mosque from the early Islamic period have also been identified. Archaeological sites are fenced off and can only be accessed by seeking permission from security.   *Julfar

The historically significant ruins of the »Palace of the Queen of Sheba«, probably built in the 16th century, are situated on a free-standing rock above the village of Shimal, 3km/2mi northeast of Ras al-Khaimah. In reality, however, the ruins date back to a hill fort and are completely unconnected to the legendary queen who lived in South Arabia about two millennia before the fort was even built. Today, all that is left of the fortifications are a few foundation walls. It is still possible to see the remains of a drinking water cistern which was equipped with a barrel-shaped roof to keep the water clean and protect it from the sun.   Sheba's Palace

In the second millennium BC, copper deposits were found in what we now call Northern Oman. Copper was extracted and transported   Shimal

Vengeful Ships of the Desert

Of all mammals in the United Arab Emirates, camels cope best with the extreme aridity. Fatty humps help the animals survive without water for several days; in emergencies, they will even drink saline water.

Wide foot pads allow the camel to walk in deep sand without sinking. Long eyelashes and closable nostrils prevent sand from getting into the camel's eyes and nose.

The Art of Survival

In extreme heat, a camel can increase its body temperature to 42°C/107°F to avoid losing too much water through sweating. Likewise, on cold desert nights, the animal can lower its body temperature to 34°C/93°F so that it doesn't catch cold. Camels are able to survive without eating or drinking for long periods of time, and when they do, they can drink 100 litres/26 US gal of water within a mere 15 minutes, a supply which will last them for up to three weeks. These ruminant animals have three stomachs in which they store water and food. They are also able to expand their red blood corpuscles to store fluid. Camels are herbivores and feed on shrubs, thorn bushes and desert grass. Camels can cover up to 50km/31mi per day and carry loads of up to 250kg/550lb. However, these animals are not completely robust. They quickly fall sick from polluted water, and if they are not given enough rest after a strenuous tour they can suddenly drop dead. It takes a very long time before camels accept their owners. These extremely vengeful animals will remember bad treatment for their entire lives, and will take revenge with kicks or bites even years later. Various different breeds of dromedary can be found on the Arabian Peninsula. Some are suited to racing, others as providers of milk and meat. The act of sexual reproduction is less than straightforward for the awkwardly long-legged beasts. They mate sitting down in a rather cumbersome fashion. Trainers interested in offspring generally have to lend a helping hand. Mares only give birth to a foal every two to three years, hence artificial insemination has become common in breeding.

Desert Joy

These frugal animals have been known on the Arabian Peninsula for 4,000 years. It is no exaggeration to claim that the settlement of the region was only possible due to camels. The word »camel«, however, is not entirely correct, for it is the single-humped dromedary, the »gamal«, which is domesticated on the Arabian Peninsula. In former times the animals were particularly valued for their milk and meat; their dung served as heating material, their leathery hide was processed to make sandals and water jugs, and their hair and fur was used to make tents, rugs and clothing. Even their

Last preparations before the start of a camel race in Digdagga

shoulder blades were put to good use, serving as writing boards for children.

The mare gives birth to her foal after twelve months. In order to get the calves accustomed to humans, the Bedouins used to take the young with them into their tents. For these sons of the desert, camels were their most precious property. They had hundreds of poetic pet names for their four-legged companions, such as »miracle of beauty«, »dauntless courage« or »desert joy«. Today camels mainly function as status symbols. A young camel costs as much as a used car: between 1,500–5,000 Euro. Visitors can often observe large herds grazing behind the fencing along motorways or in the desert.

Camel Races

Attending one of the many camel races during winter is a captivating experience. The sport's greatest fan is Sheikh Khalifa of Abu Dhabi, owner of several hundred racing camels, some of which are worth half a million Euro. Each race involves around three dozen camels. The jockeys wear headphones through which they receive instructions from the camel owners following them in their jeeps alongside the racetrack. Racing can be quite tricky as camels are very hard even to steer in the desired direction, let alone getting them to trot or gallop. Some won't budge at the start of the race, while others run wrong way or even go backwards. Races are sometimes shown on television.

along the caravan route to Shimal, 5km/3mi north of what is now Ras al-Khaimah, and shipped from there to Mesopotamia (now Iraq). The archaeological site extends over more than 3km/2mi and includes a settlement and the remains of a large burial site. These burial sites consisted of large, overground communal graves, as well as individual graves up in the mountains, which increased in number from the 2nd millennium BC. One of the graves held about 40 bodies and contained valuable burial objects, including ceramic pots, stone-carved jugs, silver earrings and numerous pearls. The openly accessible excavation site is signposted from the Al-Rams Road, the highway leading north. The walk up the steep, rocky trail to the graves can be a strenuous undertaking.

The village of Dhayah lies north of the capital, nestled between mountains and the sea. From the fort of the same name, scene of a battle between the British and the inhabitants of Ras al-Khaimah in the year 1819, wonderful views of palm groves and the coast may be savoured. **Dhayah**

Up until the second half of the 20th century, the wide and easily accessible Al-Qor Wadi was a preferred caravan route for traversing the Hajar Mountains. Pack camels transported merchants' goods from the Gulf Coast to the Batinah Coast in Oman. Only with the development of a road between Hatta and the Batinah coast did the old route lose its significance. A wadi tour promises not only beautiful landscapes, but also enters a region which was inhabited thousands of years ago. Archaeologists found a horseshoe-shaped communal grave built deep into the rock. The sensational discovery of a grave situated near Naslah (east of Huwaylat) unearthed more than 2,000 burial objects: elaborately crafted vases, jugs and storage vessels made of malleable chlorite stone from the surrounding area. Near **Rafaq**, the ruins of a fortified village were found on both sides of the wadi. Based on ceramic shards, the settlement has been dated to the 2nd millennium BC. The best way to reach the Al-Qor Wadi is to set out from Hatta. At the Hatta Fort Hotel, take the asphalt road to Huwaylat that turns into a dirt road leading to the wadi. **Wadi al-Qor**

Huwaylat, an old oasis located in the wadi, was once a traditional transit town for caravans on their way to the Batinah coast. Today Huwaylat is a popular weekend destination its streets lined with numerous holiday homes. The old rest house and a general store, which also serves tea and coffee, are reminders of former times. Falaj channels (MARCO POLO Insight p.230) outside the town and parallel to the wadi conduct water to the gardens of oasis dwellers. **Huwaylat**

View from the Dhayah fort, looking across to the village of the same name with a lush palm grove, nestling between mountains and sea

Camel trekking in the nature reserve of Banyan Tree Al-Wadi

Munay
From Huwaylat, an approximately 8km/5mi stretch of road leads northward to the magnificent palm gardens at the small oasis town of Munay. Here, time seems to have stood still: men in long white garments promenade leisurely down the street, meeting for tea or a game of cards. The womenfolk wear veils, hurrying on their way when they encounter strangers. The ruins of an old fort and watchtower remain from earlier centuries.

*Wadi Asimah
A trip into the mountains along the lush, green Wadi Asimah is very popular with the locals. Accessible via the village of Al Ghail, it is situated on the road traversing the Jeri plain, between Ras al-Khaimah and Manama. The dusty route leads through quaint mountain valleys and past steep ravines. The landscape around Asimah is not just stunningly beautiful, it also bears evidence of ancient settlements.

Graves
In 1972, the remains of nearly 20 graves from the 2nd millennium BC were found, furnished with an abundance of burial objects. Among the most significant and precious finds, all of which can be viewed at the museum in Ras al-Khaimah, is an approximately 4,000 year old filigree bronze mug, as well as several gold necklaces from the 1st century AD. It is only possible to visit the fenced-in excavation site as part of a tour booked with a local travel organization.

Fans of the sport consider the camel racetrack in Digdagga, 10km/6mi south of Ras al-Khaimah, to be the most picturesque. Situated in beautiful surroundings, it has managed to maintain its charm by forgoing ugly concrete stands or terraces. Every Thursday and Friday during the racing season between October and April, hundreds of dromedaries are to be seen here. Fed on a diet of fresh hay, honey, dates, eggs and barley – quite unlike pack animals or animals for slaughter – and kept under constant veterinary supervision, the racing dromedaries are ready to run at the age of three or four (►MARCO POLO Insight p.254).

Digdagga camel racetrack

35km/22mi beyond Ras al-Khaimah, the border crossing at Tibat leads into Oman. Following a road which runs between the sea and the mountains, the town of Khasab is reached 40km/25 further on. Excursions to the Musandam Peninsula leave from here (►p.142, 245).

Excursion to Musandam

Sharjah

SHARJAH

Area: 2,600 sq km/1,004 sq mi	**Emir:** Sheikh Dr. Sultan Bin-Moham-
Population: 1 million	med al-Qasimi (since 1972)

Sharjah is the third largest of the seven emirates, the only one to have land on both the Arabian Gulf to the west and the Gulf of Oman to the east. The east coast is particularly attractive, with long sandy beaches at the foot of the Hajar Mountains, whose peaks rise up out of the desert to 1500m/4920ft, and blessed with diving grounds rich in fish.

Sharjah contains several geographically distinct areas. The capital of the same name, 15km/9mi north of Dubai on the west coast of the United Arab Emirates, covers the major part of the emirate. Besides this, there are exclaves on the Gulf coast of Oman – including Dibba, the holiday paradise of Khor Fakkan and the fishing settlement of Kalba – plus two larger islands in the Arabian Gulf. Sharjah only has moderate petroleum resources, and gas reserves have not yet been developed. In the late 1970s, it became the first emirate to open up its gates to tourism, but a strict ban on alcohol in 1985 saw the flow of visitors change course for the more liberal ways of Dubai. Consequently, Sharjah developed into the **»Cultural Capital of the Islamic World«**. The city centre has been restored and many historic buildings have been turned into museums. Today, Sharjah has more museums than all of the other emirates combined. The emirate has also focussed on promoting the service sector and has been so successful that it can now lay claim to being the services centre of the UAE.

Emirate of the arts

Sharjah is run by Sheikh Sultan Bin-Mohammed al-Qasimi, who is considered the most intellectual of the seven emirs of the UAE and the most interested in the arts. The ruler with a PhD in agricultural economics actively promotes agriculture in the emirate. He has also written two novels and several historical books on the Gulf region.

Ruling agricultural economist

The first colonization of Sharjah happened some 6,000 years ago. The people of the ancient town of Sarcoa lived from maritime trade and fishing; later also agriculture and pearl diving (MARCO POLO Insight p.276). The major part of its history, however, is still largely unknown due to a lack of archaeological excavation work. Beginning in 1507, the Portuguese built forts in Khor Fakkan, Khor Kalba and

History

Lovingly restored houses in the Sharjah Heritage Area

Dibba to control the spice trade. After around one hundred years they were driven away by the Dutch. In the 17th century the British arrived and began to trade with the Qawasim tribe, the ancestors of the current ruling family. In the 18th century, the Qawasim were the prevailing sea power in the southern Gulf, with harbours in Ras al-Khaimah and Sharjah. In 1803 Sheikh Sultan Bin-Saqr al-Qasimi became Emir of Sharjah and ruled the sheikhdom for 63 years. The relationship with the British suffered when they held the Qawasim responsible for pirate raids on British ships, which led to the first British attack on Ras al-Khaimah in 1809 and ended with the destruction of the entire settlement. However, several peace treaties, the first concluded in 1820, secured British supremacy in the Gulf for 150 years. From 1853, the coast was referred to as the »Trucial Coast« or »Trucial States«. Between 1823 and 1954, Sharjah was the only British base on the southern Gulf. They established their first airport here as early as 1932, used for stopovers on the way to India. In 1972, after the emirates' federal alliance, oil and later gas were found in the Mubarak Field, 80km/50mi offshore on the island of Abu Musa, instigating Sharjah's modern development.

> **MARCO POLO TIP**
>
> ! **Very Special Art Centre**
>
> *Insider Tip*
>
> The name belongs to an arts centre for the disabled, providing artist workshops at Abdullah al-Sari House. It can be visited by appointment (tel. 06 568 78 12).

** Sharjah City

✦ J 3/4

Population: 900,000

Like Dubai, the emirate's capital is a modern city with urban highways and skyscrapers, along with spacious gardens and parks, souks and malls. In the city centre, there are also districts with carefully restored Islamic buildings, including many museums. In 2014, Sharjah was named Capital of Islamic Culture.

A modern city
The city of Sharjah overlooks three man-made lagoons: Khor al-Mamzar on the border with Dubai, Khor al-Khan, which is divided into three separate inlets by sandbanks, and Khor al-Khalid, a distinctive feature of the city as it winds its way far into the town. Hotels line the esplanade on the eastern side. Jazeera Park is on one of the islands in the lagoon. Khalid Lagoon flows into Sharjah Creek which meets the ocean. As in Dubai, the original settlers made their homes on the creek. The Old Town is now a picturesque arts district. The

modern centre is located to the south of Arouba Street, whilst the suburbs and industrial zones are found further south.

WHAT TO SEE IN SHARJAH CITY

The historical Old Town is now an open-air museum. It stretches from Al-Bouheira Corniche on Sharjah Creek and Arouba Road in the south. Al-Boorj Avenue, which leads to Al-Hisn Fort, runs down the middle.

Heritage Area

The old residence of the ruling family on Al-Boorj Avenue was built in 1822 by Sheikh Sultan Bin-Saqr al-Qasimi. This two-storey mud-brick building was in use until the mid-20th century. In 1969, the entire structure was torn down, except for the 12m/39ft Al-Mahal-wasa tower. Twenty years later, the loss of this historic building was so deeply regretted that the fort was reconstructed true to the origi-

**Al-Hisn Fort

The Blue Souk is one of the most photographed buildings in the UAE

Sharjah City

INFORMATION
Sharjah Commerce & Tourism Development Authority
Buheira Corniche West
Crescent Tower, 9th floor
P.O. Box 2 66 61, Sharjah
Tel. 06 556 27 77
www.sharjahtourism.ae

MUSEUMS
Museums and historic buildings are usually open between 8am and 8pm with a couple of exceptions; Wednesday afternoons are reserved for women. On Fridays they are only open in the afternoon. Admission to museums is cheap, in some cases free (information at www.sharjahmuseums.ae).

SHOPPING
Shopping in Sharjah is a special experience.
The Blue Souk, also known as Souk al-Markazi, is the most beautiful in the UAE. The upper level is devoted to antiques and old-fashioned objects, the latter sometimes brought in from the Arabian Peninsula, but more commomly from Asia.
Books in English about the region can be found in the Book Mall at Qanat al-Qasba.

WHERE TO EAT
❶ *Caesar's Palace* ££
Marbella Resort
Buheira Corniche
Tel. 06 574 11 11
The elegant restaurant with a magnificent view of the lagoon serves international cuisine, with a focus on Italian specialities.

❷ *Fishermen's Wharf* £££
Hotel Holiday International
Khalid Lagoon Corniche
Al-Majaz
Tel.06 573 66 66
This rustic, nautical-style restaurant serves fish and shellfish, prepared according to the wishes of the guests.

❸ *Sanobar* ££
Al-Khan Road
Tel. 06 528 35 01
Popular Lebanese restaurant serving delicious stews. Wide variety of fresh fish, grilled, fried or boiled.

WHERE TO STAY
❶ *Holiday International* £££
P.O. Box 58 02
Khalid Lagoon
(Buheira Corniche)
Corniche, Al-Majaz
Tel. 06 573 66 66
www.holidayinternational.com
All 253 rooms of this particularly family-friendly hotel have a balcony overlooking either the lagoon or the city.

❷ *Radisson* £££ Insider Tip
Corniche Road
Tel. 06 565 77 77
www.radissonblu.com
This hotel, directly located on the Corniche, is especially popular with European package tourists. With 300 rooms, several restaurants, a private beach and a wider variety of options for water sports.

❸ *Carlton* ££
Sheikh Sultan Al-Awal Road
Al-Khan Corniche
Tel. 06 528 37 11

www.sharjahcarlton.com;
The hotel has 174 rooms, three restaurants, a large fitness area and a 200m/218yd beach.

❹ Nova Park ££
Al-Wadah Street
(on the corner of King Feisal Street)
Al-Qasimia
Tel. 06 572 80 00
www.mhgroupsharjah.com
Comfortable hotel with 256 rooms, swimming pool and fitness room; shuttle bus services to the city centre and Dubai.

❺ Beach Hotel ££
Al-Meena Street
Tel. 06 528 13 11
www.beachhotel-sharjah.com
A beach hotel 5km/3mi from the city centre, with 131 rooms, a pool and entertainment for children. Free transfers to the airport and city.

❻ Coral Beach Resort £
Corniche Road
Al-Muntazah
Tel. 06 522 99 99
www.coral-beachresortsharjah.com
This beach hotel with 156 rooms also features a tennis court, fitness centre, sauna and pool. Free shuttle service five times per day to Dubai and Sharjah, as well as to the airports of Dubai and Sharjah.

❼ Summerland Motel £
Al-Khan Corniche
Tel. 06 528 13 21
www.albustangroup.com
Basic hotel on Sultan Al-Awal Road. All rooms equipped with air conditioning, bathroom and TV.

nal on the initiative of the incumbent emir, Sultan Bin-Mohammed al-Qasimi. Today, the main portal is adorned with a door from the original building. Since 1997, the Al-Hisn Fort has served as Sharjah's **history museum**. The exhibitions give an insight into pearl diving on the Arabian Gulf (▶MARCO POLO Insight p.276). Pride and joy of the museum are its historical maps of the Gulf region as well as the country's oldest rifle, named Abu Fatilah (»father of the muzzle-loader«).
❶ Sat–Thu 8am–2pm, admission 5 Dh, www.sharjahmuseums.ae

Some of the historic buildings west of the fort in the **Heritage Area** have been dedicated to Arab and local writers. In the centre, a large, triangular tent provides coffee for visitors to Literature Square. The House of Poetry here features an extensive collection of Arabic poetry.

Literature Square

The Heritage Area is also where the former residence of Obaid Bin-Isa Bin-Ali al-Shamsi is to be found. The man known as Naboodah grew wealthy through trade. His house was erected in 1845 and occupied by the Naboodah family until 1980. Built using traditional methods and materials, the coral limestone and African hardwood

Bait al-Naboodah

structure has been restored and serves as a fine example of how a prosperous family lived. The two-storey building has a large inner courtyard and a gallery which runs round all sides of the first floor, providing shade. The rooms exhibit silver jewellery, toys and garments – including the »work clothes« of pearl divers. The historic

Sharjah

Maritime Museum
AL-KHAN
Aquarium
Sheikh Sultan Al-Awal Road
LAYYAH
Al-Khan Corniche
Al-Khan Road
AL-KHALDIA
AL-JUBAIL
✉
Meat & Fruit Markets
Fish Market
Arouba Road
Sharjah Bridge
Bus Station
MAR
Arouba
Khor Al-Khan
Al-Khan Corniche
Jazeerah Park
Al-Ittihad Square
Souk Al-Markazi, Blue Souk
Taxi Stand
JAZEERAH
Union Monument
AL-SOOR
Marbella Club

King Feisal Mosque

Book Mall
ℹ
Sheikh Khalid Road
Qanat Al-Qasba
Corniche Road
Expo Centre
Khor Khalid
Arab Cultural Club
King Feisal Street
AL-QASIMIA
Kuwait Road
Dubai
MAJAZ
Buheira Garden
ABU SHAGARA
Al-Wahda Road

Where to stay
 Holiday International   Carlton   Beach Hotel   Summerland Motel
 Radisson   Nova Park   Coral Beach Resort

replica of a boat, partly woven from palm branches and ropes, is on display in the courtyard.

❶ Fireij al-Souk, Al-Gharb, currently closed for renovations, otherwise Sat–Thu 8am–8pm, Fri from 4pm; admission 5 Dh; information: www. sharjahmuseums.ae

0.25 mi
©BAEDEKER

Where to eat
❶ Caesar's Palace
❷ Fishermen's Wharf
❸ Sanobar

❶ **HERITAGE AREA** - Literature Square, Bait Al-Naboodah, Souk Al-Arsah, Al-Midfah Majlis

❷ **ARTS AREA** - Art Square, Abdullah Al-Sari House

Souk al-Arsah Just a short walk away, the Souk al-Arsah is the oldest restored souk in the city. »Arsah« is the term for an open space or courtyard between buildings. Accessible through four different gates, this souk conjures up a centuries-old market atmosphere, with over 100 little shops lining its narrow alleys. Elaborately carved entrances attract customers into the diminutive stores purveying high-quality arts and crafts. Incense and spice oils waft fragrantly through the air. The narrow passageways also reveal some great opportunities for finding souvenirs: silver goods from Oman and Yemen, pearl necklaces from Dubai and hand-woven textiles from India.

❶ Daily except Fri mornings, 9am–1pm and 4.30pm–8pm

> **? Did you know**
>
> **MARCO POLO INSIGHT**
>
> In 1998 and 2014, UNESCO acknowledged Sharjah's efforts and achievements in restoring the old town and saving its widely scattered cultural assets. It also recognized the emirate's commitment to cultural and historical heritage and the establishment of several outstanding museums, designating Sharjah the »Cultural Capital of the Arab World«. This encompasses the old town centre to the east (Arts Area) and the west (Heritage Area) of Al-Boorj Avenue.

Al-Midfa Majlis North of the souk, notable for its unusual, round wind tower, stands the lovingly restored house of the highly respected Midfa family. It was built in the early 20th century by Ibrahim Bin-Mohammed al-Midfa who in 1927 founded »Oman«, the first newspaper in what is today the United Arab Emirates. Besides personal items of the former inhabitants, exhibits include tools for pearl trading, such as small storage trunks and weighing scales, as well as antique writing utensils.

❶ Currently closed for renovations, otherwise Sat–Thu 8am–8pm, Fri from 4pm, admission free; www.sharjahmuseums.ae

Arts Area The Arts Area stretches out east of Al-Boorj Avenue, the vast Arts Square its appositely named centrepiece. The renovated buildings around the square are all dedicated to art.

Sharjah Art Museum The three-storey building houses the **largest art exhibition in the UAE, primarily featuring paintings by Arab artists. Most of the exhibited paintings, historic maps and objects come courtesy of Sheikh Sultan Bin-Mohammed al-Qasimi's private collection. Eight permanent exhibitions show 300 works on the theme of the Middle East, including lithographies by David Roberts (1796–1864). Among the contemporary artists represented here are John R. Harris, Ali Darwish, I. Gilbert and Abdel Kader al-Rais. The museum is particularly proud of old documents on the al-Qasimi resistance to British colonial powers in the 19th century. Local artists are

The oldest bazaar in the city: Souk al-Arsah

granted free studio space, which in turn gives visitors the chance to watch them at work.

❶ Al-Boorj Avenue, Shewhain, Sat–Thu 8am–8pm, Fri 4pm–8pm, admission free; www.sharjahmuseums.ae

Until 1960, the Bait Al-Serkal was owned by the father of the current emir. It was then converted into an American hospital, and ultimately used as an art museum from 1995 until 1997. The three-storey palace now houses the regional art school and can be visited on request (tel. 06 568 82 00).

Sharjah Art Institute

The Emirates Fine Arts Society, opposite the Sharjah Art Museum, organizes the Emirates' entire art scene: it hosts exhibitions and promotes countless artistic activities and events.

Emirates Fine Art Society

Artists can always be found at work in the studios arranged around an inner courtyard at Obaid Al-Shamsi House.

Daily except for Mon and Fri 8am–1pm and 4.30pm–8.30pm

Sharjah Art Galleries

Museum of Islamic Civilization: presentations of Islamic history

Museum of Islamic Civilization	In a building that used to be the **Al-Majarrah Souk** on the Al-Majarrah Waterfront (Sharjah Corniche, a few yards further on), the Museum of Islamic Civilization opened in 2008. The ground floor of this magnificent, palace-like building is devoted to historic Islamic coins and exhibitions on Islamic faith and science, whilst the upper floor houses Islamic art, including old editions of the Qur'an and calligraphic decoration. There is also a cafeteria for those wishing to take a break from studying the 5,000 exhibits presented here. Sat–Thu 8am–8pm, Fri from 4pm, admission 5 Dh, families 10 Dh; www.islamicmuseum.ae
*Blue Souk	The famous **Souk Al-Markazi**, also known as the Blue Souk, can be found between Khalid Lagoon and Al-Ittihad Square. The barrel vaults inside the six elongated buildings are decorated with blue-green tiles. Wind towers lend the 1978 construction from 1978 the air of a Belle Époque train station. The two-storey souk is the landmark of Sharjah and the most photographed building of the emirate. Around 600 shops offer cosmetics, textiles and electronic devices, prayer rugs and household goods, mainly to suit the tastes of locals and Asian guest workers. The open gallery on the first floor is home

to one antique dealer after another. The souk is surrounded by lawns and gardens where locals gather for picnics.

❶ Al-Majaz, southern end of the Al-Buheira Corniche, Sat–Thu 10am–1pm, 4pm–10pm, Fri 4pm–11pm.

On Al-Ittihad Square, the tall and slender Ittihad Monument rises as a symbol of federation and union. The shells at the foot of the column stand for the seven emirates, while the bowl-shaped top holds a pearl.

Ittihad Monument

The Grand Mosque on Al-Ittihad Square, with elaborately decorated mosaics and calligraphies, was a gift from the Saudi Arabian King and duly named after him. Indeed, Sharjah and Saudi Arabia enjoy close relations. When the Emir of Sharjah introduced Sharia law in the courts and reintroduced the ban on alcohol in the emirate, this was seen as an expression of his gratitude for the gift of the mosque and further financial support from the Saudi King.

King Feisal Mosque

This lagoon was artificially enlarged and encircled by a 5.5km/3.4mi corniche with numerous hotels, restaurants and cafés as well as gardens and parks. The connection to the sea has been kept open so that boats can still come and go. A fountain at the centre of the lagoon shoots water 60m/200ft high. **Dhow trips** are offered from the shore, lasting between 15 and 60 minutes. The **Buheira Corniche** waterfront road on the east side of the Khalid Lagoon has been upgraded. The newly built **Al Noor Mosque** stands over the water and is open to visitors. A park has been laid out between the lagoon bank and the road, a restaurant on a (permanently moored) dhow serves dinner and there is a traditional coffee shop for shorter breaks. Jazeerah Island in the Khalid Lagoon is easily accessible via Al-Arouba Road. The 12 ha/30 acre **Al Montazah Park** includes an area for children, a small zoo, two swimming pools and a man-made waterfall. A miniature train transports visitors to the various attractions and the picnic grounds.

Khalid Lagoon

Al Noor Mosque: Mon 10am, information: Sharjah Centre for Cultural Communication, www.shjculture.com, tel. 06 568 00 55

Montazah Park: Sat–Wed 10am–11pm, Thu, Fri until 1am, admission 10 Dh, some attractions cost extra, between 10 and 25 Dh, Water Park 120 Dh, children 75 Dh

The Khalid and Al-Khan lagoons are linked by the Qanat al-Qasba canal, about 1km/0.5mi long and 30m/100ft wide. Little abras ferry visitors across the water and three footbridges span the canal. There are various restaurants and leisure facilities along its banks, including the Eye of the Emirates, a big wheel which offers visitors panoramic views of Sharjah from its 42 air-conditioned glass cabins and, weather permitting, Dubai from a height of 60m/200ft.

Qanat al-Qasba

❶ www.alqasba.ae

Natural Air-Conditioning

At the beginning of the 20th century, Persian traders settled in Dubai, naming their district Bastakiya (p.208) in memory of their homeland, Bastak in South Persia. They built houses of mud bricks and coral stone, adding wind towers to remarkable effect. This simple technical achievement ensured that their homes remained pleasantly cool – without electricity – in spite of the scorching heat outside.

❶ Open on all sides

Towers up to 15m/49ft and open on all sides were added to the corners of the houses.

❷ Shaft system

Insided the towers, two right-angled walls crossed to create four shafts, an X-shaped construction which caught even the lightest of breezes and channelled air through two of the shafts into the living quarters below. The air was then directed upwards through the other two shafts.

❸ Bottom funnel

The air was swept across a water basin on the ground which enhanced the cooling effect through evaporation. A pleasant indoor climate was thus achieved during the day (far superior to modern air-conditioning technology).

They provide a comfortable temperature without elaborate technology: wind towers in the United Arab Emirates

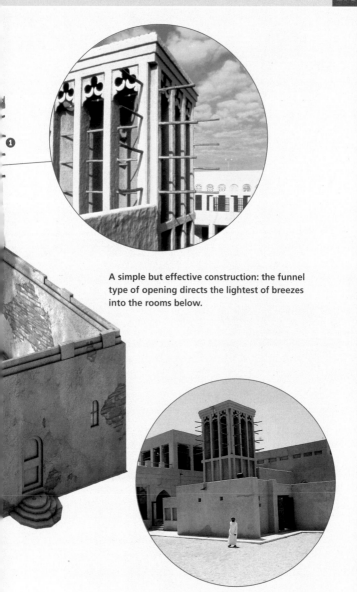

A simple but effective construction: the funnel type of opening directs the lightest of breezes into the rooms below.

Wind towers provide cool air, even in desert regions where they are especially prevalent.

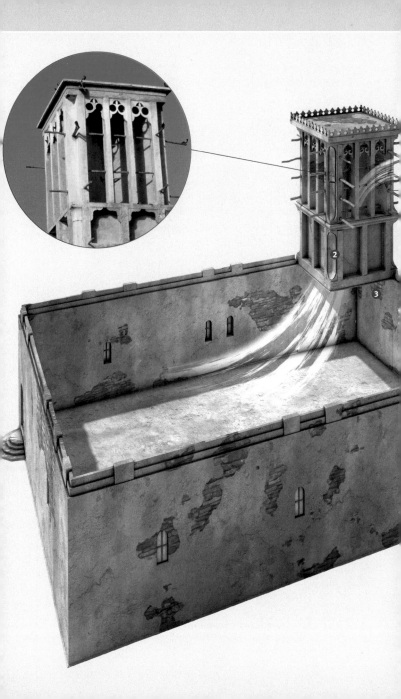

Maritime Museum	Opened in 2009 in the Al-Khan district, this architecturally striking museum offers insights into how tradtional dhows are built, the boats which have been indispensable for fishing, pearl diving and commerce. There is also much to learn about the art of sailing and pearl farming. Al-Mina Road, Al-Khan, Sat–Thu 8am–8pm, Fri from 4pm, admission 10 Dh, children 5 Dh, families 20 Dh; www.sharjahmuseums.ae
Sharjah Aquarium	Located slightly to the south, the Sharjah Aquarium presents some 250 species of sea creatures, from seahorses to sharks. A café overlooks the lagoon. Al-Khan Road, Sat–Thu 8am–8pm, Fri 4pm–10pm, Wed families only, Sun closed, admission 20 Dh, children 10 Dh, families 50 Dh; www.sharjahaquarium.ae
Beaches	Several beach hotels line Sheikh ltan al-Awal Road on the shore, complementing the most beautiful beaches of Sharjah City.
Cultural Square	Cultural Square is located in the suburb of Halwan on the way to the airport. It is visible from afar, thanks to the enormous marble monument in the shape of an open book. The Science Museum and the Archaeological Museum, two of the most prominent museums of the emirate, are situated here, as well as the Cultural Centre, which offers exhibitions on the history and culture of the emirate along with theatre and folklore performances.
Sharjah Science Museum	Surrounded by palm trees, this expansive museum, which also houses a planetarium, was built in 1996 in neo-Islamic style. The museum, entered through an elaborately carved door, is divided into three sections: the Exhibition Hall, a Learning Centre dedicated to computers and how to use them, and a lounge area with a café and souvenir shop. The Exhibition Hall is seen as a science museum, primarily aimed at children to help them grasp – literally – scientific and technical contexts by playing and experimenting with 50 interactive exhibits. The topics include building and construction, media, the human body and sports. A »motorway« and miniature cars teach children how to drive, whilst an »educational supermarket« provides »shopping practice« for youngsters. Cultural Square, next to the television station, Sun–Thu 8am–2pm, Fri, Sat 4pm–8pm, admission 10 Dh; www.sharjahmuseums.ae

! Insider Tip

Sharjah Ladies Club

MARCO POLO TIP

For women only: wellness, spa, beauty, sports, beach, restaurant and lounges where guests can chat with local women (Sharjah Corniche Road, Al-Seef, tel. 06 506 77 77, www.slc.ae; open Sat–Thu 8am–9pm, Fri from 2pm).

The Sharjah Archaeological Museum, which opened in 1997 directly next to the Science Museum, owns an excellently presented and didactically outstanding collection of exhibits, taking visitors on a journey through time from the first settlement of the Gulf region to the present. The museum features models of 3,000 year old settlements, a replica burial mound from Meleiha, in which a man was buried with his horse, as well as finds from several excavation sites, including precious burial objects. A walk through the exhibition traces the emirate's 6,000 year old history. Its trade relations with Mesopotamia are illustrated with shells, necklaces and ceramics. The tools of shepherds, farmers, hunters and fishermen show the lifestyles of people over the last few thousand years.

Sharjah Archaeological Museum

Al-Hizam Al-Akhdar Road, on the corner of Sheikh Zayed Road, Cultural Square, Sat–Thu 8am–8pm, Fri 4pm–8pm, admission 5 Dh; www.archaeologymuseum.ae

Cultural Square – sculpture in front of the cultural palace

Harvesting The Oyster Beds

The museums in Sharjah, Dubai and Ras al-Khaimah are highly dedicated to the history of pearl diving, and for a good reason: until the discovery of crude oil and the emergence of Japanese cultured pearls, trade with pearls was one of the most significant economic activities on the Gulf coast.

Around 1900, the heyday of the pearl-diving industry, the Sheikhdom of Abu Dhabi had the largest pearl diving fleet on the Arabian Gulf – with more than 400 boats. However, diving for pearls had been going on here over 1,000 years ago.

Oyster banks at depths of up to 30m/98ft were located off the Gulf coast. Pearl divers went out to sea between May and September, when the ocean was calm and storms unlikely.

At Sea with Prayer Leader and Cook

On board every boat were around ten divers and the same amount of helpers. A cook and often a prayer leader, singer and drummer accom-

Fascinating variety of pearls

sia. Magnifying glasses, scales and other mechanical devices specially built for the purpose determined the quality and size of the pearls. Traders sold the precious pearls to India and Europe. In the 1920s, jewellers from as far away as New York sent requests to purchase the highly valued pearls from the Arabian Gulf. The wealth created from pearl exports led to a building boom in the sheikhdoms – sandy hut villages evolved into small harbour towns. The 1930s, the Great Depression and competition from Japanese cultured pearls marked the decline of the pearl diving industry. Eventually, the Second World War made the export of pearls virtually impossible. Those interested in learning more about pearl diving should pay a visit to the museum at Al-Hisn Fort in Sharjah City (▶p.263).

panied the crew. The captain's task was to find a suitable diving ground. Once an oyster bed was discovered, all other boats were notified as well. Oyster fields of up to 200 sq km/77 sq mi ensured a rich harvest.

Gloves and Nose Clips

Equipped with leather gloves, a wooden nose clip and a rope tied around the hips, men dived down to the bottom of the sea to collect oysters into a basket.

Each dive lasted approximately three minutes. On command, the helpers would then pull the divers up from the depths. A working day, starting at sunrise and ending at sunset, comprised up to 100 dives. The boats only returned to their home harbour at the end of a pearl diving season.

Harvests were stored in precious teakwood chests with ivory intar-

AROUND SHARJAH CITY

*Sharjah Natural History Museum & Desert Park
Roughly halfway between Sharjah and Al-Dhaid, the wide open spaces of the Sharjah Desert Park stretch out. The nature reserve, established by Sheikh Sultan Bin-Mohammed al-Qasimi in 1992, began life as a small protected area for endangered lizards. At the Natural History Museum, accommodated in a large modern building, visitors can learn more about the fauna and flora of the United Arab Emirates. One exhibition room illustrates the human impact on desert landscapes, while the geology of the region is exhibited on two floors, featuring fossils and sparkling crystals. The museum is especially proud of its herbarium, with its almost complete documentation of all plants found in the United Arab Emirates.

> **!** MARCO POLO TIP
>
> *Searching for shells in the desert* Insider Tip
>
> Turn off at the first roundabout in Al-Dhaid and continue 12km/7.5mi towards Al-Madam. The road eventually leads to Mileiha where »Fossil Rock«, a rugged limestone rock, rises above the golden desert (access from the south). The hike is rewarded with stunning views. Be sure to take a look at the maritime fossils inside the rock: sea snails and shells that are over 100 million years old. It is, however, prohibited to take anything away.

At the **Children's Farm**, located across the way from the museum, kids can see animals at close quarters and feed sheep, lambs, goats, ponies and chickens. The Reptile House exhibits both common and rare species of snakes, lizards and insects. The enclosures of the Arabian Wildlife Centre accommodate desert foxes, jackals and porcupines. Visitors can observe the animals through the large windows of an air-conditioned hall, which provides various information panels for orientation.

The Breeding Centre of Endangered Wildlife is not open to the public. As the name suggests, the centre is dedicated to the breeding of endangered species.

❶ Sharjah Airport Road, Dhaid Highway, Junction no. 8; Su, Mon, Wed, Thu 9am–5.30pm, Fri from 4pm, Sat from 11am, admission 15 Dh; www.breedingcentresharjah.com

Al-Dhaid
The Al-Dhaid oasis, situated 50km/31mi east of Sharjah, is heralded as the »fruit basket« of the Emirates. The city is surrounded by numerous springs and groundwater reserves which are used to irrigate large agricultural areas. More than 4,000 farms are located here, some with cattle, others producing fruit, vegetables and grain. The large souk in the city centre sells ceramics, rugs, spices and many kinds of dates. The **Old Fort** stands at the northwestern edge of the city. In winter, the **camel racetrack** on the road to Sharjah hosts races every Friday morning.

Khor Fakkan

✦ L 3

Population: 55,000

The exclave of Khor Fakkan is situated on the east coast between the northern Hajar Mountains and the Gulf of Oman. Its sandy beaches and colourful underwater world have turned the town into a popular bathing and diving resort. Fortunately, it has managed to retain its calm, unspoiled character.

The city is of strategic importance to the government, as a natural harbour south of Khor Fakkan allows import and export activities to continue, even in the event of the Strait of Hormuz coming under threat or being closed. An ongoing expansion programme is reflected by the constant presence of huge container ships transporting oil and freight. A cruise terminal has also been added.

Important UAE harbour

Khor Fakkan on the east coast of the UAE is a holiday paradise

Khor Fakkan

WHERE TO EAT
Bab al Bahar £££
Oceanic Hotel, Corniche
Tel. 09 238 51 11
Al fresco restaurant offering internatio-
nal cuisine, fish, seafood and Italian spe-
cialties. No alcohol served.

Irani Pars ££
Corniche
Tel. 09 238 77 87
Persian cuisine with an Arabic influence,
always well attended.

Taj Khorfakkan £ Insider Tip
Corniche
(opposite the Safir Centre)
Tel. 09 237 00 40
www.grouptajmahal.com
Best spot on the promenade. This Indian
restaurant offers inexpensive lunch deals
(12pm–3pm) and dinners from 7pm. The
fish and prawn curries are absolutely delicious.

Golden Fork £
Corniche Road
Tel. 09 238 70 85
www.goldenforkgroup.com

Restaurant chain serving primarily Philippine cuisine, with a particularly wide variety of fish dishes and seafood. Diners
love the fish soup and prawn curries.

WHERE TO STAY
Oceanic Hotel £££
Corniche
Tel. 09 238 51 11
www.oceanichotel.com
Comfortable hotel with 162 rooms, a
beautiful private beach and plenty of
water sports facilities, including a dive
platform.

Holiday Beach Motel ££ Insider Tip
Dibba – Khor Fakkan Highway
Tel. 09 244 55 40
www.holidaybeachmotel.com
In Al-Fuqait, north of Khor Fakkan and
5km/3mi from Dibba, this new motel
has 41 bungalows, lined up between
the steeply rising Hajar Mountains and
the beach. The small houses arranged
around a pool are equipped with one or
two bedrooms, a living room, terrace,
kitchenette and bathroom. Restaurant,
bar and nightclub also on site, as well as
a PADI diving centre.

»Creek of Two Jaws« Khor Fakkan, the »creek of two jaws«, is located in a gently rounded bay at the foot of the Hajar Mountains. The landmark of Khor Fak-kan, an emir's palace, stands high above the city – empty for most of the year. Below the palace is the popular Oceanic Hotel. Several small cafés and restaurants line the seaside promenade, landscaped as a park. Several years ago, the rising number of visitors led to the con-struction of a traditional-style souk selling food and textiles as well as electronic devices, arts and crafts. The main shopping street is Sheikh Khalid Road, off Corniche Road, near the roundabout.

History In the 16th century, Khor Fakkan became one of the most significant hubs for dhow traffic; from here ships left for Africa and India. The

Portuguese established a base in the early part of the 16th century and built several watchtowers along the coast, only one of which still exists today.

WHAT TO SEE IN KHOR FAKKAN

The Rifaisa Reservoir is situated a little further inland in the mountains. Locals say that there is a sunken village at the bottom of the lake, visible when the water is clear.

Rifaisa Reservoir

The Oceanic Hotel, located at the northernmost end of the bay, is central to the city's tourist and social life. Hotel guests come here for the calm atmosphere and for the relatively low prices compared to Abu Dhabi and Dubai. Between the palm trees and the white sandy beach there are several tennis courts and a swimming pool. A rock emerges from the water of the bay, which is protected from heavy swells, making for ideal snorkelling conditions.

Oceanic Hotel

A diving club directly next to the hotel even has offers for beginners to explore the Gulf's rich underwater world and observe morays, butterfly fish or hakes. Dive spots include the Anemone Gardens, the Martini Rocks, the Hole in the Wall and the waters around the small **Shark Island**, a short boat trip from the shore. Those interested can either book an organized tour at the hotel or a travel agency, or ask a fisherman for a ride.

Umm al-Quwain

Umm al-Quwain

Area: 750 sq km/290 sq m
Population: 60,000

Emir: Sheikh Saud Bin-Rashid
al-Moalla (since 2009)

The country's second smallest emirate is also the one which has changed the least. Situated north of Ajman, between Sharjah and Ras al-Khaima, it occupies a long and narrow sandy spit on the Arabian Gulf.

Umm al-Quwain means »mother of two powers«, a reference to the long seafaring tradition of its people. Three quarters of them are Emirati who have been making their living from fishing and trade for as long as anyone can remember. Boat building also has a long tradition here.
The eponymous capital is situated at the end of a 12km/7.5mi land spit, populated by flat buildings and garage stores which – unlike the metropolises of the Emirates of Abu Dhabi, Dubai or Sharjah – lend the impression of a village or small town.

»Mother of two powers«

In 1976, small deposits of oil as well as larger gas deposits were discovered 22km/13.5mi off the shore. As per an agreement with Dubai, Umm al-Quwain supplies the wealthier emirate with natural gas, needed for one of the industrial plants in the Jebel Ali free trade zone.

Oil and gas deposits

The oasis town of Falaj al-Moalla, located 55km/34mi southeast of the capital in the Emirate of Sharjah, also belongs to the sheikhdom of Umm al-Quwain. It stretches 40km/25mi between the coast and the hinterland. Local farmers profit from the rich supply of water to cultivate date palms, fruit and vegetables. Cows provide the emirate with milk and dairy products, and a poultry farm provides chickens; surplus produce is exported to the other emirates.

Falaj al-Moalla oasis

Ten islands with mangrove forests lie off the emirate's coast. The largest, with an area of 90 sq km/35 sq mi, is Siniyah, an ideal destination for birdwatchers and nature enthusiasts.

Siniyah

**The Old Fort of Umm al-Quwain
is now a museum**

Umm al-Quwain City

✧ J/K 3

Population: 35,000

The capital of the emirate is situated on a 12km/7.5mi long peninsula, roughly 1km/less than a mile wide, between the Arabian Gulf and the lagoon of Khor Umm al-Quwain.

City on the largest lagoon in the UAE

Reaching far inland with many indentations, sandbanks and a number of small islands covered with mangroves, this is not only the largest lagoon in the emirates, but also a paradise for nature enthusiasts and birdwatchers.

The city itself is divided into the Old Town in the northern part of the peninsula, with narrow winding alleys and harbour, and the New Town in the south. Predominantly older houses line the perfectly straight roads here, skyscrapers are few and far between. Numerous small shops, cafés and simple restaurants lie along King Feisal Road, which runs to the centre from the south and is subdivided by the Musalla and the Shabiyah roundabouts. The tourist centre, fruit and vegetable market, fish market, dhow yard and marine club can all be found by the lagoon.

WHAT TO SEE IN UMM AL-QUWAIN CITY

*Old Town

Lazimah, the Old Town of Umm al-Quwain which covers the northern tip of the peninsula, is well worth visiting. The streets are filled with old, mostly derelict houses, traditionally constructed using coral and shell limestone. Some even still have their old wooden window frames. Lacking the necessary funds to build new houses, Umm al-Quwain has not demolished its older building stock. As awareness for the beauty and unique historical value of traditional architecture grew in the wealthy emirates of Dubai and Abu Dhabi, new traditional-style houses have been erected everywhere – not least to satisfy the tourists' perception of old Arabia – and Umm al-Quwain now also plans an extensive restoration of its old town. Unfortunately, the high city wall which once surrounded it no longer exists and only three old watchtowers remain.

> **!** *A dip in the lagoon*
>
> MARCO ⊕ POLO TIP
>
> The large lagoon, Khor Umm al-Quwain, is ideal for all kinds of water sports. The necessary equipment can be obtained from Flamingo Beach Resort or the UAQ Marine Club near the fish market. Spontaneous travellers should therefore consider setting a few hours aside for a dip when visiting the old town.

Traditional techniques are used to make dhows

The historic Old Fort is still in good condition, thanks to restoration works in recent years. Built from mud bricks in the mid-18th century, the building was long used as the Emir's residence. Today the fort houses a small museum, relating the history of Umm al-Quwain.
Sun–Thu 8am–1pm and 5pm–8pm, Fri 5pm–8pm; admission 4 Dh

Old Fort

The Khor Umm al-Quwain lagoon provides a habitat for numerous (aquatic) birds. Bird life is particularly manifold in winter, when flocks migrating from European regions arrive here. Thanks to the United Arab Emirates' increasing environmental awareness, the entire lagoon has been designated a protected area.

Khor Umm al-Quwain

Umm al-Quwain

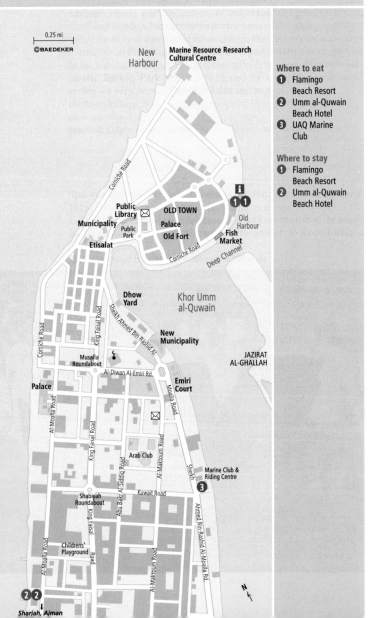

0.25 mi
©BAEDEKER

New Harbour

Marine Resource Research Cultural Centre

Corniche Road

Public Library

OLD TOWN

Municipality

Palace

Public Park

Old Fort

Etisalat

Old Harbour

Fish Market

Corniche Road

Deep Channel

Dhow Yard

Khor Umm al-Quwain

Sheikh Ahmed Bin-Rashid Al-

King Faisal Road

New Municipality

Corniche Road

JAZIRAT AL-GHALLAH

Musalla Roundabout

Al-Diwan Al-Emiri Rd.

Palace

Emiri Court

Al-Moalla Road

King Faisal Road

Mo'alla Road

Abu Bakr Al-Siddiq Road

Arab Club

Al-Maktoum Road

Sheikh

Marine Club & Riding Centre

Shabiyah Roundabout

Kuwait Road

King Faisal

Ahmed Bin-Rashid Al-Moalla Rd.

Childrens' Playground

Al-Moalla Road

Al-Maktoum Road

N

Shariah, Ajman

Where to eat
1 Flamingo Beach Resort
2 Umm al-Quwain Beach Hotel
3 UAQ Marine Club

Where to stay
1 Flamingo Beach Resort
2 Umm al-Quwain Beach Hotel

Umm al-Quwain City

INFORMATION
UAQ Tourist Centre
at the Flamingo Beach Resort
Tel. 06 765 00 00
www.flamingoresort.ae

WATER SPORTS
At the tip of the peninsula, the tourist centre at Flamingo Beach Resort offers a restaurant, boat and surfboard rentals and diving. The local dive area is by a small rocky island off the coast. The lagoon, which provides a habitat for a large variety of birds, can be explored with pedalos or little sailing boats. The shores of the small lagoon islands are equally fascinating; some of them are surrounded by mangroves.

WHERE TO EAT
❶ Flamingo Beach Resort ££
UAQ Tourist Club, tel. 06 765 00 00
www.flamingoresort.ae
The Flamingo Café hotel restaurant serves fish dishes.

❷ Umm al-Quwain Beach Hotel ££
Corniche / Muroor Road
Tel. 06 766 66 47
The hotel restaurant serves Lebanese cuisine; on Fridays there is live music.

❸ UAQ Marine Club ££
UAQ Lagoon

Tel. 06 766 66 44
www.uaqmarineclub.com
A club restaurant which is also open to non-members.

WHERE TO STAY
❶ Flamingo Beach Resort ££
UAQ Tourist Centre
Tel. 06 765 00 00
www.flamingoresort.ae
The leisure and water sports club on the northern tip of the peninsula has 48 rooms, a pool and a beautiful garden.

❷ Umm al-Quwain Beach Hotel ££
Corniche / Muroor Road
Tel. 06 766 66 47
www.uaqbeachhotel.com
When driving onto the Umm al-Quwain Peninsula, the beach to the left of the road is lined by several palaces belonging to the members of the emirate's ruling family. The Beach Hotel can also be found here, comprising 38 rooms and apartments

At the dhow yard, south of the Old Town, shipbuilders still employ traditional techniques to make the wooden ships which centuries ago secured the Arabs' maritime supremacy. The boatbuilders have relaxed as far as visitors are concerned, having nothing against a few spectators as they go about their work (▶MARCO POLO Insight p.289).

*Dhow yard

Sambouks, Booms, Baghalas ...

Arabs have been sailing the seas for thousands of years. As early as 2500 BC they dominated the transfer of goods across the Indian Ocean. After the spread of Islam and the associated creation of a world empire, Arab sailors established trade routes to Canton.

A return trip took around 18 months – one of the longest sea journeys at that time. Even today, the Emirates' ports are almost like a picture from the past: dozens of anchored dhows are loaded with foodstuffs, furniture or electronic goods.

Centuries-old Shipbuilding Tradition

The name »dhow« was coined by Europeans and used to denote the various types of traditional Arab wooden ship. Eventually the term was adopted in Arabic. Even in pre-Islamic times, dhows were built entirely from wood and without the use of nails; instead the ship's planks were sewn together with coconut fibre. The round-shaped hull and relatively short keel are characteristics seen in larger dhows. Further distinct features are the forward leaning main mast and a vertical mizzen mast. Three differently sized, trapeze-shaped sails were taken on a voyage and exchanged according to the wind conditions. Some ships carried an additional triangular foresail.

Ocean-going Sambouks

There are several types of dhow: pearl divers and pilgrims to Mecca mainly used sambouks with a square stern. Sambouks were approx. 25m/27yd long and 6m/6.5yd wide and known to be particularly fast and agile. The cabins for the captain and crew were in the elevated rear deck area. To this day, these ocean-going vessels are used as freight ships.

Dhows are still constructed by hand without any blueprints

Booms and Baghalas

The largest Arab dhows, with an average length of 30m/33yd and a width of approx. 7m/7.7yd, were called booms. Narrowing at the bow and stern, the most characteristic feature of a boom is the rounded extension of the stern. In the rear third of the ship, there was another elevated deck, the poop. This was where the coxswain stood, and where particularly important goods were stored.

The most magnificent dhow is the baghala, an ocean-going trade ship of up to 40m/44yd in length and with a loading capacity of up to 500 tons. The carved false galleries attached to the side of the stern have a merely decorative function and – along with the high poop deck and the richly ornamented transom stern – reveal the influence of 18th century European shipbuilding. By the middle of the 20th century, the two or three sail baghala was superseded by the faster and cheaper boom due to the baghala's elaborate and costly manufacture.

Dhow Building

Today the shipyards of Abu Dabi, Dubai and Ajman mainly hire carpenters from India and Pakistan. Fewer and fewer craftsmen have mastery of the art of traditional dhow building since there have never been any tutorial books or manuals, all knowledge being orally conveyed. Also, dhows are now equipped with diesel engines and modern radio and radar systems. The dhow's accompanying dinghy is often a teakwood log boat (maschwa or hori) with an outboard engine.

Siniyah The 85 sq km/33 sq mi Siniyah Island is situated opposite the city in the Arabian Gulf. Ceramic relics suggest that Siniyah was already colonized in the 7th century – during the time of Islamization. The island is privately owned by Sheikh Saud Bin-Rashid-Ahmed al-Moalla, who has family homes and a private zoo there.

AROUND UMM AL-QUWAIN

Al-Dhour Al-Dhour (»the houses«) lies south of the headland on the road to Ajman. In pre-Christian times it had one of the biggest harbours in the region. The settlement used to be situated right on the coast, but sand drifts have shifted the coastline. The archaeological site is now about 3km/2mi east of Umm al-Quwain. Among the most precious finds are coins from the 2nd century BC, bearing witness to the economic heyday of Al-Dhour. Ceramic shards, possibly stemming from the same vessels as once produced in Rome, are an indication of early trade relations. The approx. 1 x 3km (0.6 x 1.9 mile) archaeological site is openly accessible. Now in poor condition, it has been adopted by locals as a picnic ground. Further excavations are planned, but have not yet begun, due to a lack of funds.

> **!** MARCO ⦿ POLO TIP
>
> *Dreamland Aqua Park* Insider Tip
>
> The Emirate's biggest attraction stretches along the coast, 14km/8.5mi north of the city: Dreamland Aqua Park features various pools and slides, monster waves and baby pools, restaurants, cafés and picnic areas. As beautiful as Wild Wadi and Aquaventure in Dubai but less crowded and not as pricey (daily 10am–6pm, Fri from 2pm; Tel. 06 768 18 88, www.dreamlanduae.com; admission 135 Dh, children up to 1.2m/3ft 11in 85 Dh).

Falaj al-Moalla The centre of Umm al-Quwain's agricultural production is the oasis of Falaj al-Moalla, situated 55km/34mi southeast of the capital in the Emirate of Sharjah. Visitors are primarily attracted to the valley, known as **Wadi Al-Batha**, whose impressive, enormously high mountains of sand begin to glow a deep copper red with the rising and setting of the sun.

Falaj al-Moalla is a modern oasis. The town, characterized by its well-trimmed parks and wide roads, is especially proud of its local camel racetrack, where the menfolk gather to attend races during the winter months. People here live in simple houses built several decades ago. The most significant employer is one of the largest poultry farms in the United Arab Emirates: the National Company for Poultry and Foodstuff, founded in 1977, has been modernized several times at a cost of millions of Dirham. In 1980, Friesian and Jersey cows were imported to start a dairy farm in Falaj al-Moalla. Keeping the animals proved to be unproblematic, so the herds were increased and several farms established. Since then, several thousand litres of milk have been produced every day. Eventually a pasteurization and filling plant went into production on an area of almost 100ha/247acres. In recent years, agricultural productivity has improved significantly thanks to the use of fertilizers as well as efficient water extraction and the use of high performance pumps to draw water out of the ground and transport it directly to the farms.

PRACTICAL INFORMATION

How do you travel to the United Arab Emirates? Where can you find information on the UAE before travelling? How do you travel around Dubai, with a water taxi or a metro? Read it here – best before the trip.

Arrival · Before the Journey

TRAVEL OPTIONS

A variety of airlines offer many daily flights to Abu Dhabi and Dubai from London Heathrow. Direct flights are offered by British Airways (2 flights a day), Virgin Atlantic, Emirates, Royal Brunei, Gulf Air and Etihad Airways (London and Manchester), indirect flights by for example Kuwait Airways (via Kuwait), Air France, KLM and others. Qatar Airways flies direct from London and Manchester. Emirates also provides a non-stop service to Dubai from New York as well as from Sydney. The duration of a flight from London Heathrow to Dubai is approximately seven hours.

?

Tour operators

Various tour operators offer all-inclusive trips to the United Arab Emirates, often combined with excursions to Oman. Emirates Tours UK (www.emiratestours.co.uk) is one of many offering special deals. Organized excursions within the Emirates and to Oman can also be booked on location.

ENTRY AND DEPARTURE REGULATIONS

Travel documents

Upon arrival at an airport in the United Arab Emirates – usually Abu Dhabi, Dubai, or Sharjah – UK residents receive a free visa which is valid for 60 days (»visa on arrival«), which can be extended for another 30 days for a fee of 500 dirham. A passport valid for at least another six months, which must not contain any Israeli stamps, is required.

A further 33 countries are now treated in the same way as the UK; these include the USA, Canada, Australia, New Zealand and the Republic of Ireland. To cross a border with Oman, for example during an excursion, a valid visa from one of the two countries is sufficient for the other. The return flight must be re-confirmed within 72 hours of departure (except for Gulf Air).

Customs regulations

Personal items are not subject to any customs regulations when entering the UAE. 200 cigarettes (Abu Dhabi: 800) or 50 cigars or 250g of tobacco and 2 litres of wine (4.2 US pints) of spirits as well as 2 litres (4.2 US pints) of wine can be imported duty free. The import of all alcoholic drinks to the Emirate of Sharjah is prohibited.

Returning to the UK

Goods up to a total value of £390 are duty free, including perfume or eau de toilette. 200 cigarettes or 100 small cigars or 50 cigars or

250g/9oz tobacco, and 2 litres/3.5pt (4.2 US pints) of wine or other beverages containing up to 22% alcohol, or 1 litre/1.7pt (2.1 US pints) of spirits containing over 22% alcohol, are also free of duty.

VACCINATIONS

Vaccinations are not mandatory when entering the UAE, but being protected against polio, tetanus and diphtheria is recommended. Al-though hygiene standards are very good, a preventive hepatitis A vaccination is recommended, especially for those planning excursions to Oman.

TRAVEL INSURANCE

In order to avoid potential financial risk, obtaining private travel health insurance (for a defined period of time) is recommended to cover any costs for doctors and medication.

MARCO POLO TIP

Stopover in Kuwait Insider Tip

On flights to or from Abu Dhabi or Dubai, Kuwait Airways offers a stopover in Kuwait with an inexpensive overnight stay. The visa is obtained from Kuwait Airways or the hotel, and is also available after arriving at the airport.

AIRLINES
British Airways
Tel. +44 (0) 844 / 493 0787
www.britishairways.com or
www.ba.com

Emirates Airlines
Tel. +44 (0)844 / 800 277
www.emirates.com

Etihad Airways
Tel. +44 (0) 203 / 450 7300
www.etihadairways.com

Gulf Air
Tel. +44 (0) 844 493 1717
www.gulfairco.com/uk

Kuwait Airways
Tel. +44 (0)20 741 200 06
www.kuwait-airways.com

Qatar Airways
Tel. +44 (0)870 389 8090
www.qatarairways.com

Royal Brunei
Tel. +44 (0)20 7584 6660
www.bruneiair.com

Virgin Atlantic
Tel. +44 (0)844 209 7777
www.virgin-atlantic.com

FLIGHT INFORMATION
IN THE UAE
Abu Dhabi
Tel. 02 / 5 75 76 11

Dubai
Tel. 04 / 2 06 66 66

Electricity

The voltage in the United Arab Emirates and Oman is 220/240 volts, 50 Hertz. Adapters can be obtained in electronics stores and supermarkets for a few dirham.

Emergency

GENERAL EMERGENCY
Police
Tel. 999

Ambulance
Tel. 998 and 999
Only in Abu Dhabi, Al Ain and Fujairah;
in the other emirates Tel. 999

Red Crescent
Tel. 998

Fire Service
Tel. 997

BREAKDOWN SERVICES IN UK
RAC
Tel. 08705 722 722
(customer services)
Tel. 0800 82 82 82
(breakdown assistance)

AA
Tel. 0800 88 77 66
(emergency breakdown)
Tel. +44 161 495 8945
(international enquiries)

INTERNATIONAL AIR
AMBULANCE SERVICES
Cega Air Ambulance (worldwide service)
Tel. +44(0)1243 621097
Fax +44(0)1243 773169
www.cega-aviation.co.uk

US Air Ambulance
Tel. 800/948-1214 (US; toll-free)
Tel. 001-941-926-2490
(international; collect)
www.usairambulance.net

Etiquette and Customs in Dubai

TABOOS IN THE ISLAMIC WORLD

Although at first glance it may not seem that way, in Dubai, the metropolis with international flair, visitors are expected to act in a manner adapted to the rules of conduct in an Islamic country. This includes the selection of proper clothing: although scantily-clad tourists are increasingly appearing outside the beach hotels, it is better to adapt to Islamic customs and dress correctly in public. Therefore, men should avoid shorts and muscle shirts when strolling through the city; on the other hand, Bermuda shorts that reach the knee and polo shirts are acceptable in Dubai. Women should leave tight skirts and slacks as well as translucent tops or those that expose the midriff or highlight the décolleté at the hotel. Moreover, clothing that covers the body offers better protection from the intense sunlight.

In Islamic countries, wearing your hair open is considered a provocative act – those who have shoulder-length or longer hair should tie it up during excursions outside of Dubai. Couples should also refrain from showing affection in public.

RESTRAINT REGARDING ARAB WOMEN

Arab women and girls neither want to be photographed nor approached by foreigners, even if it is just to ask for directions. Also, women are greeted without a handshake.

A DRINK ANYTIME?

Drinking alcohol in public is not permitted. The consumption of alcoholic beverages is limited to hotels, licensed restaurants, bars and discos. In the Emirate of Sharjah, alcohol is totally prohibited. Driving under the influence of alcohol is subject to stiff penalties and should therefore be avoided under all circumstances. During the month of fasting, tourists also should not eat, drink or smoke in public.

PHOTOGRAPHY PROHIBITED

Some government buildings, port facilities, oil installations and military facilities are »restricted areas« where photography is prohibited. Before photographing the palaces that belong to members of the ruling class, ask permission from the guards. Locals should be asked for permission before their picture is taken.

PRIVATE VISITS IN THE EMIRATES

Should you receive a private invitation to the house of a local – which is unlikely to happen to tourists very often – it is polite to bring a gift

for the children but not for the wife; also, it is not done to inquire about the woman of the house. It is customary to remove footwear in private residences. When sitting, ensure that the soles of the feet do not point at another person.

SERVICE CHARGE AND TIPPING

On hotel bills, a service charge of 10 to 15% is added in addition to taxes between 8 and 10%; therefore, tipping is not required. However, these fees are not passed on to personnel, so in exceptional cases when extremely good service has been provided a small tip is appropriate. Restaurants are also increasingly following the practice of adding »Service« or »Tip« to the bill amount in addition to taxes. In this case, additional tipping is not required.

Health

MEDICAL ASSISTANCE

In the United Arab Emirates, the supply of hospitals and clinics is excellent; the doctors usually speak English. In emergencies, tourists also receive treatment in state-run hospitals for moderate fees. When visiting a clinic, a consultation including initial treatment costs about 100 to 200 AED.

Medical care

Hospitals

ABU DHABI
Central Hospital
Tel. 02 / 6 21 46 66

Mafraq Hospital
Tel. 02 / 51 23 10 00

Salam Clinic
(Outpatient centre and dentist)
Tel. 02 / 6 71 12 20

DUBAI
Al-Wasl Hospital
Tel. 04 / 2 19 30 00

American Hospital Dubai
Karama, tel. 04 / 3 36 77 77
www.ahdubai.com

Rashid Hospital
Tel. 04 / 3 37 11 11

Students on the AUS campus, the American University of Sharjah

PHARMACIES

Pharmacies or chemist's are found in commercial areas and shopping centres. Almost all medications are available, many without a pres-cription and quite inexpensive; however, they are often sold under other names, so regular medication should be taken along on the trip. **Opening hours** Pharmacies are usually open from 8am or 9am until 8pm, with a lunch break of approximately two hours between 1pm and 5pm. To find out which pharmacies offer services at night, on Fridays and during holidays, call tel. 04 / 2 23 22 32.

PREVENTIVE HEALTHCARE

Protection
from the sun

Sufficient protection from the sun is essential. At temperatures as high as those in the UAE during the day, it is important to drink plenty of liquids in order to compensate for the body's water loss.

Risk of colds

Almost all public buildings, hotels and restaurants in the United Arab Emirates are kept quite cool by air conditioning systems. Since there is a significant temperature difference – often more than 15 °C – compared to outside, one can easily catch a cold. Therefore tourists are advised to always bring a light jacket or sweater along on excursions and sightseeing tours.

Information

The Government of Dubai has a Department of Tourism & Commerce Marketing (DTCM) whose mission is »to position Dubai as the leading tourism destination and commercial hub in the world«. Information is also available from travel agencies – both at home and in the sheikdoms – and from airlines such as Emirates and Gulf Air as well as the press offices of the embassies.

TOURIST INFORMATION
Dubai Tourism and Commerce Marketing
4th floor, Nuffield House
41–46 Piccadilly, London W1J 0DS
Tel. +44 (0)20 7321 6110
Fax +44 (0)20 7321 6111
www.dubaitourism.ae

Abu Dhabi Tourism Authority
No. 1 Knightsbridge
London SW1X 7LY
Tel: +44 (0)207 201 6400
Fax: +44 (0)207 201 6426
www.exploreabudhabi.ae

EMBASSIES

Embassy of the United Arab Emirates, UK
30 Princes Gate
London SW7 1PT
Tel: 020 7581 1281 Fax: 020 7581 9616
www.uaeembassyuk.net

Consulate of the United Arab Emirates, UK / Visa Section
48 Princes Gate
London SW7
Tel: 020 7808 8307

Embassy of the United Arab Emirates, Republic of Ireland
(accredited in London)
30 Princes Gate
London SW7 1PT
Tel: +44 20 7581 1281
Fax: +44 20 7581 9616
www.uaeembassyuk.net

Embassy of the United Arab Emirates, USA
3522 International Court, NW Suite
Washington, DC 20008
Tel: 202 243 2400
Fax: 202 243 1029
www.uae-embassy.org

Embassy of the United Arab Emirates, Canada
125 Boteler Street
Ottawa, Ontario
Tel: 613-565-7272 Fax: 613-565-8007
www.uae-embassy.ae/Embassies/ca

Embassy of the United Arab Emirates, Australia
12 Bulwarra Close
O'Malley ACT 2606
Tel: 61-2-6286 8802
Fax: 61-2-6286 8804
www.uae-embassy.ae/Embassies/au

EMBASSIES IN THE UAE

British Embassy, Dubai
Al Seef Road P.O. Box 65, Dubai
Tel. 04 309 4444
Fax 04 309 4257
http://ukinuae.fco.gov.uk

British Embassy, Abu Dhabi
Khalid bin Al Waleed St (Street 22)
P.O. Box 248, Abu Dhabi
Tel. 02 6101100
http://ukinuae.fco.gov.uk/en/

Embassy of the United States, Abu Dhabi
P.O. Box 4009, Abu Dhabi
Tel. 02 414 2200
http://abudhabi.usembassy.gov

The Embassy of Canada to the United Arab Emirates
9th & 10th Floor, West Tower
Abu Dhabi Trade Towers
(Abu Dhabi Mall)
P.O. Box 6970, Abu Dhabi
Tel. 02 694 0300, fax 02 694 0399
www.canadainternational. gc.ca/
uae-eau

Australian Embassy in the United Arab Emirates
8th floor, Al Muhairy Centre
Sheikh Zayed the First Street
P.O. Box 32711, Abu Dhabi
Tel. 02 401 7500, fax 02 401 7501
www.uae.embassy.gov.au

Irish Embassy, Riyadh, Saudi Arabia (also responsible for UAE)
P.O. Box 94349
Riyadh 11693
Saudi Arabia
Tel. +966 (0)1 488 2300
Fax +966 (0)1 488 0927
www.embassyofireland.org.sa

INTERNET
www.arabianwildlife.com
Belongs to the magazine of the same name, and offers videos, images and information regarding flora and fauna and, in particular, bird-watching tips.

www.sharjah-welcome.com
This website is primarily directed at tourists and visitors to the emirate.

www.uaeinteract.com
The website of the Ministry of Information and Culture offers current news and a lot of mainly tourism-related information regarding the United Arab Emirates.

www.dubaicityguide.com
Colourful site overflowing with information and tips on restaurants, hotels, nightclubs and sightseeing.

Language

Official language
The official language in the UAE is Arabic, but due to the British influence on the Emirates in the past and the especially close relationship with Great Britain, most locals also understand English – at least in Abu Dhabi and Dubai. English has also established itself as the language of commerce. Most street and building signage is bilingual, in Arabic and English.

Language of the Prophet
Arabic is the language of the prophet, so it is said with self-confidence on the Arabian peninsula. The Arabic language spread to the entire peninsula during the 7th century in parallel with the spread of Islam. Numerous regional languages with various dialects that differ from classic high Arabic developed over subsequent centuries. In general, the following applies: the closer the respective language area is to Mecca and Medina, the centre of Islam, the more prevalent high Arabic is.

Family of languages
The Arab language is a member of the Semitic group of languages. It is based on the ancient Semitic consonant script of the Nabataeans and is comprised of 28 characters that are based on just 17 different shapes. These are further differentiated by one or more dots above or below the letters. It is written from right to left. Arab numbers are an exception, since they are read from left to right. There are two different styles of lettering: an angular monumental script that was common into the 12th century and the round cursive style used to-day. Currently, Arab lettering is the second most used in the world after Latin.

Arab names
The names on the Arabian peninsula are unusual for visitors from the West ; they are always comprised of several components. In addition to the given name and surname, a full name also includes the name of the father (and often the grandfather), and sometimes even the name of the tribe. These elements are joined by »Bin ...«, »son of ...«, or »Bint ...«,

»daughter of ...«. Thus women keep their name even after marriage. For the rulers of the emirates, the name of the tribe is also part of their full name: Sheikh Zayed Bin-Sultan Bin-Khalifa Bin-Zayed al-Nahyan al-Bu Falah means: Sheikh Zayed, son of the sultan, son of Khalifa, son of Zayed from the Nahyan family of the tribe of Bu Falah.

Literature

The Arabian Nights; Everyman's Library (1992). The stories in this volume, which are over 700 years old, were translated by Husain Huddawy from the oldest Arabian manuscript by Muhsin Mahdi. The translator has produced a clear, fluent and readable version.

Jelaluddin Rumi: The Essential Rumi: Selected Poems. Penguin Books Ltd; New Ed edition (24 Jun 2004). Coleman Barks has produced exquisite translations of the 13th-century Persian mystic's words.

Fatima Mernissi: Islam and Democracy: Fear of the Modern World; Perseus Books, US (1994). For those wishing to acquire understanding of the Muslim heart and mind, this is essential – and provocative – reading.

Albert Hourani: A History of the Arab Peoples; Faber and Faber (2005). In this hefty tome, Hourani relates the definitive history of the Arab peoples from the seventh century, when the new religion of Islam began to spread from the Arabian Peninsula westwards, to the present day.

Fazlur Rahman: Islam; University of Chicago Press (1979). A rather academic but comprehensive history and analysis of Islam. Rahman has been widely praised as one of the world's most incisive scholars in this field.

Walter M. Weiss: Islam (Crash Course Series); Barron's Educational Series (2000). A crash course in Islam: the author describes 13 centuries of Islamic history, art, and culture on less than 200 easily comprehensible pages with just as many photos.

Edward W. Said: Orientalism; Vintage Books (1979). A provocative critique of Western attitudes about the Orient which has become a modern classic.

Keith Critchlow: Islamic Patterns: An Analytical and Cosmological Approach; Inner Traditions (1999). The geometry and underlying

---

Fiction

History and politics

Islam, Cultural History

The best books on Arabia **Insider Tip**

Sultan Bin Muhammad Al-Qasimi (ed.): The Gulf in Historic Maps 1493 – 1931, Leicester, UK, Haley Sharpe (1996). A unique collection of historic maps of the Emir of Sharjah (available only in bookshops in the UAE).

Walter M. Weiss (author), Kurt-Michael Westermann (photographer): The Bazaar: Markets and Merchants of the Islamic World, Thames & Hudson (2001).

Stefano Bianca: Urban Form in the Arab World, Verlag der Fachvereine Hochschulverlag AG an der ETH Zurich (1994). Palaces and gardens between desert and oasis.

Walter M. Weiss (author), Kurt-Michael Westermann (photographer): The United Arab Emirates and Oman: Two Pearls of Arabia, Art Books Intl Ltd (2000).

cosmological principles of Islamic patterns explained.

Attilio Petruccioli (Editor), Khalil K. Pirani (Editor): Understanding Islamic Architecture; Routledge-Curzon (2000). Architects and academics discuss how it is possible to build in the spirit of Islam. **Wiebke Walther:** Women in Islam; Wiener (Markus) Publishing Inc., US (1995). Stories from the classical period to the present day of Muslim warriors, poets, slaves and dancers – all of whom are women. Images of Dubai and the UAE (Photography Book); Explorer Publishing (2006). Stunning prize-winning views of the Emirates, city and country, ancient and modern.

Ross E. Dunn: The Adventures of Ibn Battuta: A Muslim Traveler of the Fourteenth Century; University of California Press (2004). Ibn Battuta, the »Arab Marco Polo«, jurist, pilgrim, adventurer, and diplomat, travelled as far as India and China on his journeys that lasted 27 years. Dunn's classic retelling of his accounts makes the legendary traveller's story accessible to a wide audience.

Wilfred Thesiger: Arabian Sands; Penguin Books Ltd (1984). This report by Wilfred Thesiger is a great work of travel literature: from 1947 to 1950, the British researcher and explorer crossed the desert of Rub al-Khali, the »empty quarter« of the Arab peninsula, with a group of Bedouin.

Arab cuisine   **Lutz Jakel:** Dubai New Arabian Cuisine; Parkway Publishing (2007). A well-illustrated cookery book whose combination of traditional Arab ingredients with elements of European cuisine represents a mix of cultures typical of Dubai.

ROAD MAPS AND CITY PLANS

Maps and plans from geological projects and from Fairey/Falcon are available for the individual sheikdoms in branches of Family Bookshop, the bookshops in the luxury hotels, and in some specialized bookstores. Since new roads and highways are always being built, it is very important to ensure maps are current.

Media

RADIO · TELEVISION

There are numerous English-language radio stations in the UAE, including Channel 4 FM 104.8 (music, news, sport and competitions), Dubai 92 (the Gulf's longest-established radio station playing hits of today and the past; 92.0 FM), Dubai Eye 103.8 FM (the official broadcaster for the Arabian travel market; news, business, talk, music), Emirates Radio 1 FM (contemporary dance and R&B music) and Emirates Radio 2 (caters for a more mature audience with musical tastes from the 1960s onwards).

The BBC World Service (Dubai: 87.9 FM; Abu Dhabi 90.3 FM) offers news as well as cultural and entertainment programmes.

Abu Dhabi, Dubai, Sharjah and Ajman have their own television stations with various programmes, including some in English.

Satellite TV is very common, and most hotels offer a large selection of television programmes.

NEWSPAPERS · MAGAZINES

The magazines Time Out Abu Dhabi, Time Out Dubai and What's On appear monthly and provide information about all events in the UAE, including the entertainment programmes offered by the larger hotels.

The quarterly brochure Sharjah What Where contains information regarding attractions, hotels, restaurants and events in the Emirate of Sharjah. The English-language newspapers Gulf News, Khaleej Times, and Emirates News are available at most hotels. Foreign daily newspapers and magazines can be found in hotel bookshops and supermarkets, with a day's delay.

Money

The national currency is the dirham (AED, also Dh), divided into 100 Fils. Coins in 1, 5, 10, 25, and 50 Fils as well as 1 AED denominations

National currency

CONTACT DETAILS FOR CREDIT CARDS

In the event of lost bank or credit cards you can contact the following numbers in UK and USA (phone numbers when dialling from abroad). Have the bank sort code, account number and card number as well as the expiry date ready.

Eurocard/MasterCard
Tel. 001 / 636 7227 111

Visa
Tel. 0800 / 811 84 40

American Express UK
Tel. 0044 / 1273 696 933

American Express USA
Tel. 001 / 800 528 4800

Diners Club UK
Tel. 0044 / 1252 513 500

Diners Club USA
Tel. 001 / 702 797 5532

The following numbers of UK banks can be used to report and cancel lost or stolen bank and credit cards issued by those banks:

HSBC
Tel. 0044 / 1442 422 929

Barclaycard
Tel. 0044 / 1604 230 230

NatWest
Tel. 0044 / 142 370 0545

Lloyds TSB
Tel. 0044 / 1702 278 270

and notes in 5, 10, 50, 100, 200, and 500 AED denominations are in circulation. The dirham is fixed to the US currency at 3.67 AED per 1 US$. Money can be changed at banks, in hotels and at bureaux de change. Cash can be obtained at automated cash machines, by debit or credit card.

Credit cards Credit cards are the most common form of payment in the UAE. Some small stores add a surcharge of 3 to 5% for credit card payments as opposed to cash. In case of loss or other credit card problems in Dubai (area code: 04), contact: American Express tel. 3 36 50 00; Diners tel. 3 49 82 00; Master Card Tel. 3 32 29 56; or Visa tel. 2 23 68 88. See the information box for international numbers for lost bank and credit cards.

Most banks are open Sun–Thu 8am–noon/1pm; some banks are also open from 4pm–5.30pm. The money exchanges are open 9am–1pm and 4pm–8pm daily.

? | MARCO ⊕ POLO INSIGHT

Rates of exchange

1 AED = £0.20
£1 = 4.91 AED
1 AED = €0.24
€1 = 4.07 AED
1 AED = US$0.27
US$1 = 3.67 AED
Current exchange rates at
www.oanda.com/convert/classic

Nature Reserves

The UAE is increasingly making efforts to conserve nature and protect wildlife; therefore, some desert and lagoon areas have been declared nature reserves.

ABU DHABI
Al-Wathba Wetland Reserve
A bird sanctuary covering 5 sq km/2 sq mi located 40km/25mi south-east of Abu Dhabi; approximately 200 species of bird live and nest here.

Sir Bani Yas
On this island off Jebel Dhanna in the west of the emirate of Abu Dhabi oryx antelopes and many other Arabian and African animals can be seen.

DUBAI
Al-Maha Desert Resort
The luxury eco-hotel is located 65km/40mi south-east of Dubai in a 25 sq km/10 sq mi nature reserve (▶Baedeker Special, p.215).

Ras Al Khor Wildlife & Waterbird Sanctuary
This bird sanctuary is located at the end of the Creek, to the east of Dubai.

FUJAIRAH
Khor Kalba Mangrove Reserve
Khor Kalba
Swamp and mangrove landscape with bird sanctuary located south of Kalba.

SHARJAH
Sharjah Desert Park
Sharjah Airport Road
Junction No. 8
Dhaid Highway
Nature reserve halfway between Sharjah and Al-Dhaid.

Hatta Oasis belongs to Dubai and is a popular weekend excursion venue

Personal Safety

The United Arab Emirates are among the safest countries in the world. Pickpocketing or carjacking, fraud at restaurants or while shopping and in particular theft and violence are practically unheard of, either in the Emirates or for that matter on the entire Arabian peninsula. Visitors can move around freely anywhere around the clock without cause for nervousness; this also applies to women travelling alone. In case of complaints or doubts, the Tourist Security Department of the Municipality of Dubai is available at tel. 800 4438.

Post · Communications

POST

Postage   A postcard to Europe costs 3 AED, an airmail letter 3.50 AED; mailing time to Europe is 5 to 7 days. Stamps are also available in hotels and shops.

Opening hours   Post offices are open Sat–Wed 8am–1pm and 4pm–7pm, main post offices until 10pm.

MAIN POST OFFICES AND
AREA CODES
Abu Dhabi
East Road (between Al-Falah and Zayed
2nd Street)
Tel. 02 / 6 21 16 11

Dubai
Zabeel Road, Umm Hureir
Tel. 04 / 3 37 15 00

Country codes
From UK and Republic of Ireland ...
... to the UAE: 00 971
From USA, Canada and Australia...
... to the UAE: 0011 971
The 0 that precedes the subsequent local area code is omitted.
From the UAE ...

... to the UK: 00 44
... to the Republic of Ireland: 00 353
... to the USA/Canada: 00 1
... to Australia: 00 61
The 0 that precedes the subsequent local area code is omitted.

Local area codes
Abu Dhabi: 02
Ajman: 06
Al Ain: 03
Dubai 04
Fujairah: 09
Ras al-Kaimah: 07
Sharjah: 06
Umm al-Quwain: 06

Directory inquiries
180 (no charge)

TELEPHONE CALLS

Almost every street corner has a public telephone that accepts phone and credit cards. Phone cards for 30 and 50 AED are available in many shops. The **mobile phones** common in western Europe work in the United Arab Emirates without any problems. The national phone company Etisalat sells tourists a SIM card for the duration of their stay in the UAE: this **Ahlan card** is available at airports in the duty-free shops and in the Etisalat outlets. It costs 60 AED, which includes a credit for phoning of 25 AED.

Prices · Discounts

During the summer, the hotels reduce their prices significantly and frequently even offer »special rates or packages« with half or full board. Due to the very low ticket and admission prices (1 to 5 AED; 14 to 70 pence), public transport and museums do not offer any special discounts.

Time

The United Arab Emirates is four hours ahead of Greenwich Mean Time, and in summer only three hours ahead of British Summer Time (there is no adjustment for daylight saving in the UAE).

Transport

ROAD TRAFFIC

The road network in the UAE is in excellent condition. The city motorways and highways have four to six lanes, and signposting is generally in English.

Road network

The UAE has right-hand traffic. Seat belts must be worn when driving; children under the age of ten are required to sit in the back seat. Traffic coming from the right has right-of-way unless signpost-ed otherwise. Typically, there are numerous roundabouts (R/A) rather than traffic lights in the UAE: here the circling traffic has right of way.

Traffic regulations

Distances

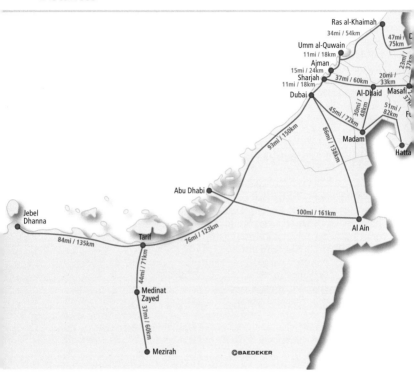

Driving while under the influence of alcohol is severely punished, as is speeding. Tourists are usually required to pay the fine straight away. Maximum speed for passenger cars: 25–38mph/40–60kmh within city limits, 44–56mph/70–90kmh on country roads, 75mph/120kmh on motorways. Cars (even rental cars) driving faster than 75mph/120kmh have a warning signal to warn the driver that the speed limit has been exceeded.

CAR RENTAL

The minimum age for renting a car is 21 (for four-by-fours 25). An international or a national driver's licence is required. A small car with air-conditioning costs between 150 and 250 AED per day. Since larger hotels pick up their guests at the airport and usually provide a car rental service, it is normally not necessary to rent a car at the airport.

With a visa from the UAE or Oman, a visa from the respective other country can be obtained at the border. When entering Muscat (►p.138) from Al Ain, an Omani visa costing 6 OR (60 AED) is obtainable after paying a UAE vehicle fee of 20 AED. When driving from Dubai to Hatta or vice versa, the visa fee is waived, but there is a vehicle fee of 2 OR (20 AED).

To cross the border between the UAE and Oman with a hire car, it is necessary to pay additional insurance fees (approx. 8–10 OR, or 80–100 AED per day). This has to be agreed and a certificate ob- tained when first hiring the car, as the insurance offices at the border are only for residents of the UAE. Those who enter Oman from Ras al-Khamaih at Tibat (heading for Khasab) must leave by the same route.

BREAKDOWN SERVICE

In the event of a car accident the police should be immediately informed (tel. 999). The vehicle must not be moved until the accident has been recorded. Also, a vehicle may not be repaired without a police accident report. What to do in the event of an accident with a rental car is explained in the documents for the rental car. In the event of a breakdown, it usually only takes a few minutes before a police car stops to organize assistance.

TAXIS

In Abu Dhabi, all taxis run on a taximeter. The basic fee is 3 AED including 3km/2mi; each additional kilometre (0.6mi) costs 1 AED. A trip from the airport to the city centre costs about 70 AED. In Abu Dhabi and Al Ain, it is best to use the Al-Ghazal taxis with the gazelle logo; their drivers usually speak English (tel. 4 44 77 87).

In Abu Dhabi

In Dubai, there are taxis with and without a meter. The beige-coloured taxis of the Dubai Transport Corporation (tel. 2 08 08 08) cost 3.50 AED basic fee and 1.60 AED per kilometre (0.6mi); night fares are slightly higher. Expect to pay between 35 and 40 AED for a trip from the airport to the city centre.

In Dubai

In all other emirates, the fare must be negotiated beforehand. Prices are low, but it is best to ask your hotel for a benchmark. A trip within the city limits usually costs just under 10 AED. The drivers are mostly Asian and often don't speak English. It helps to name a prominent building (e.g. a hotel) close to the desired destination.

In the other emirates

Share taxis   Share taxis or service taxis (sometimes called collective taxis) are vehicles for four to six people. Parked at specific locations in the cities, they only leave with a full load, which means a bit of waiting around at first.

The taxi is crowded when full, but in return a trip to another emirate costs next to nothing. From the service taxi stations in Dubai a trip to the northern emirates on the west coast costs between 5 and 20 AED per person, 25 to 30 AED to the east coast, 60 AED to Abu Dhabi or Al Ain.

PUBLIC TRANSPORT

Abu Dhabi and Dubai are the only emirates with a regular public bus service. The destinations of the buses are not always signposted in English. The Transport Department in Dubai (tel. 8 85 94 01) operates about 20 routes from 6am to 11pm every day. A single tick-et costs on average between 1 and 4 AED; it is 5 AED to Jebel Ali (40km/15mi) and 12 AED for a 100km/62mi bus ride to Hatta. Tickets are available from the driver.

The Emirates Express runs every hour between Dubai and Abu Dhabi (6am–9pm, journey time 2 hrs, fare 20 AED.

Twice daily a bus runs from Dubai to Muscat via Hatta and Sohar (journey time 6 hrs).

In Abu Dhabi and Al Ain there are fewer public buses. However, they run around the clock. One trip on the island of Abu Dhabi costs between 2 and 5 AED, and 15 AED to Al Ain.

The other emirates are served by minibuses of the Dubai Transport Corporation (tel. 2 27 38 40).

BUS STATIONS
Abu Dhabi
Hazza Bin-Zayed Road

Dubai
Al-Khor Street, Al-Ras
(between the Hyatt Hotel and Gold Souk)
Al-Sabkha Road (Bur Deira)
Al-Ghubaiba Bus Station, Al-Rifa Street, Bur Dubai

SERVICE TAXIS
Dubai
Al-Ghurair Shopping Complex

ABRAS LANDING STAGES
Ajman
Khor Ajman

Dubai
Bandar Talib Station on the Al-Khor Corniche in Bur Deira;
Abra Docks in the Bastakiya district in Bur Dubai

Ras al-Khaimah
Al-Khor, between the western part of the old town and the eastern part of the Nakheel district

Travellers with Disabilities

Overall, the United Arab Emirates – particularly the sheikdoms of Dubai, Abu Dhabi and Sharjah – are quite easily accessible for those with disabilities. In public buildings, airports, shopping malls and hotels in the four and five-star category, special parking spaces, ramps, wide doors, lifts with low-mounted buttons and toilets for the disabled can be found. The cruise ship harbour in Dubai is also properly equipped for the needs of disabled individuals. The museums are a different matter; with the exception of the Dubai Museum, they are usually not wheelchair accessible.

Access for individuals with disabilities

There are various institutions that organize group trips; trained travel agents arrange individual trips and provide assistance.

Organizations

ORGANIZATIONS FOR
THE DISABLED
Tourism for All
c/o Vitalise, Shap Road Industrial Estate,
Kendal LA9 6NZ
Tel. (08 45) 124 99 71
www.tourismforall.org.uk
Click on Where to Go, and Overseas Travel.

Mobility International USA
132 E. Broadway, Suite 343
Eugene, Oregon USA 97401
Tel. Tel: (541) 343-1284
www.miusa.org

MossRehab ResourceNet
MossRehab Hospital
1200 West Tabor Road
Philadelphia, PA USA
Tel. 215 456 9900
www.mossresourcenet.org

Accessible Travel (UK)
Avionics House
Naas Lane
Quedgeley
Gloucester GL2 2SN
Tel. 01452 729 739
Fax 01452 729853
www.accessibletravel.co.uk

When To Go

With a relatively short flight of approximately 7 hours from London and the pleasant temperatures between October and April, the UAE is an ideal winter travel destination. The months of November through to March are the best time to travel, but Christmas, Easter, and in Dubai also the »Shopping Festival« taking place from mid-January to mid-February are regarded as the peak seasons when the hotels are largely booked out. Many locals leave the Emirates during the hot summer months, and hotels lower their prices starting in May. But since temperatures rise as high as 50°C, visiting the UAE

Winter travel destination

during these months is not recommended. Ramadan, the month of fasting (►Festivals, Holidays and Events) when rules of conduct are very strictly interpreted, is also unsuitable for a visit. During these four weeks, restaurants do not open until after dusk, and business and public life is reduced to a minimum. In Dubai however, the restrictions related to Ramadan are less pronounced.

CLIMATE

The climate of the UAE is arid year-round. Rain usually falls only during the winter months. The average amount of annual precipitation is less than 100mm/4in. Temperatures seldom fall below 20°C. During the **summer months** between May and August, the thermometer climbs above 40°C; sometimes, it even goes as high as 50°C in the shade. The average amount of daily sunshine is eleven hours (eight hours during winter). Relative humidity is low; in the interior of the country, where it sometimes does not rain for years, it is around 20%. Therefore, the streets are practically deserted on a typical summer day; the locals fly to cooler regions during this time.
During the **winter months**, daytime temperatures decrease to values between 20° and 30°C. During this time of »increased rain«, relative humidity is often considerable and can even reach 90% on some days. The notorious wind known as **Shimal**(»north«) which blows from the north-west between May and June can be accompanied by sandstorms and occasionally by rain. The Shimal causes severe discomfort for sensitive individuals, caus-ing headaches and sometimes breathing problems.

The **sea** is warm enough for swimming all year. The water temperature reaches 20°C even in January and February. During the following months, the water temperature increases gradually and reaches an average of 31°C in August.

Index

List of Maps and Illustrations

Photo Credits

Publisher's Information

1st Edition 2017
Worldwide Distribution: Marco Polo
Travel Publishing Ltd
Pinewood, Chineham Business Park
Crockford Lane, Chineham
Basingstoke, Hampshire RG24 8AL,
United Kingdom.

Photos, illlustrations, maps::
149 photos, 30 maps and and
illustrations, one large map
Text:
Dr. Manfred Wöbcke and
Birgit Müller-Wöbcke
Editing:
John Sykes, Robert Taylor, Michael
Scuffil
Translation: David Andersen, Gareth
Davies, Barbara Schmidt-Runkel, John
Sykes, Robert Taylor, Michael Scuffil
Cartography:
Christoph Gallus, Hohberg;
MAIRDUMONT Ostfildern (large map)
3D illustrations:
jangled nerves, Stuttgart
Infographics:
Golden Section Graphics GmbH, Berlin
Design:
independent Medien-Design, Munich
Editor-in-chief:
Rainer Eisenschmid, Mairdumont
Ostfildern

Printed in China

Despite all of our authors' thorough
research, errors can creep in. The pub-
lishers do not accept any liability for thi
Whether you want to praise, alert us to
errors or give us a personal tip Please
contact us by email or post:

MARCO POLO Travel Publishing Ltd
Pinewood, Chineham Business Park
Crockford Lane, Chineham
Basingstoke, Hampshire RG24 8AL
United Kingdom
Email: sales@marcopolouk.com

FSC
www.fsc.org
MIX
Paper from
responsible sources
FSC® C011918

MARCO POLO

HANDBOOKS

 ANDALUCÍA

 BALI

 BARCELONA

 BERLIN

 DRESDEN

 DUBAI

 FLORIDA

 GRAN CANARIA

 ICELAND

 IRELAND

 LONDON

 NEW YORK

 NEW ZEALAND

 PARIS

 PRAGUE

 ROME

 TUSCANY

VENICE

www.marco-polo.com

Curious Facts United Arab Emirates

Names of metro stations that are auctioned off, 20 tons of snow over-night, a falcon on the seat next to you in Business Class – the UAE have some curious facts on offer.

▶Drastic measures
The names of the metro stations in Dubai were auctioned off to the highest bidders. If the winner did not pay in time the station names were changed.

▶Wedding presents
The emir gives every native man money and a house as a wedding present for his first, second and third weddings; and with the fourth wife he still gets a house.

▶Snow and sledding
Dubai gets more than 20 tons of snow a night – in the world's largest indoor ski park.

▶Falcon on the next seat
On flights between the Gulf States it can happen that a falcon is seated on the seat next to its owner.

▶Fashionable abaya
The women's black cloaks, called an abaya, has long since become a fashion accessory in the UAE that is designed by local designers and decorated with sequins and embroidery.

▶Nearby mosques
No Muslim in Dubai and Abu Dhabi should have to walk more than 10 minutes to a mosque – there is a correspondingly large number of mosques in the UAE cities.

▶Culinary trends in the desert
Along with camelburgers (with camel meat) the sale of chocolate made with camel's milk is flourishing – nicely wrapped in foil and shaped like a camel.

▶Super rich
The nearby oil wells made it possible: 68,000 millionaires live in Dubai – the ruler's wealth is estimated at US$ 16 bil.

▶Question of status
Nanny, cook, cleaning women, gardener and driver are part of the local living standard in Dubai and Abu Dhabi.

▶Kaaba compass
So that the direction to Mecca is always clear there is a compass next to the mileage counter in UAE cars, on cell phones and on signs in hotel rooms.